★Stars★

by
Naoko Takeuchi

2

Stars 4	6
Stars 5	51
Stars 6	92
Rini's Picture Diary	133

TOKYOPOP®
Manga

TOKYOPOP Presents
Sailor Moon StarS 2 by Naoko Takeuchi
TOKYOPOP is a registered trademark and
TOKYOPOP Manga is a trademark of Mixx Entertainment, Inc.

ISBN: 1-892213-70-2
First Printing June 2001
12   11   10   9   8   7   6   5   4   3   2

This volume contains the SAILOR MOON StarS installments from Smile
No. 3.4 through No. 3.6 in their entirety.

Translator - Anita Sengupta. Retouch Artist - Wilbert Lacuna.
Graphic Assistants - Steve Kindernay, Dao Sirivisal. Graphic Designer - Akemi Imafuku.
Associate Editor - Katherine Kim. Editor - Michael Schuster.
Senior Editor - Jake Forbes. Production Manager - Fred Lui.

Email: editor@Press.TOKYOPOP.com
Come visit us at www.TOKYOPOP.com
TOKYOPOP
Los Angeles - Tokyo

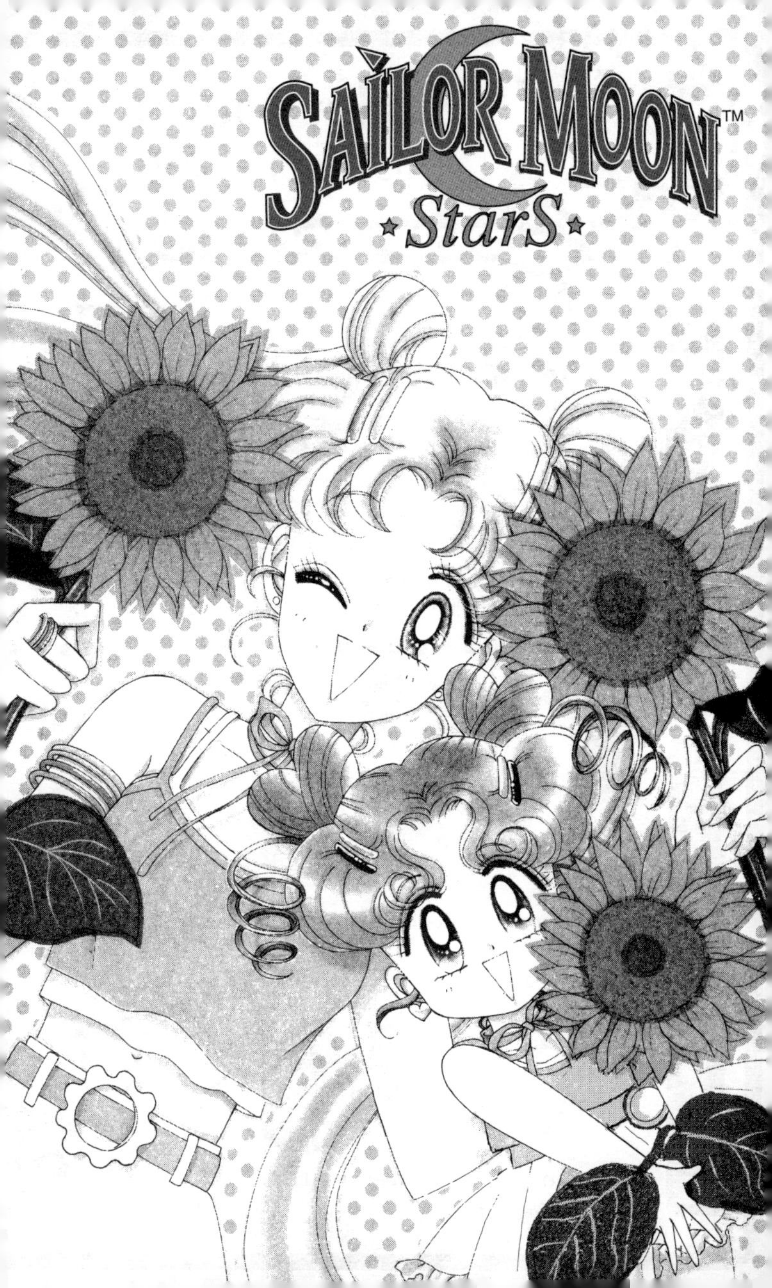
Sailor Moon™
StarS

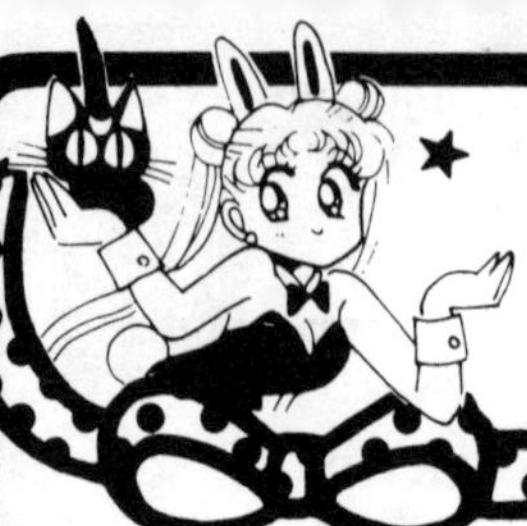

Sailor Moon
Instant Replay

The Main Characters

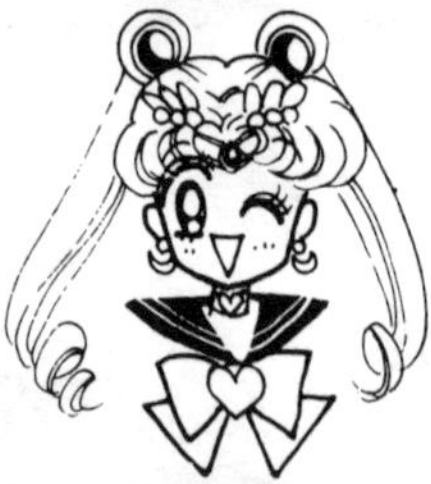

Sailor Moon

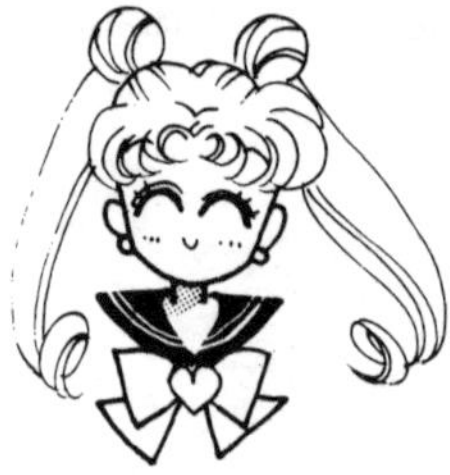

Bunny

Bunny transforms into Sailor Moon to fight evil!

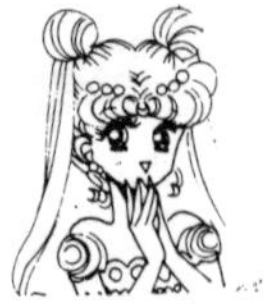

Princess Serenity

Bunny's former life.

The Sailor Scouts who join Bunny's fight.

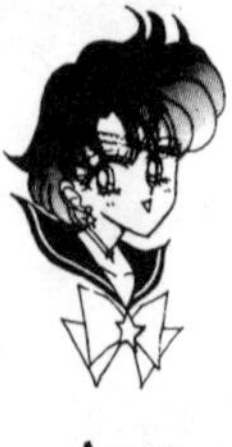

Amy
Sailor Mercury

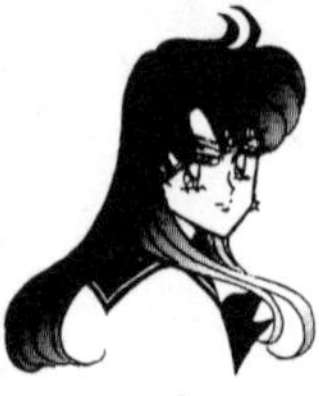

Raye
Sailor Mars

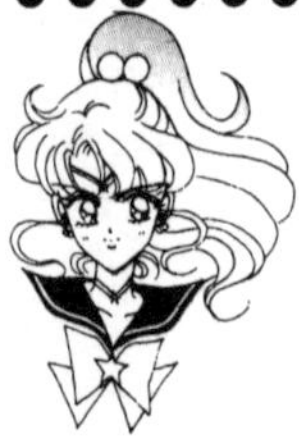

Lita
Sailor Jupiter

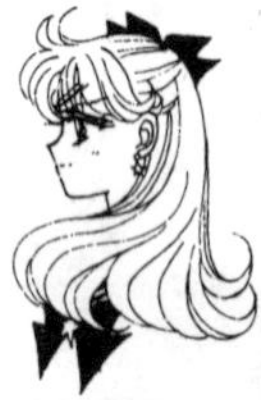

Mina
Sailor Venus

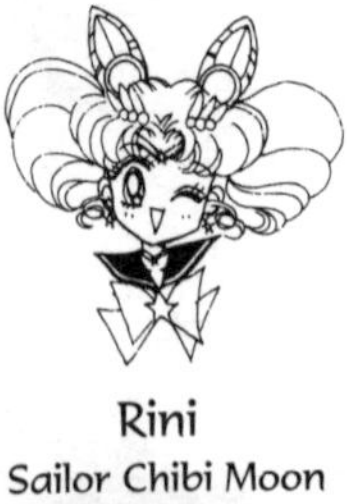

Rini
Sailor Chibi Moon

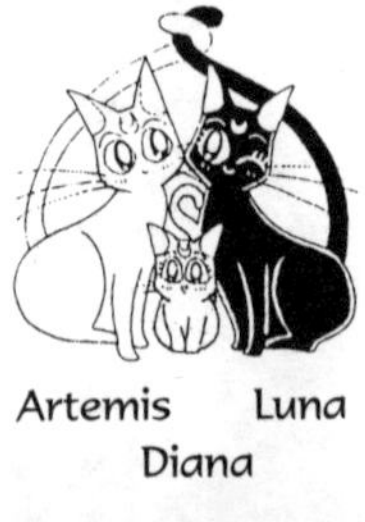

Artemis Luna
Diana

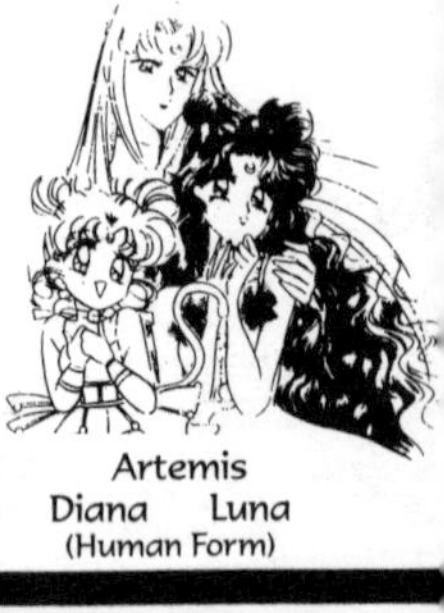

Artemis
Diana Luna
(Human Form)

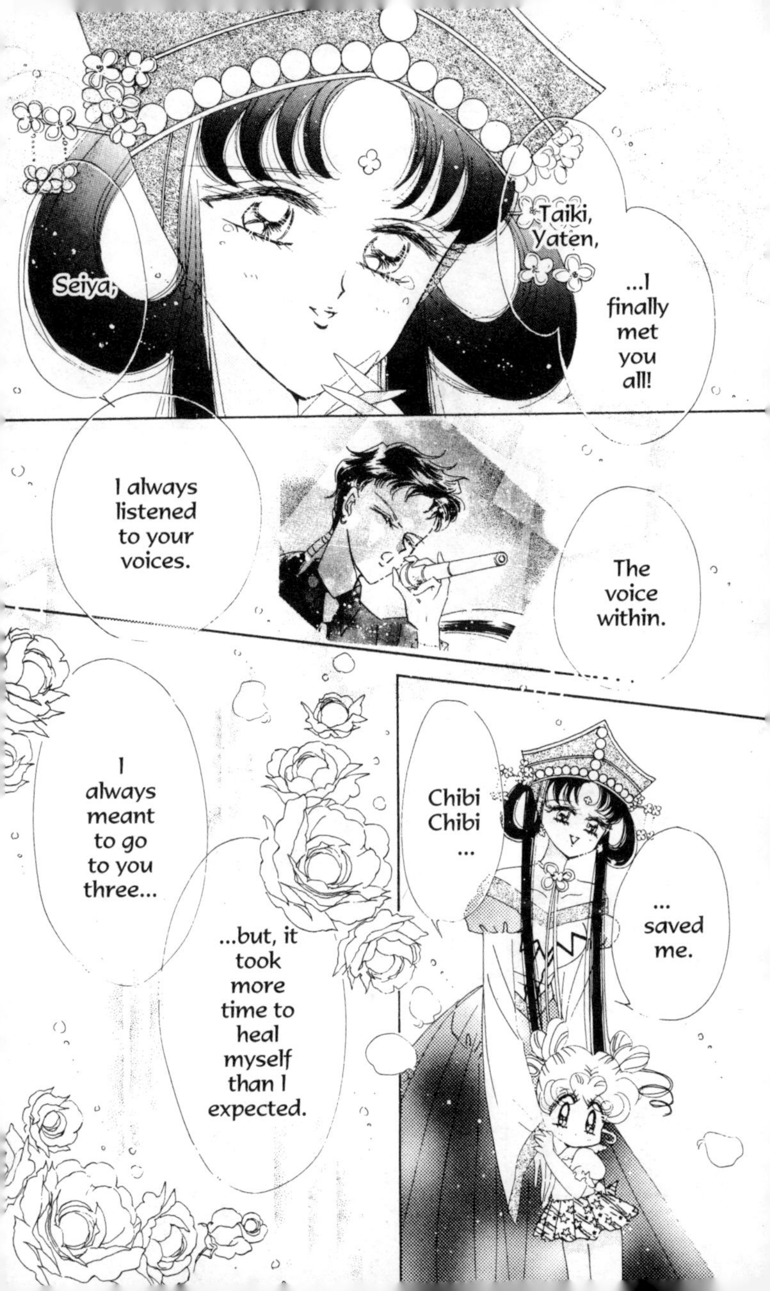
Seiya,
Taiki, Yaten,
...I finally met you all!
I always listened to your voices.
The voice within.
I always meant to go to you three...
...but, it took more time to heal myself than I expected.
Chibi Chibi ...
... saved me.

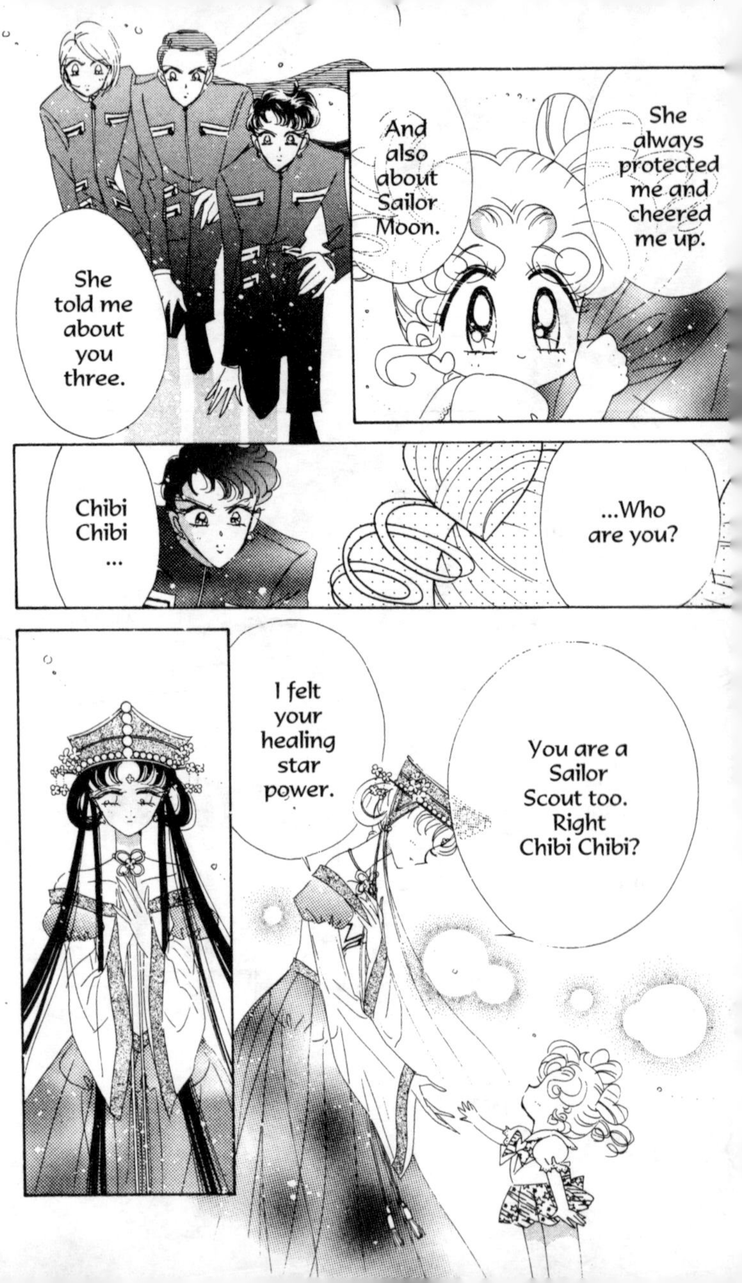
She told me about you three.
And also about Sailor Moon.
She always protected me and cheered me up.
Chibi Chibi ...
...Who are you?
I felt your healing star power.
You are a Sailor Scout too. Right Chibi Chibi?

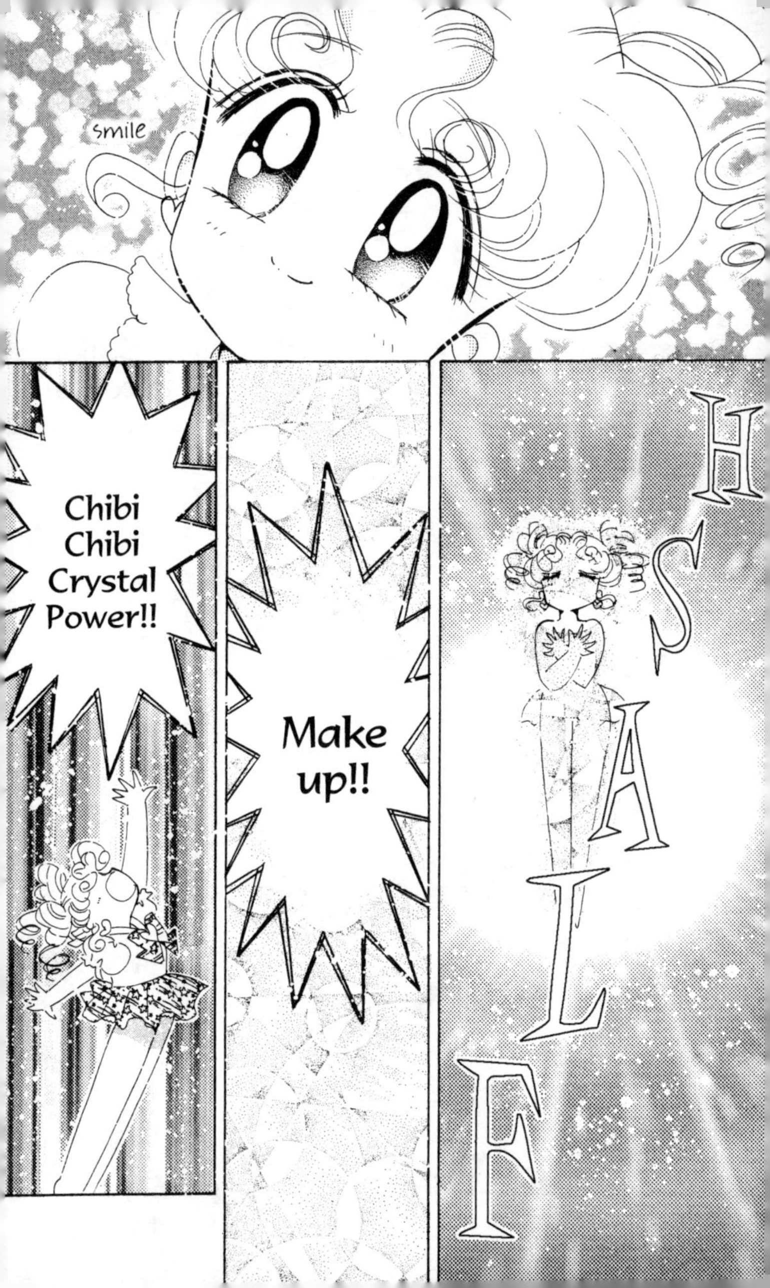

smile
Chibi Chibi Crystal Power!!
Make up!!
HSALF

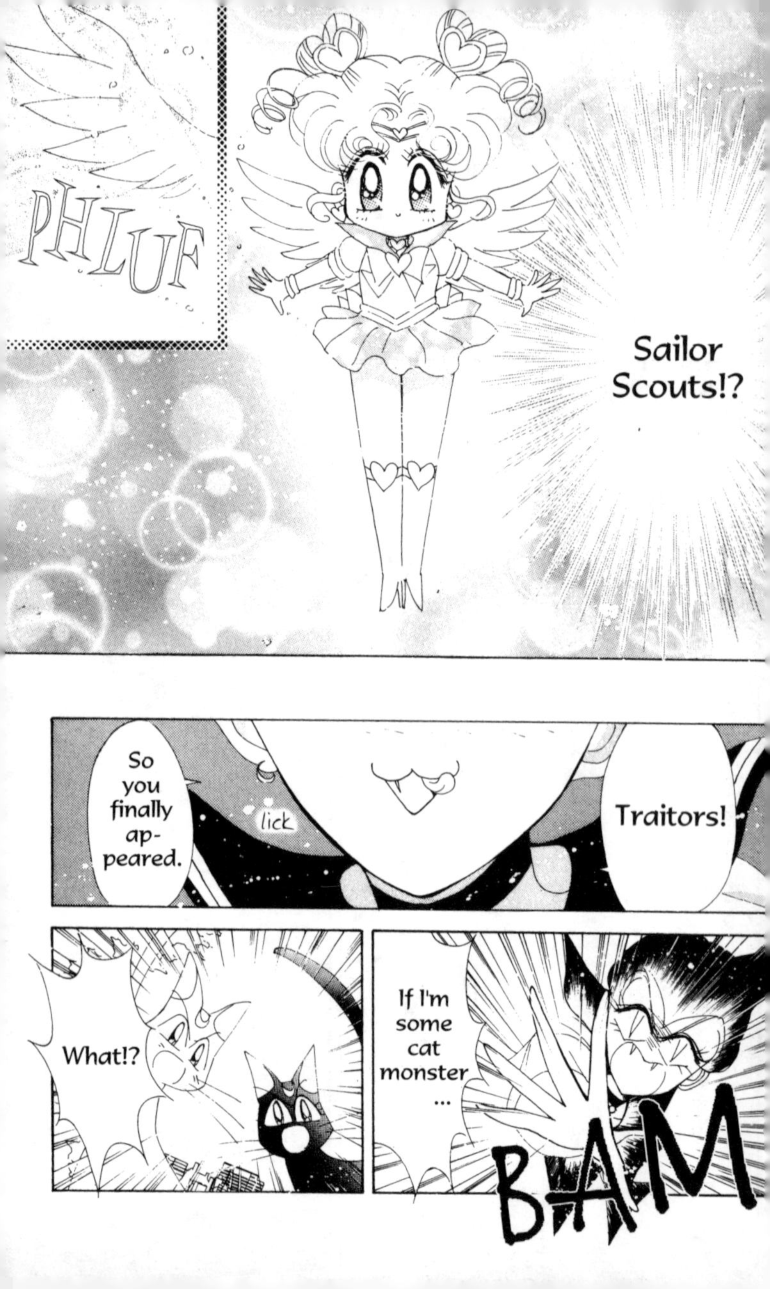
PHLUF
Sailor Scouts!?
So you finally ap-peared.
lick
Traitors!
What!?
If I'm some cat monster ...
BAM

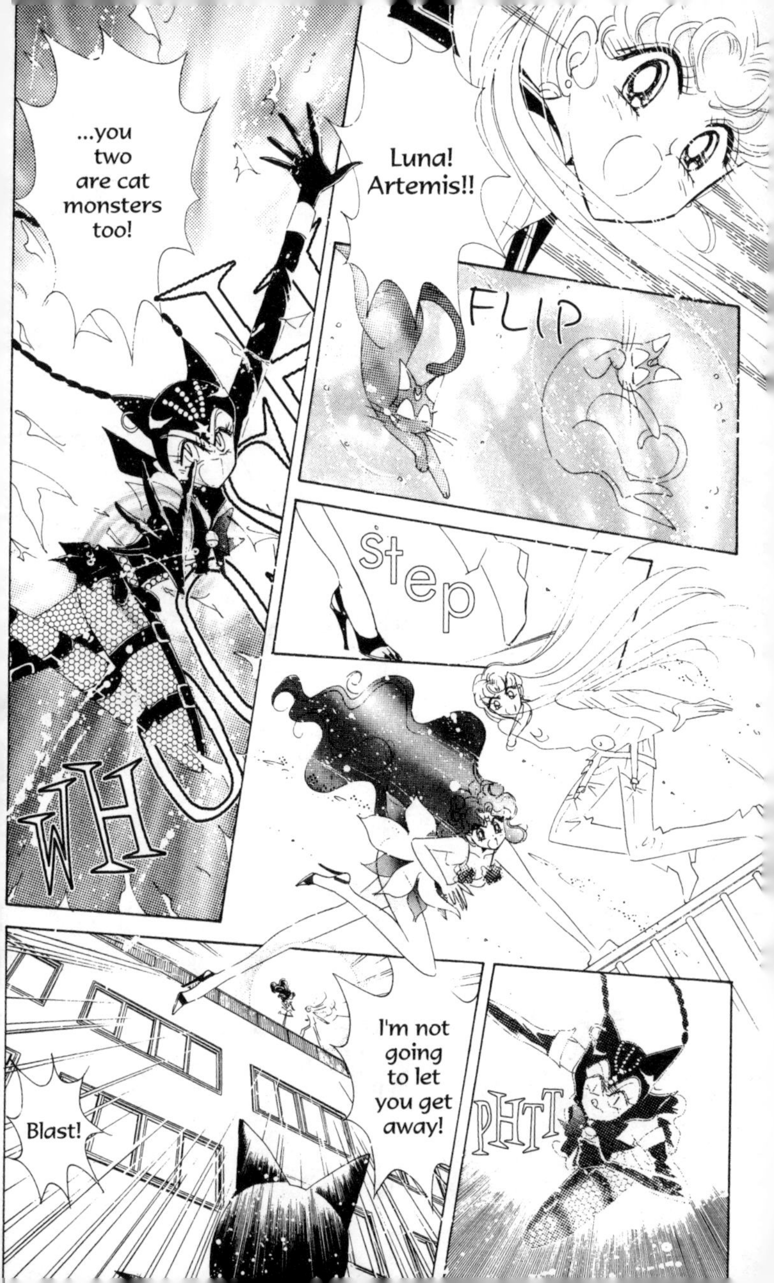
...you two are cat monsters too!
WH
Luna! Artemis!!
FLIP
step
Blast!
I'm not going to let you get away!
PHTT

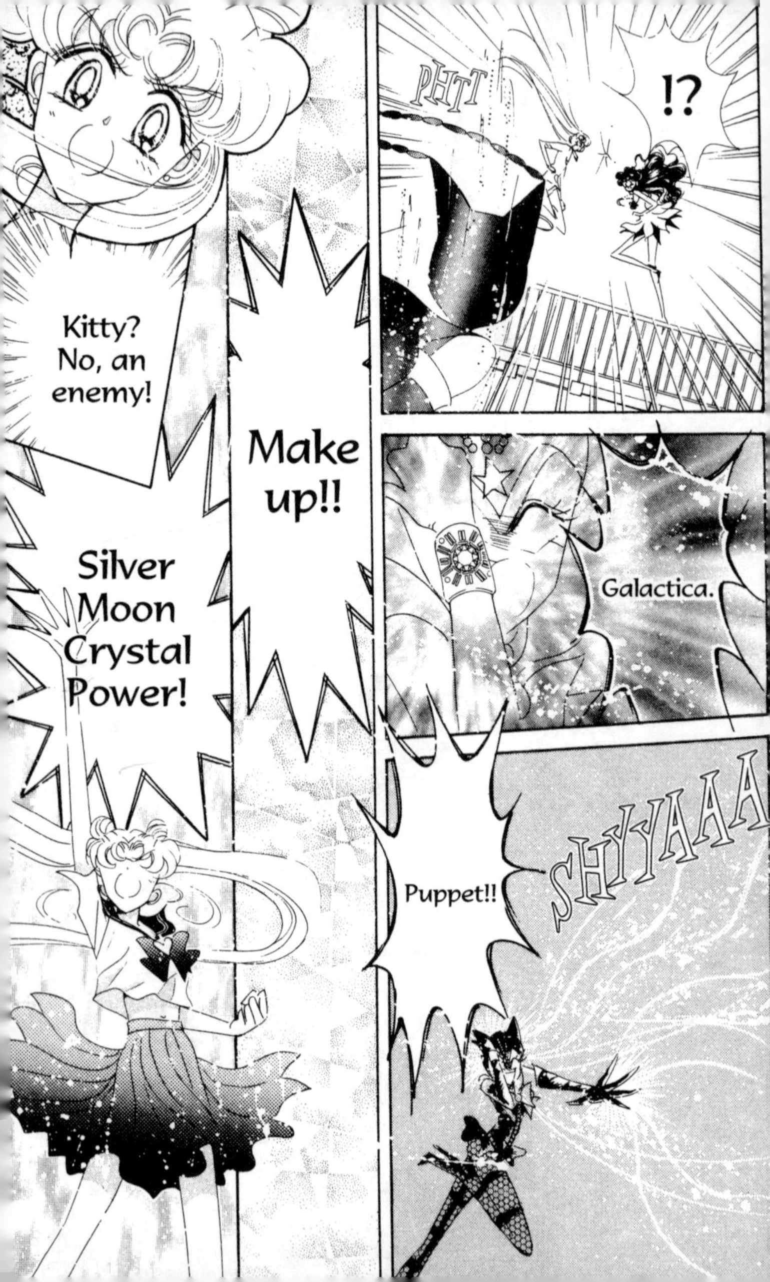
Kitty? No, an enemy!
Silver Moon Crystal Power!
Make up!!
PHTT
!?
Galactica.
Puppet!!
SHYYAAA

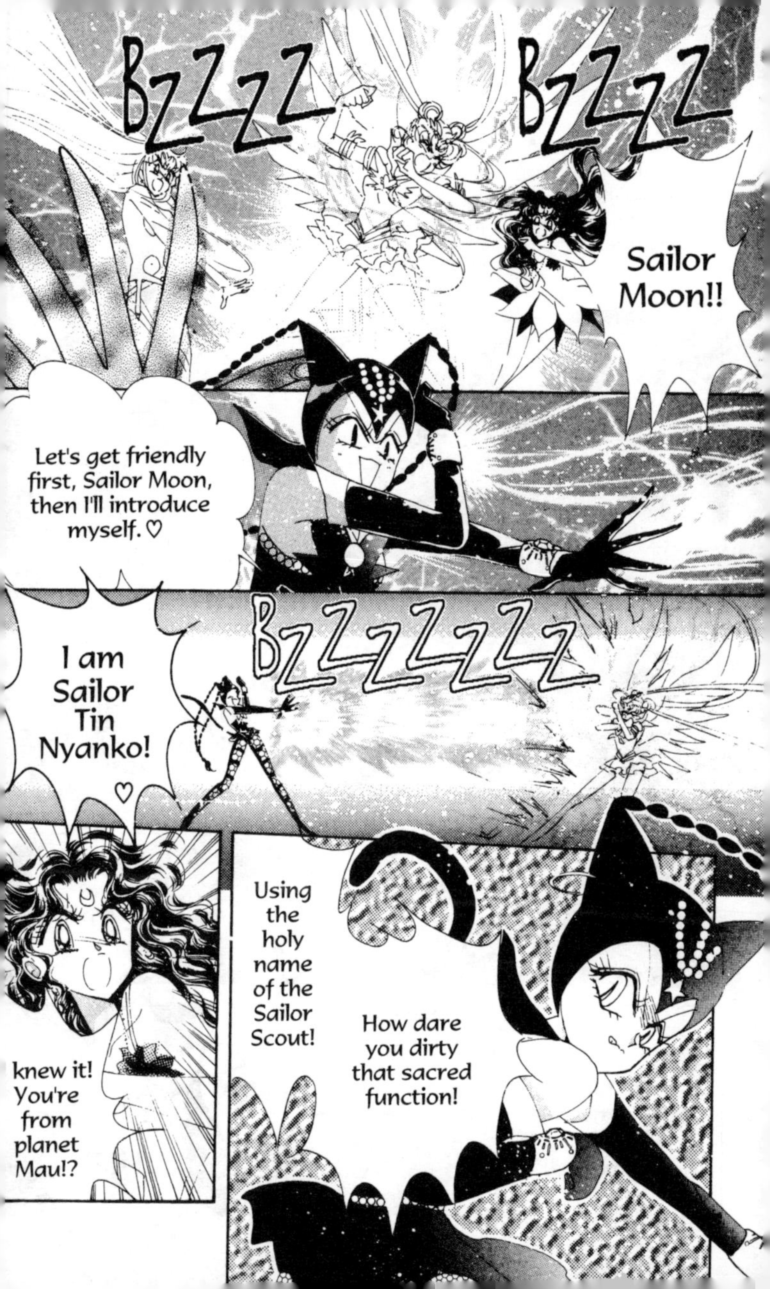
BZZZZ
BZZZZ
Sailor Moon!!
Let's get friendly first, Sailor Moon, then I'll introduce myself. ♡
I am Sailor Tin Nyanko! ♡
BZZZZZZZ
knew it! You're from planet Mau!?
Using the holy name of the Sailor Scout!
How dare you dirty that sacred function!

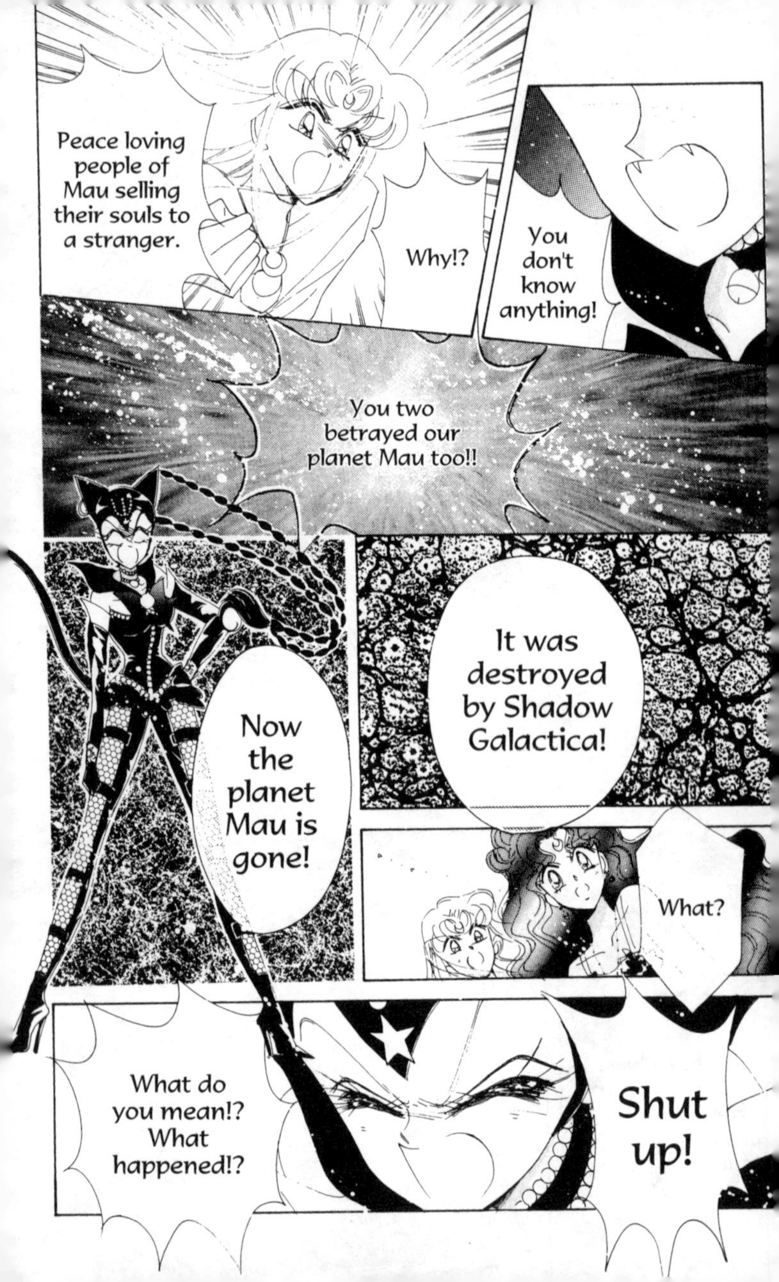
Peace loving people of Mau selling their souls to a stranger.
Why!?
You don't know anything!
You two betrayed our planet Mau too!!
Now the planet Mau is gone!
It was destroyed by Shadow Galactica!
What?
What do you mean!? What happened!?
Shut up!

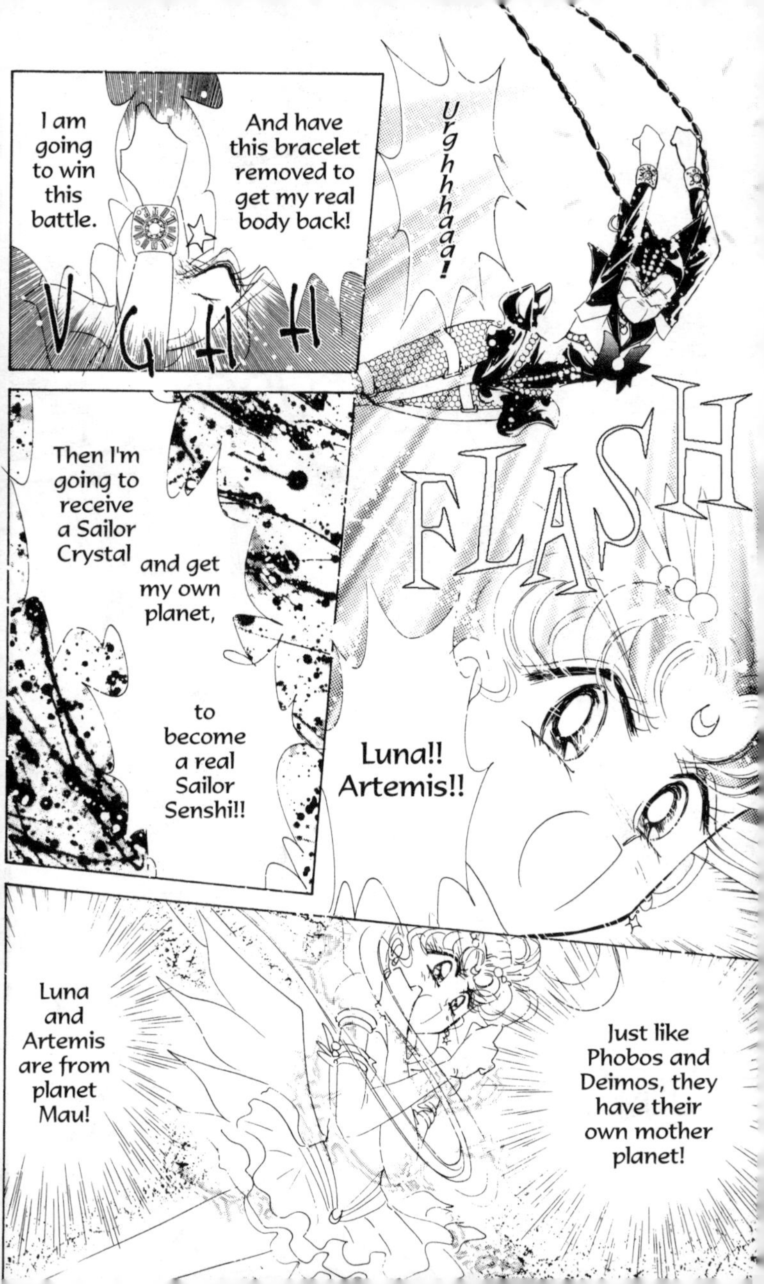
I am going to win this battle.
And have this bracelet removed to get my real body back!
VGHH
Urghhhaaa!
Then I'm going to receive a Sailor Crystal
and get my own planet,
to become a real Sailor Senshi!!
FLASH
Luna!! Artemis!!
Luna and Artemis are from planet Mau!
Just like Phobos and Deimos, they have their own mother planet!

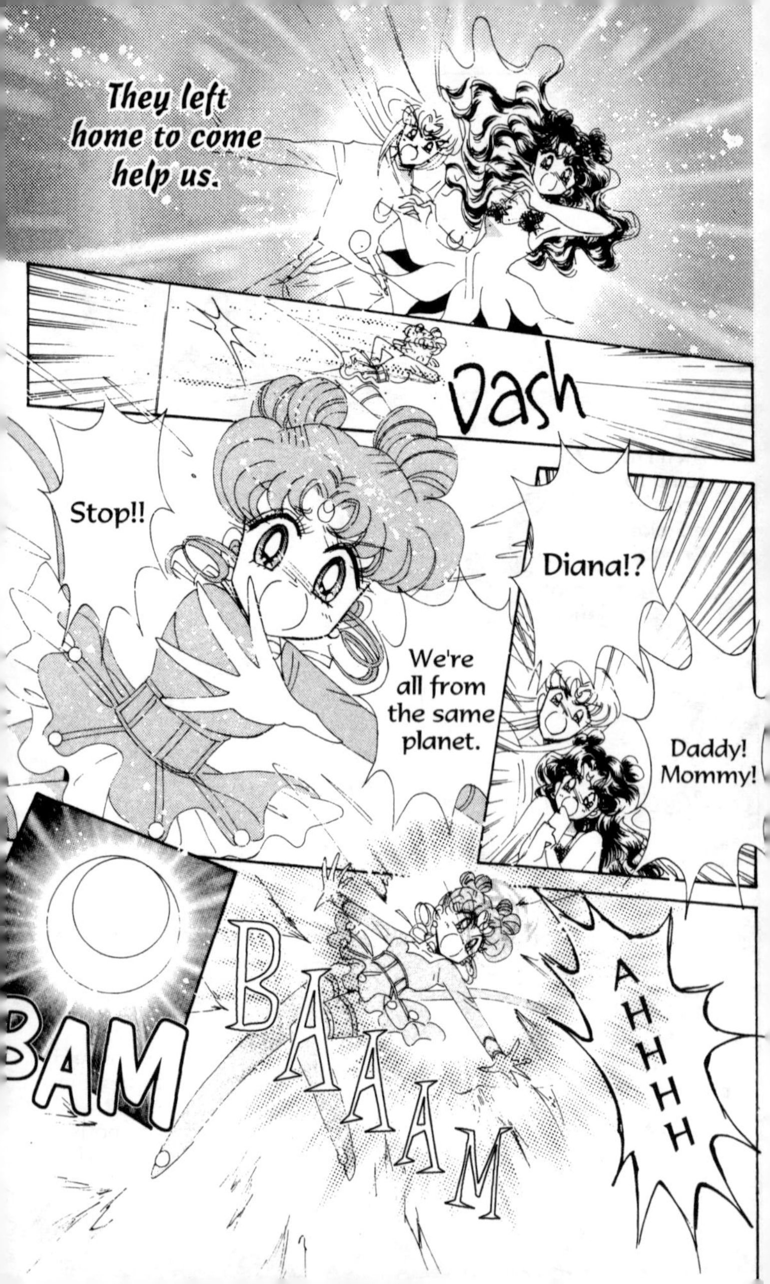
They left home to come help us.
Dash
Stop!!
We're all from the same planet.
Diana!?
Daddy! Mommy!
BAM
BAAAM
AHHHH

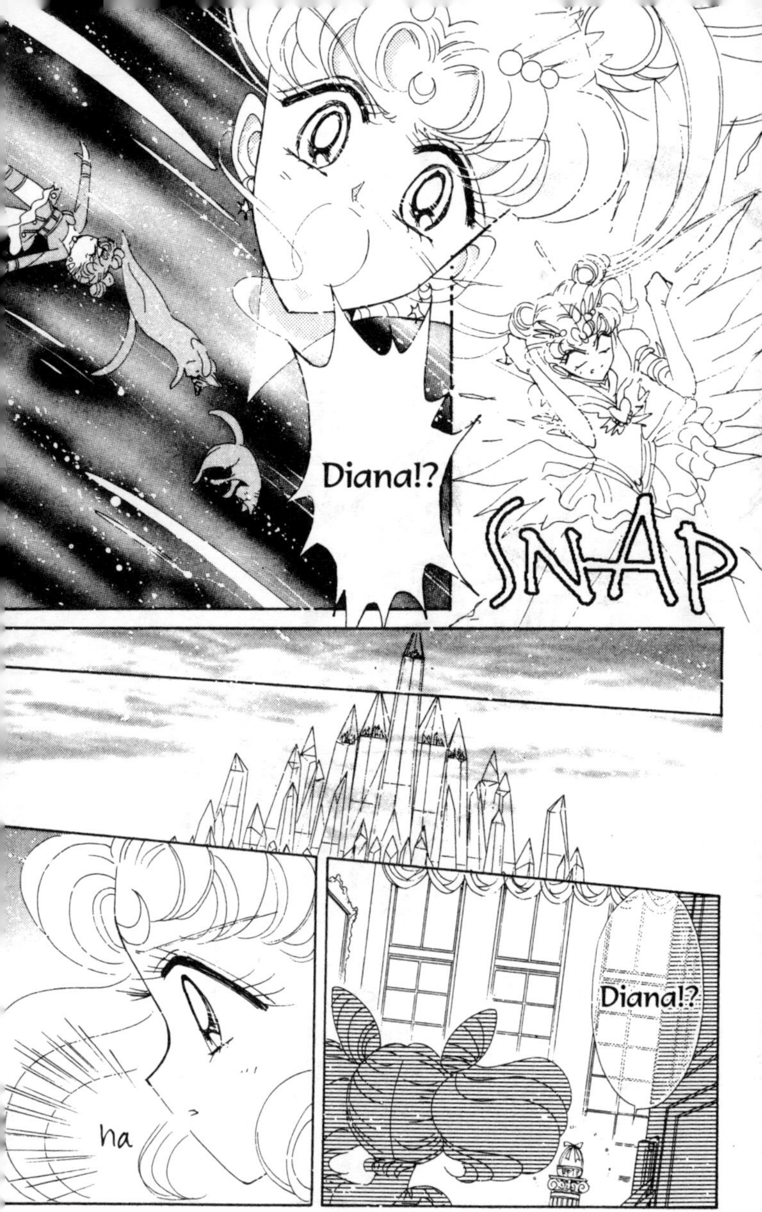
Diana!?
SNAP
ha
Diana!?

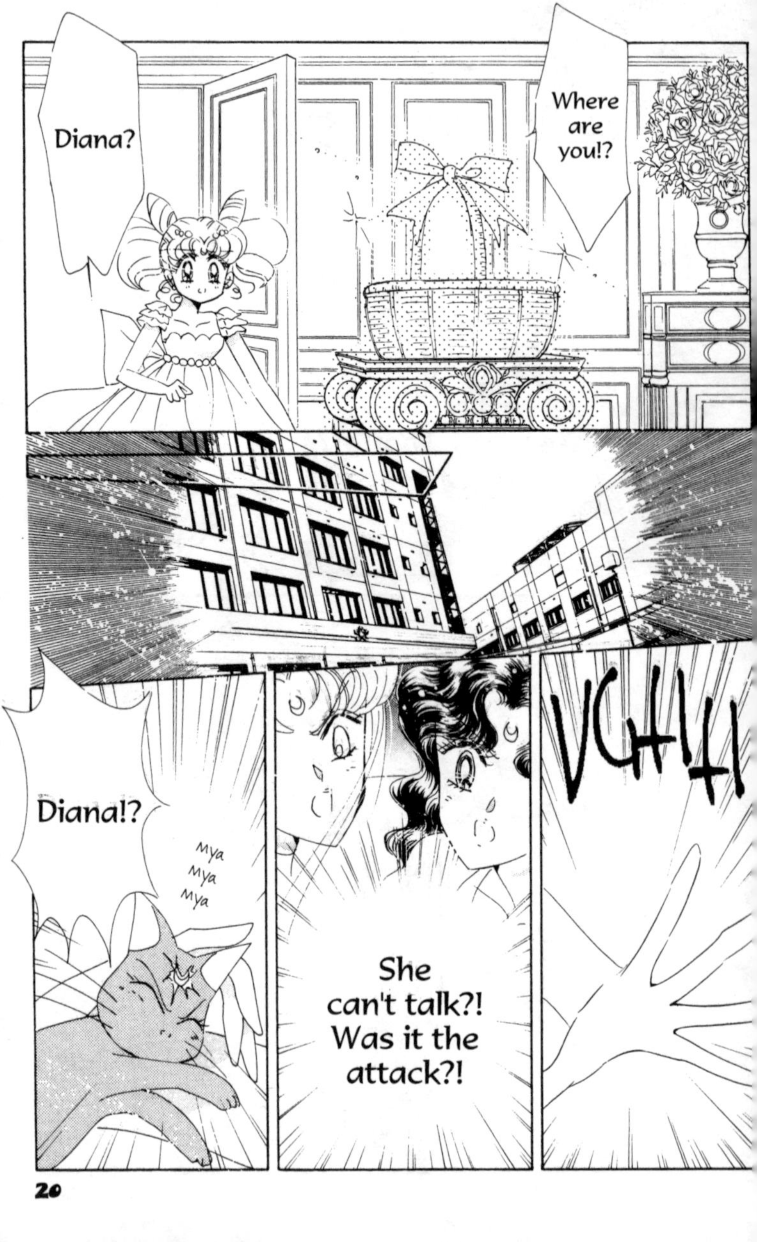
Diana?
Where are you!?
Diana!?
Mya Mya Mya
She can't talk?! Was it the attack?!

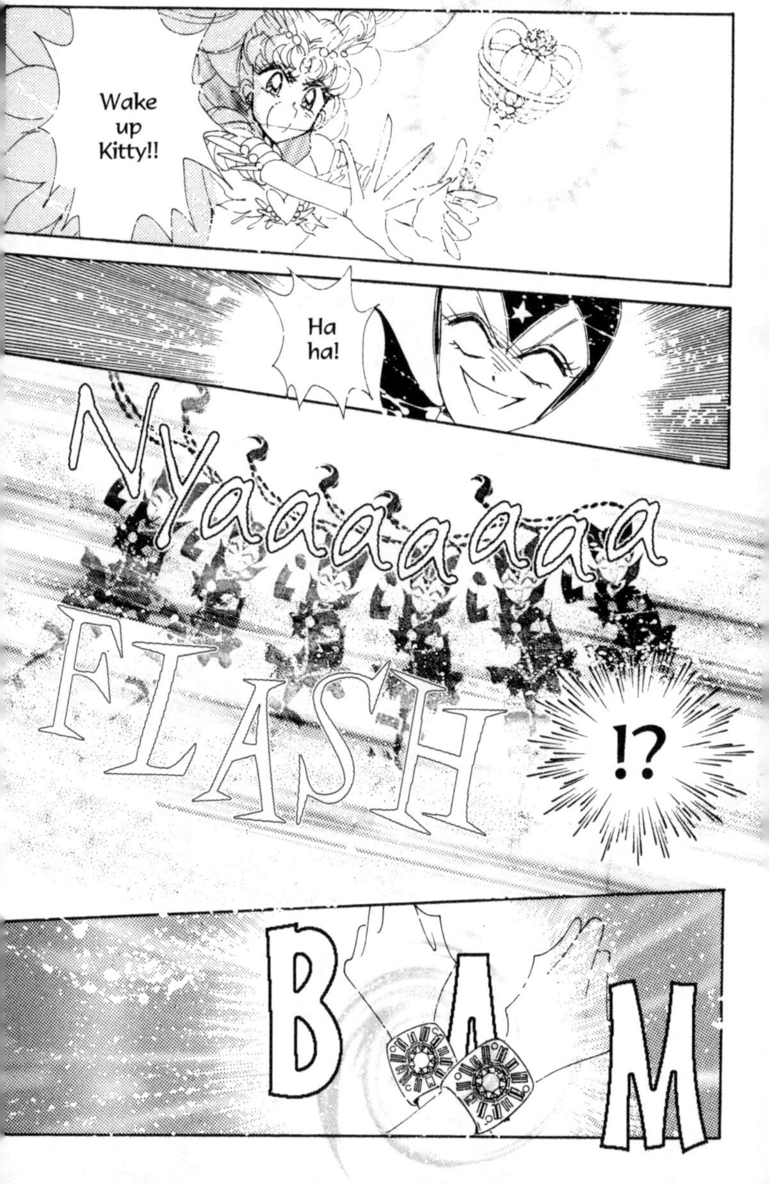

Wake up Kitty!!
Ha ha!
Nyaaaaaaa
FLASH
!?
BAM

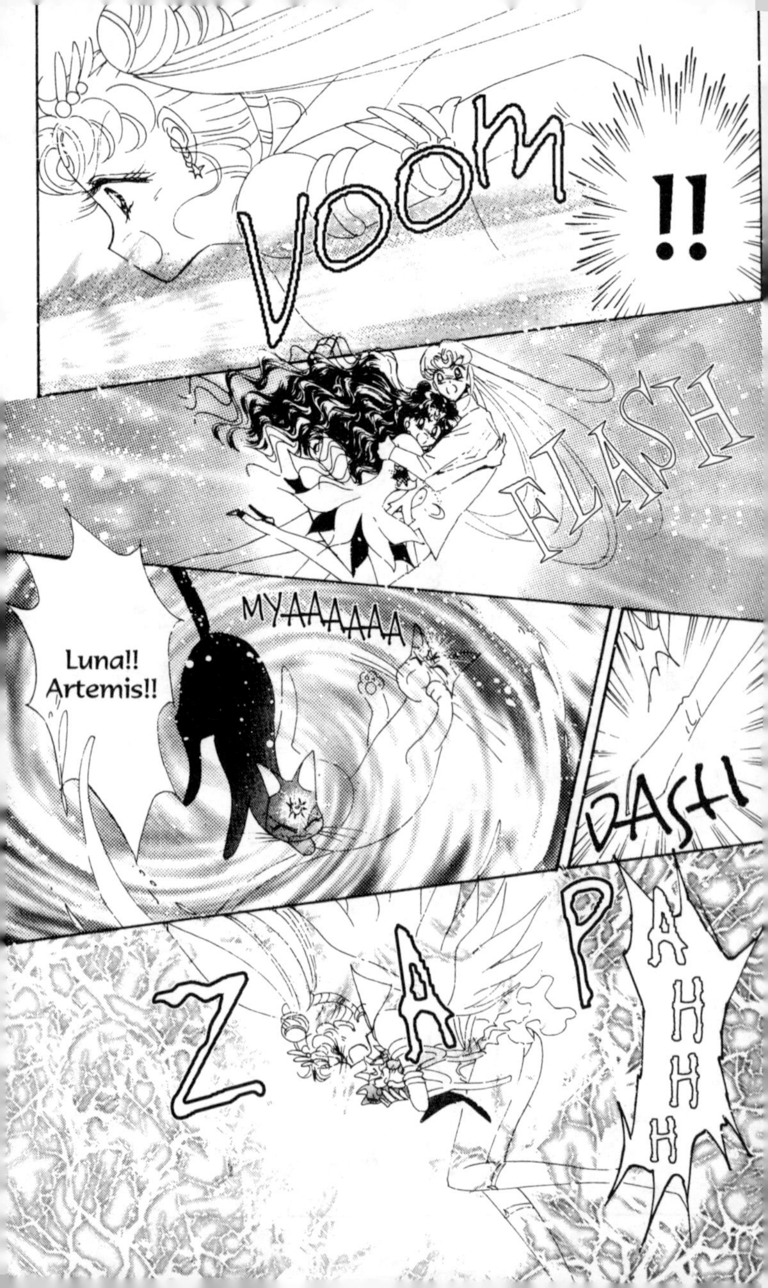
VOOM
!!
FLASH
Luna!!
Artemis!!
MYAAAAAAA
DASH
ZAP
PAHHHH

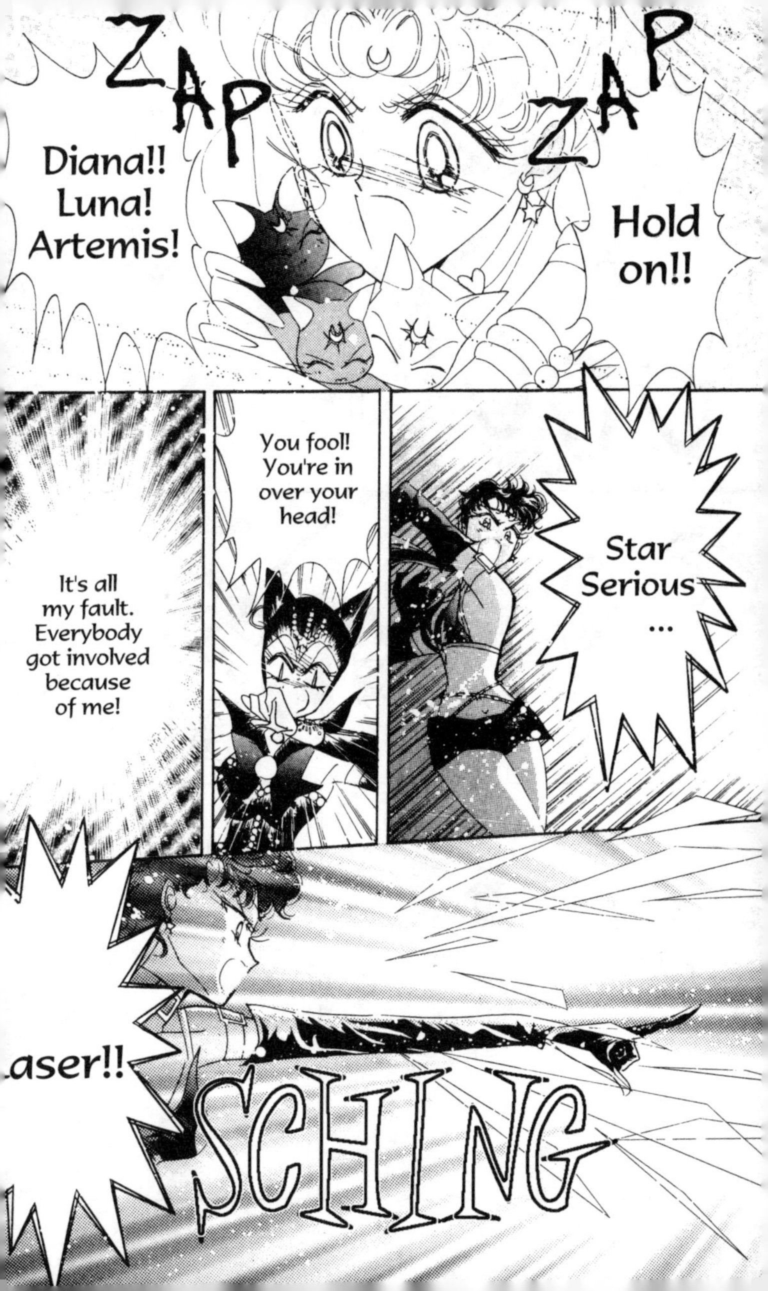

ZAP
Diana!! Luna! Artemis!
ZAP
Hold on!!
It's all my fault. Everybody got involved because of me!
You fool! You're in over your head!
Star Serious ...
aser!!
SCHING

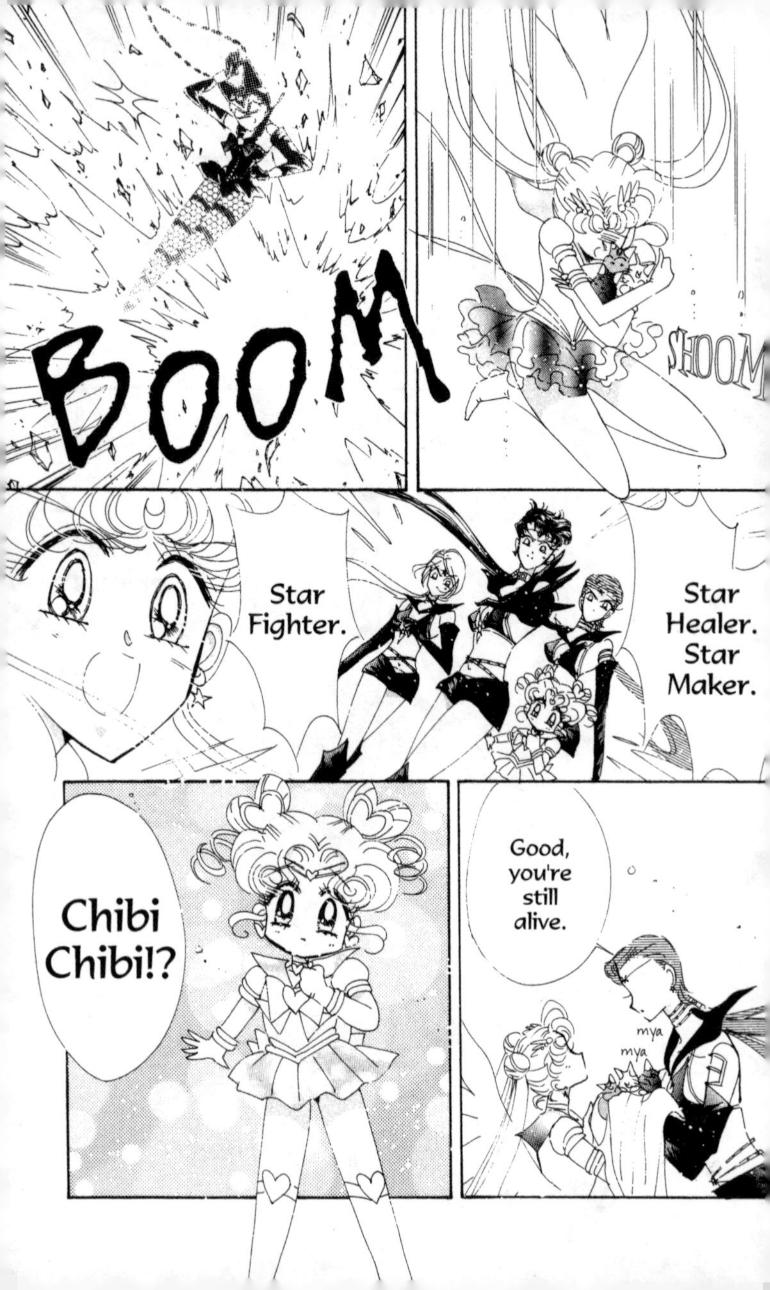
BOOM
SHOOM
Star Fighter.
Star Healer. Star Maker.
Chibi Chibi!?
Good, you're still alive.
mya
mya

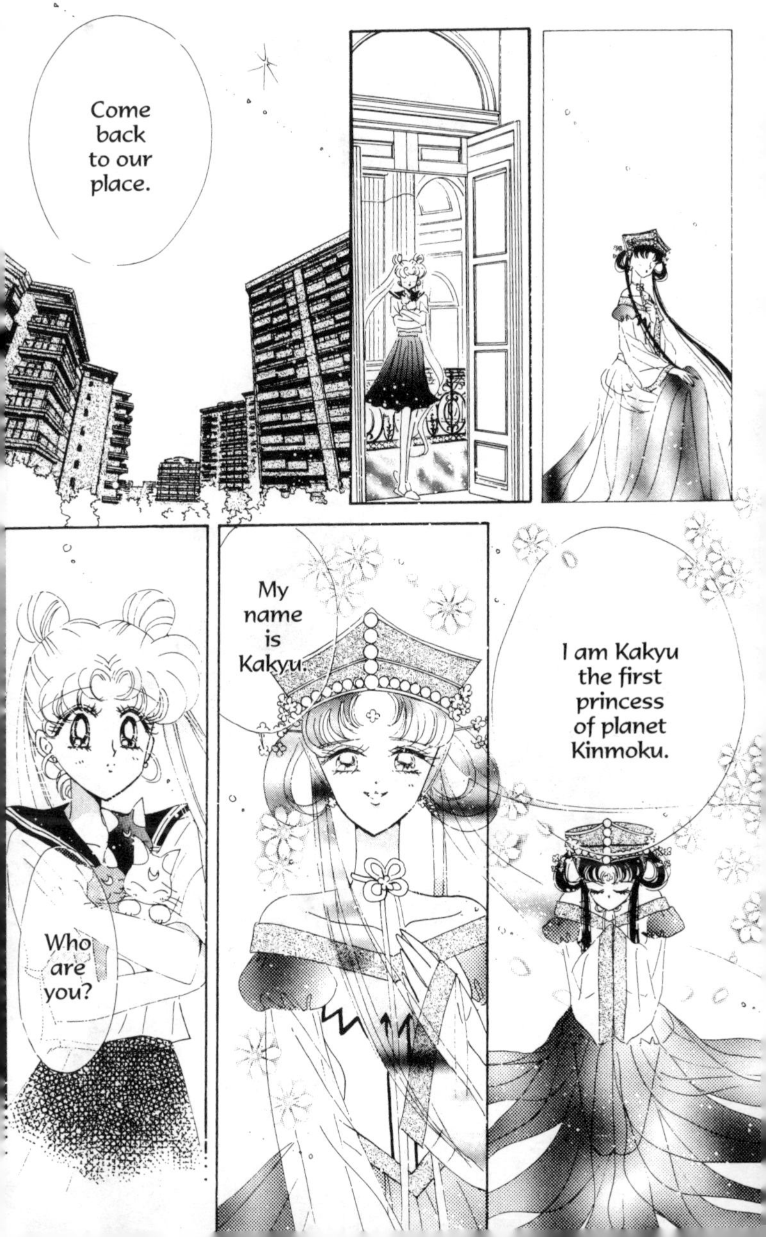
Come back to our place.
Who are you?
My name is Kakyu.
I am Kakyu the first princess of planet Kinmoku.

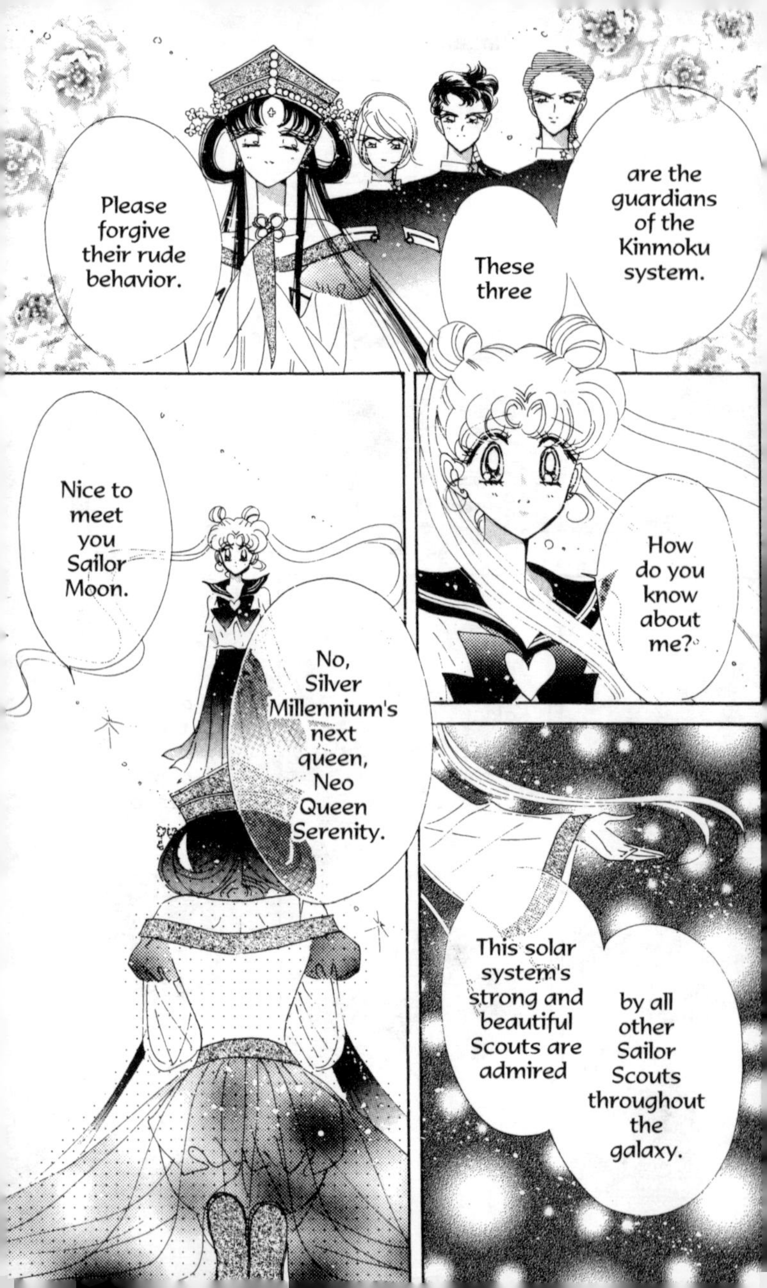
Please forgive their rude behavior.
These three
are the guardians of the Kinmoku system.
Nice to meet you Sailor Moon.
No, Silver Millennium's next queen, Neo Queen Serenity.
How do you know about me?
This solar system's strong and beautiful Scouts are admired
by all other Sailor Scouts throughout the galaxy.

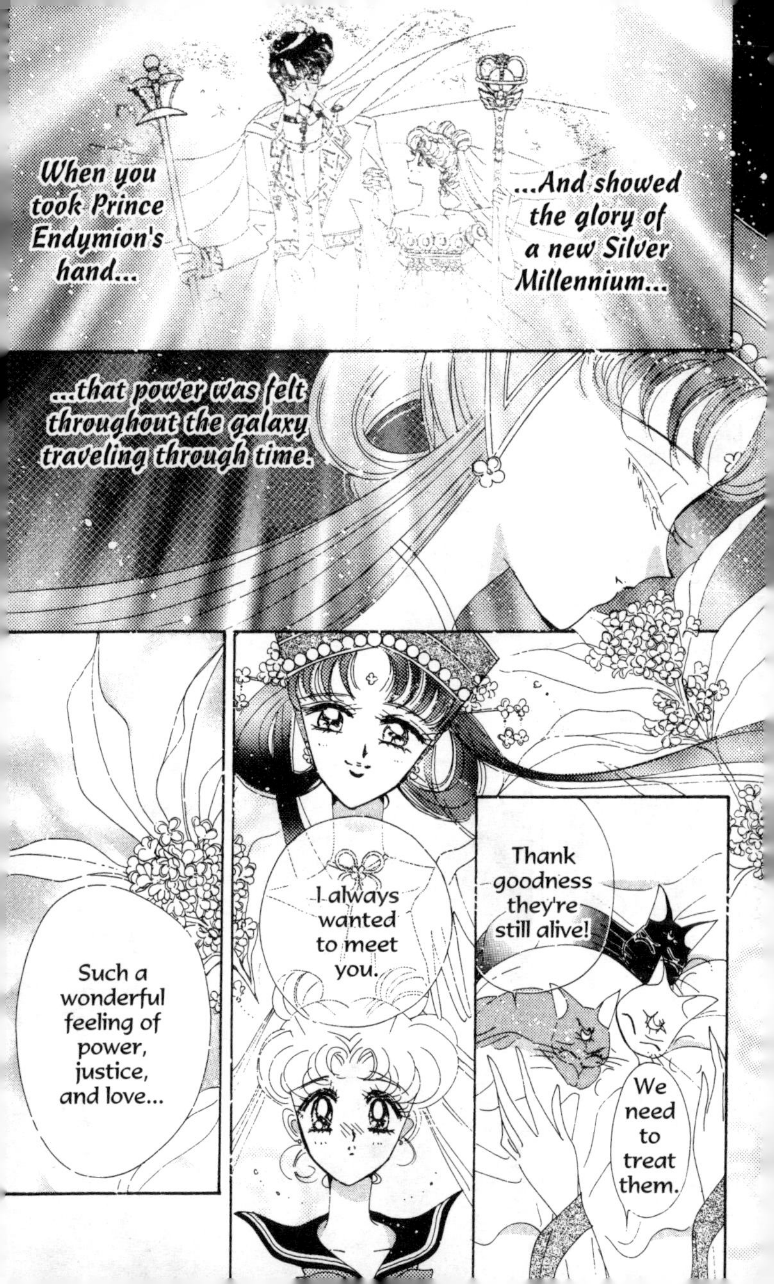
When you took Prince Endymion's hand...
...And showed the glory of a new Silver Millennium...
...that power was felt throughout the galaxy traveling through time.
Such a wonderful feeling of power, justice, and love...
I always wanted to meet you.
Thank goodness they're still alive!
We need to treat them.

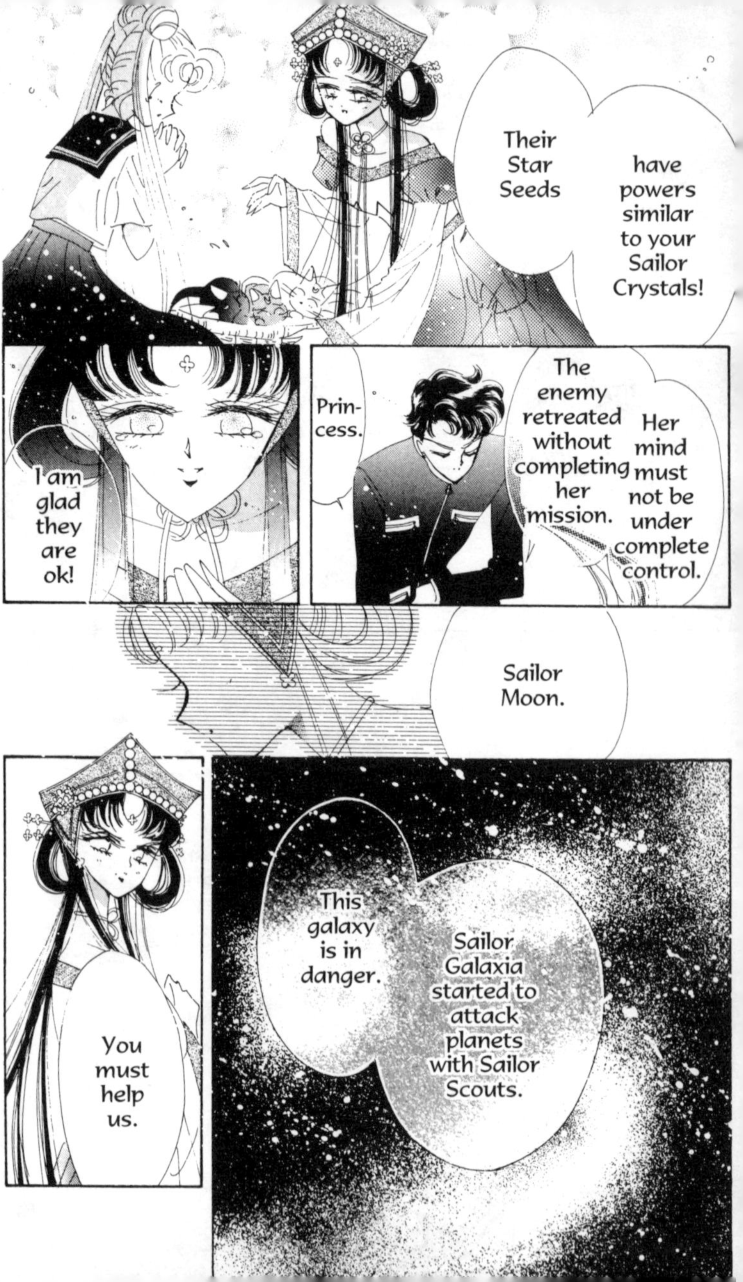
Their Star Seeds
have powers similar to your Sailor Crystals!
I am glad they are ok!
Prin-cess.
The enemy retreated without completing her mission.
Her mind must not be under complete control.
Sailor Moon.
You must help us.
This galaxy is in danger.
Sailor Galaxia started to attack planets with Sailor Scouts.

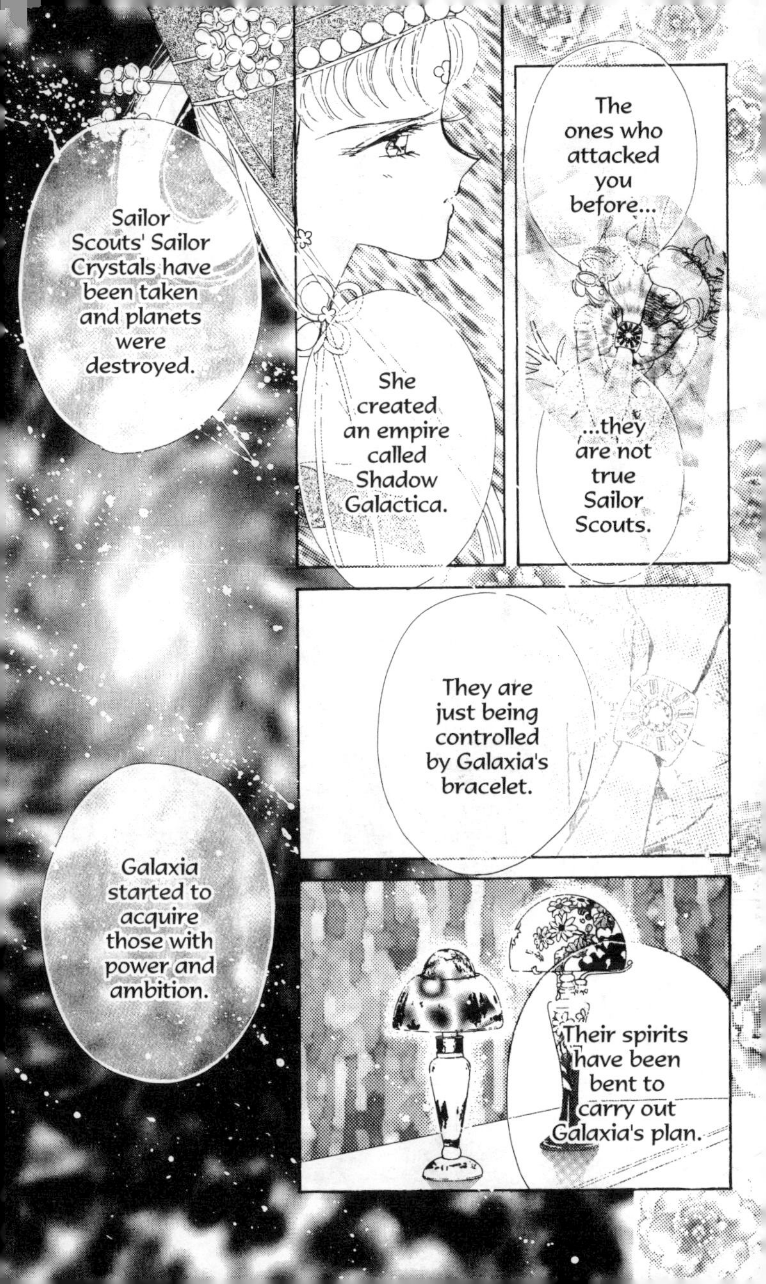

Sailor Scouts' Sailor Crystals have been taken and planets were destroyed.
Galaxia started to acquire those with power and ambition.
She created an empire called Shadow Galactica.
The ones who attacked you before...
...they are not true Sailor Scouts.
They are just being controlled by Galaxia's bracelet.
Their spirits have been bent to carry out Galaxia's plan.

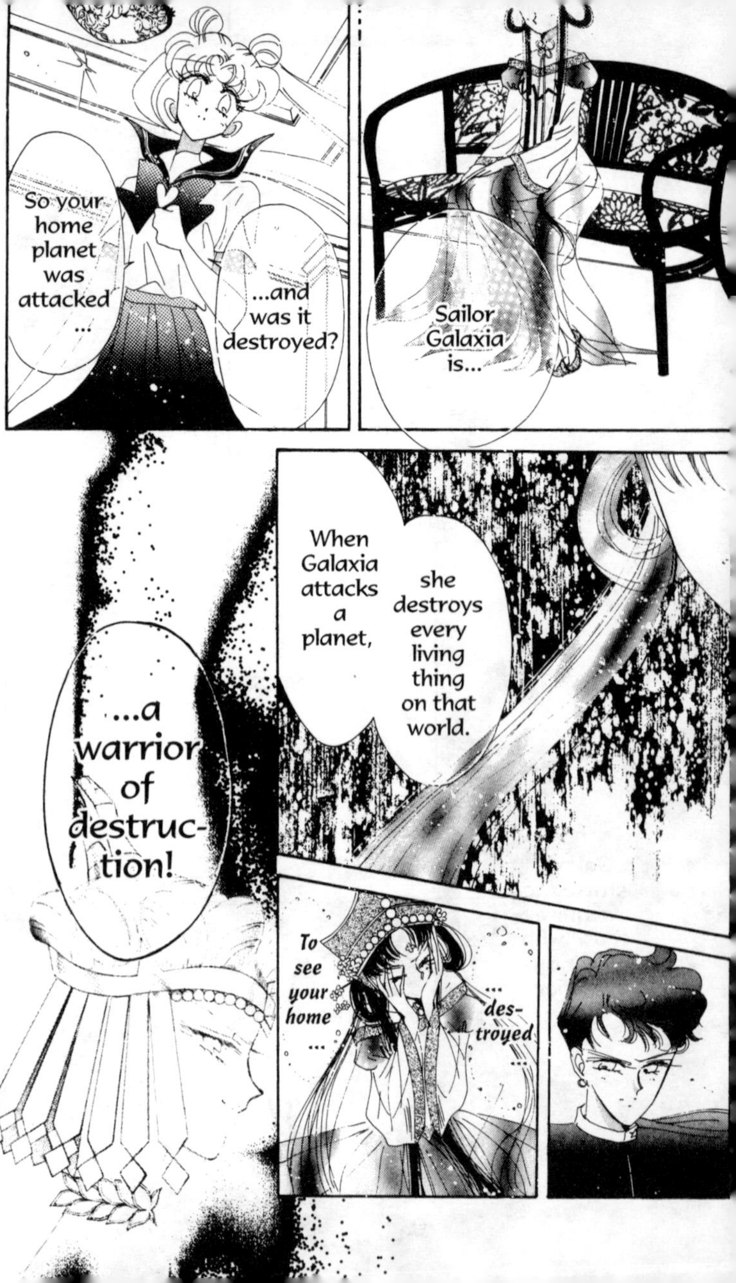

So your home planet was attacked ...
...and was it destroyed?
Sailor Galaxia is...
...a warrior of destruc-tion!
When Galaxia attacks a planet,
she destroys every living thing on that world.
To see your home ...
... des-troyed ...

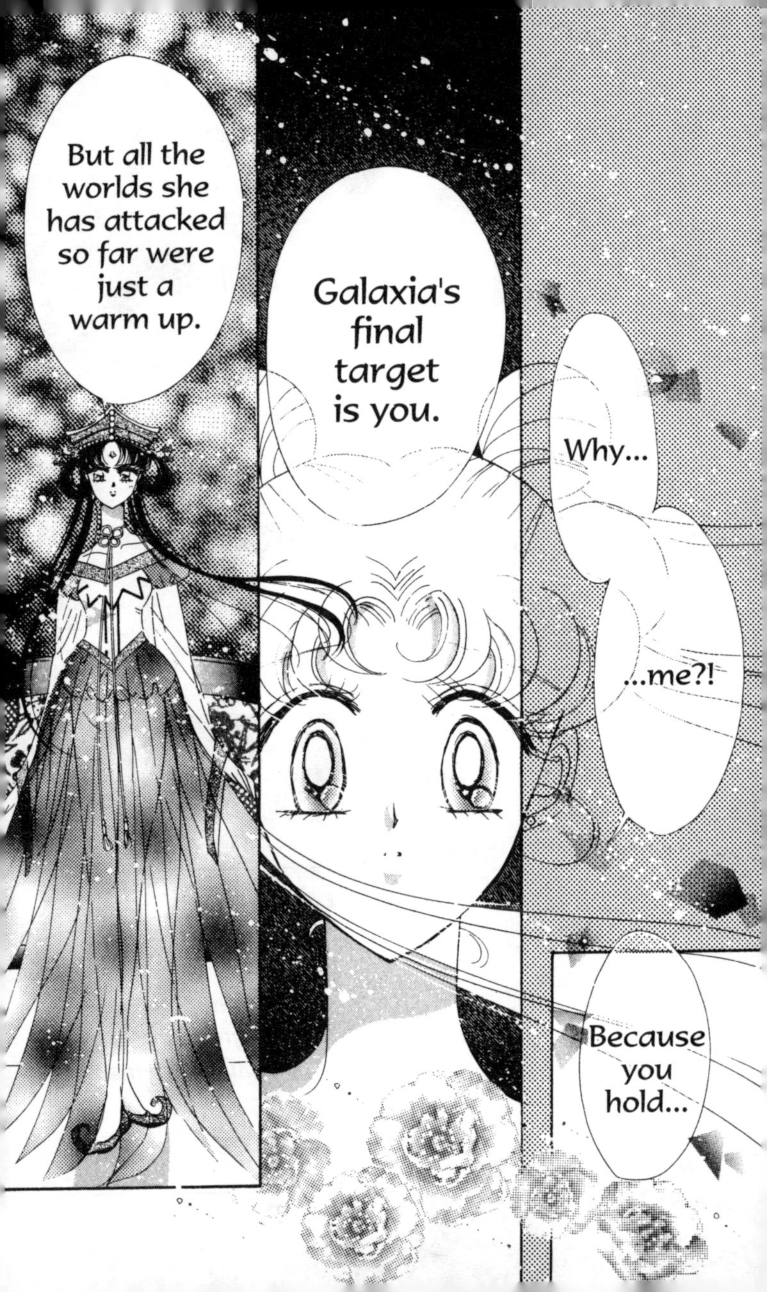

But all the worlds she has attacked so far were just a warm up.
Galaxia's final target is you.
Why...
...me?!
Because you hold...

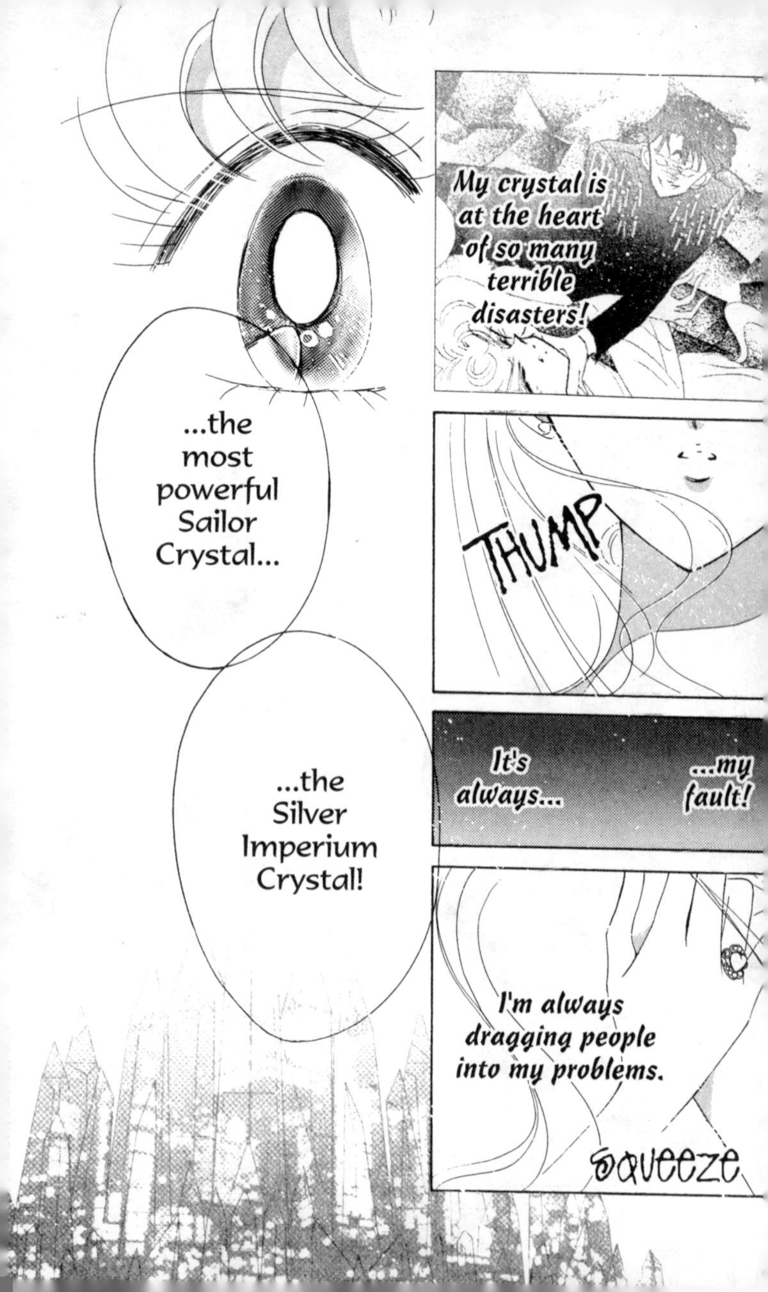
...the most powerful Sailor Crystal...
...the Silver Imperium Crystal!
My crystal is at the heart of so many terrible disasters!
THUMP
It's always...
...my fault!
I'm always dragging people into my problems.
SQUEEZE

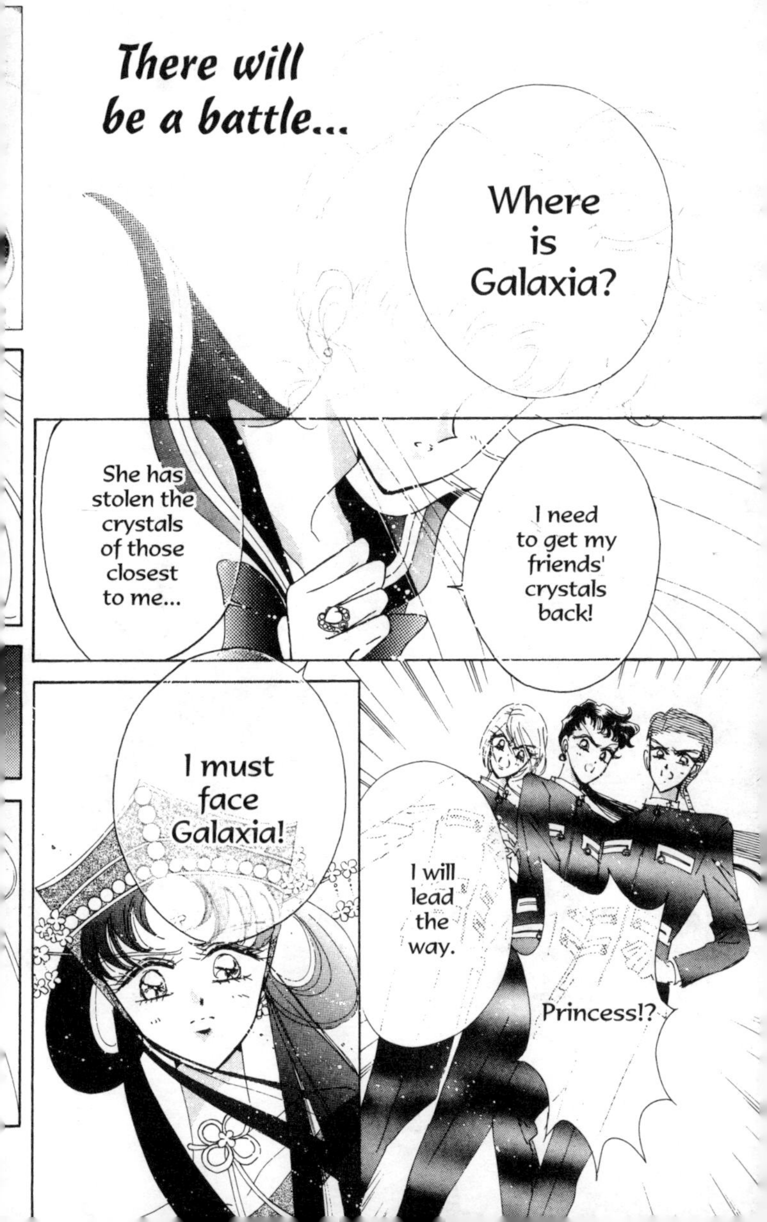
There will be a battle...
Where is Galaxia?
She has stolen the crystals of those closest to me...
I need to get my friends' crystals back!
I must face Galaxia!
I will lead the way.
Princess!?

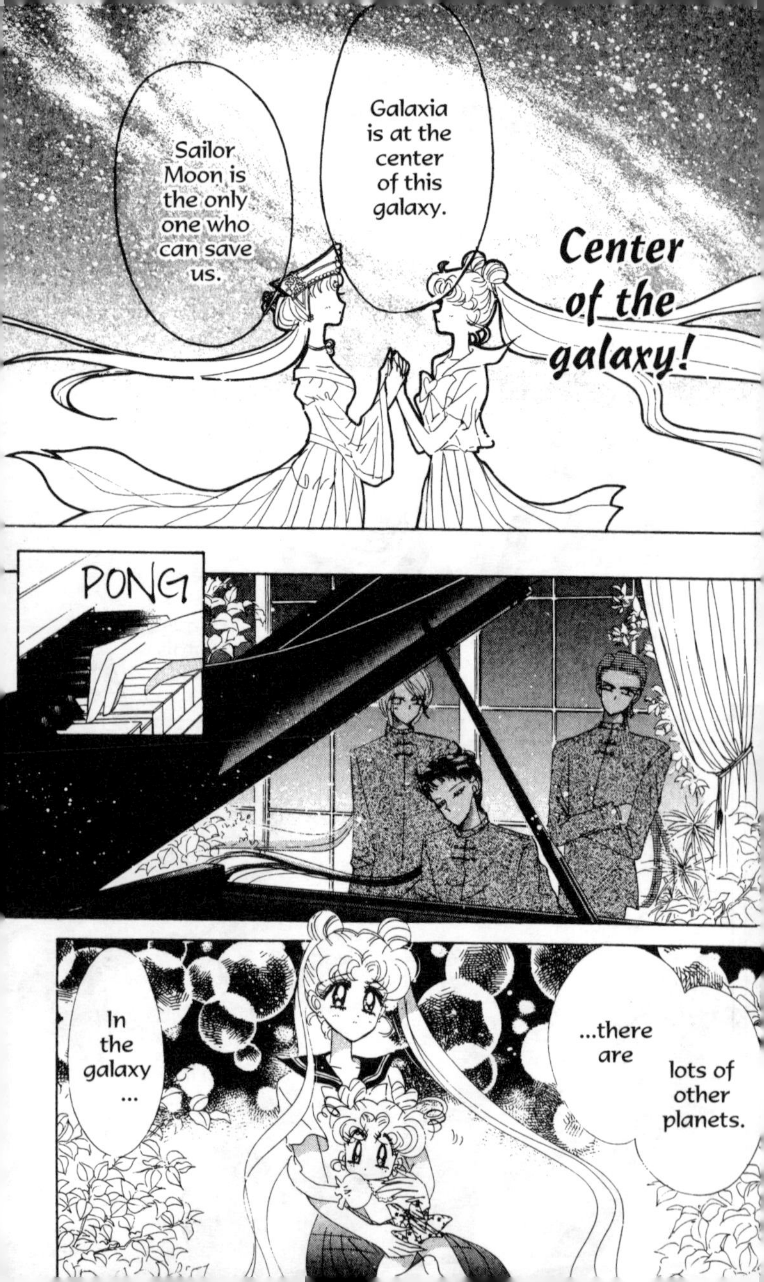

Sailor Moon is the only one who can save us.
Galaxia is at the center of this galaxy.
Center of the galaxy!
PONG
In the galaxy ...
...there are
lots of other planets.

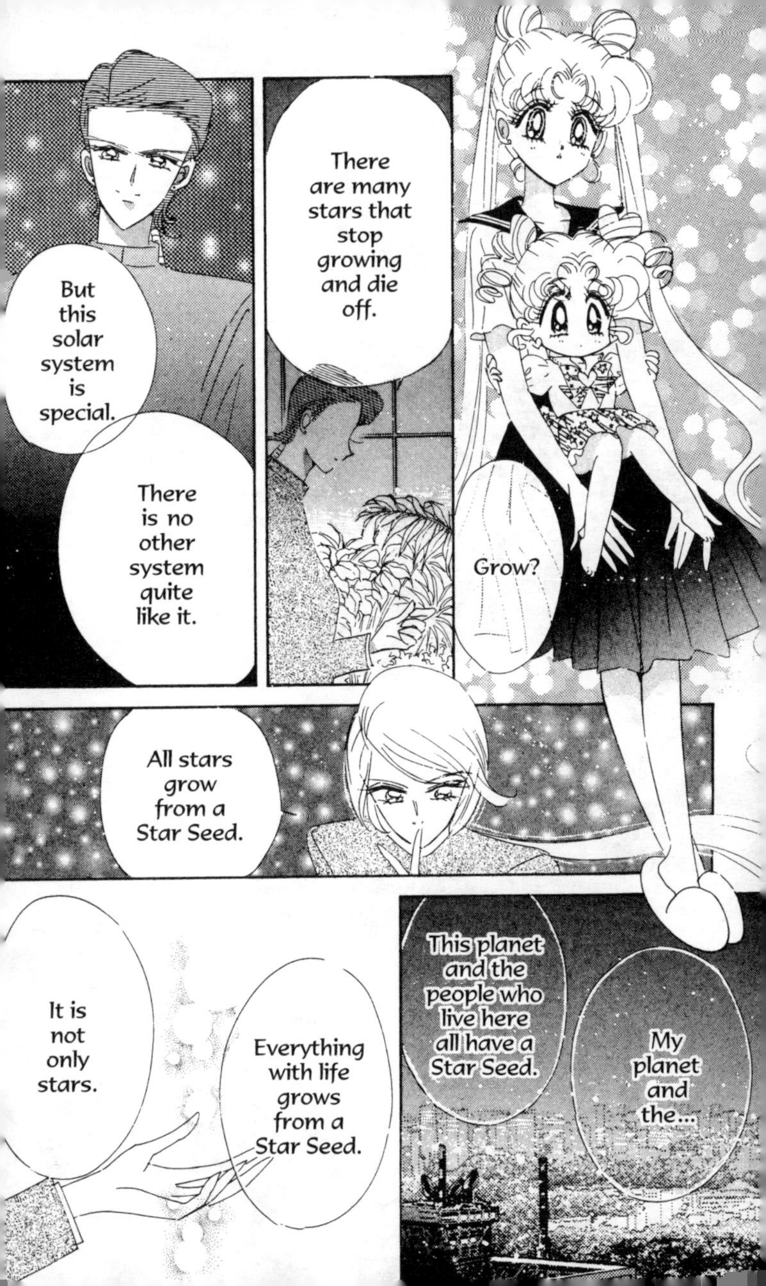

But this solar system is special.
There is no other system quite like it.
There are many stars that stop growing and die off.
Grow?
All stars grow from a Star Seed.
It is not only stars.
Everything with life grows from a Star Seed.
This planet and the people who live here all have a Star Seed.
My planet and the...

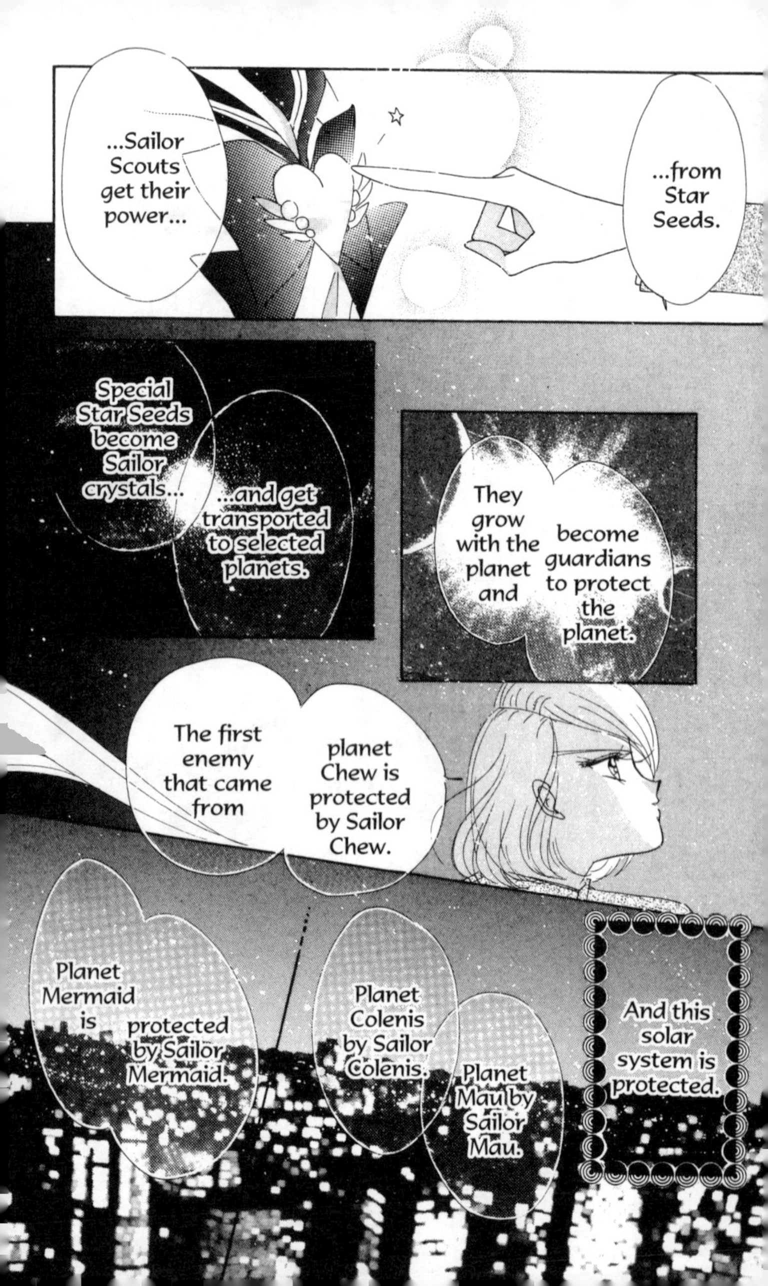
...Sailor Scouts get their power...
...from Star Seeds.
Special Star Seeds become Sailor crystals...
...and get transported to selected planets.
They grow with the planet and
become guardians to protect the planet.
The first enemy that came from
planet Chew is protected by Sailor Chew.
Planet Mermaid is
protected by Sailor Mermaid.
Planet Colenis by Sailor Colenis.
Planet Mau by Sailor Mau.
And this solar system is protected.

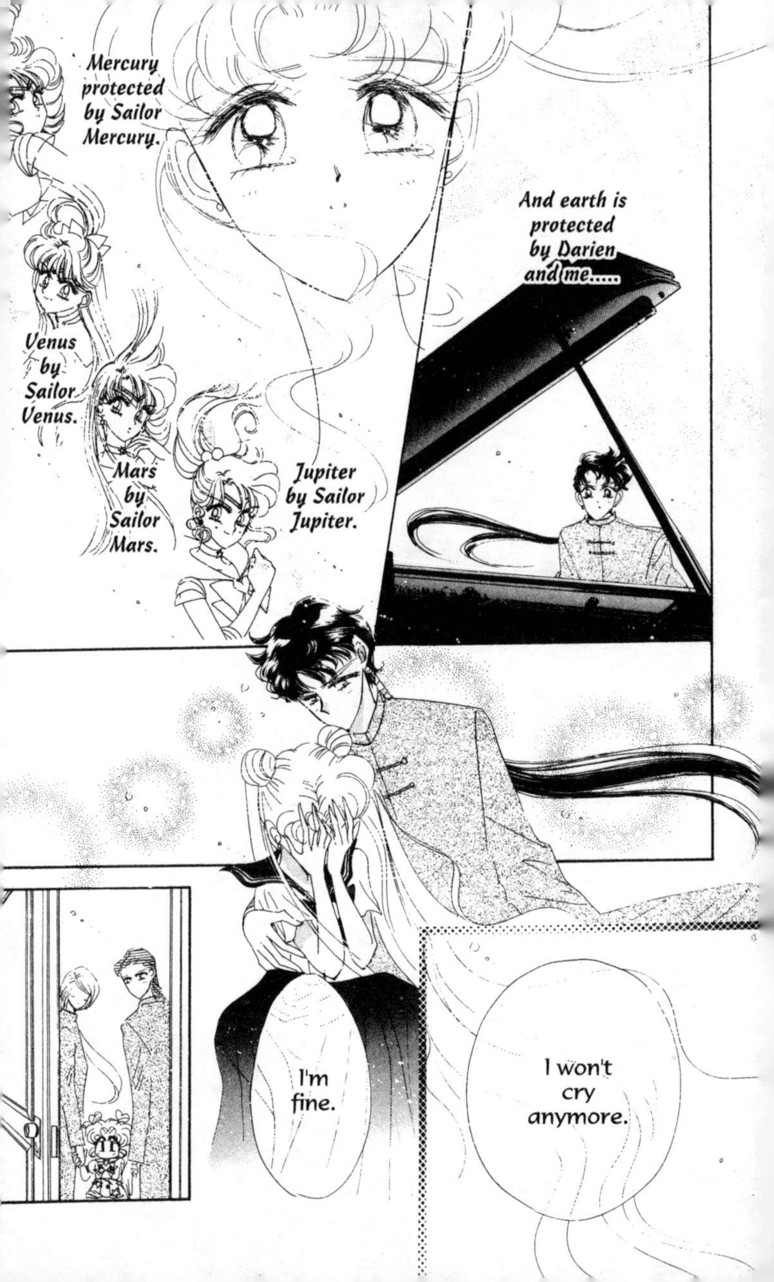

Mercury protected by Sailor Mercury.
Venus by Sailor Venus.
Mars by Sailor Mars.
Jupiter by Sailor Jupiter.
And earth is protected by Darien and me.....
I'm fine.
I won't cry anymore.

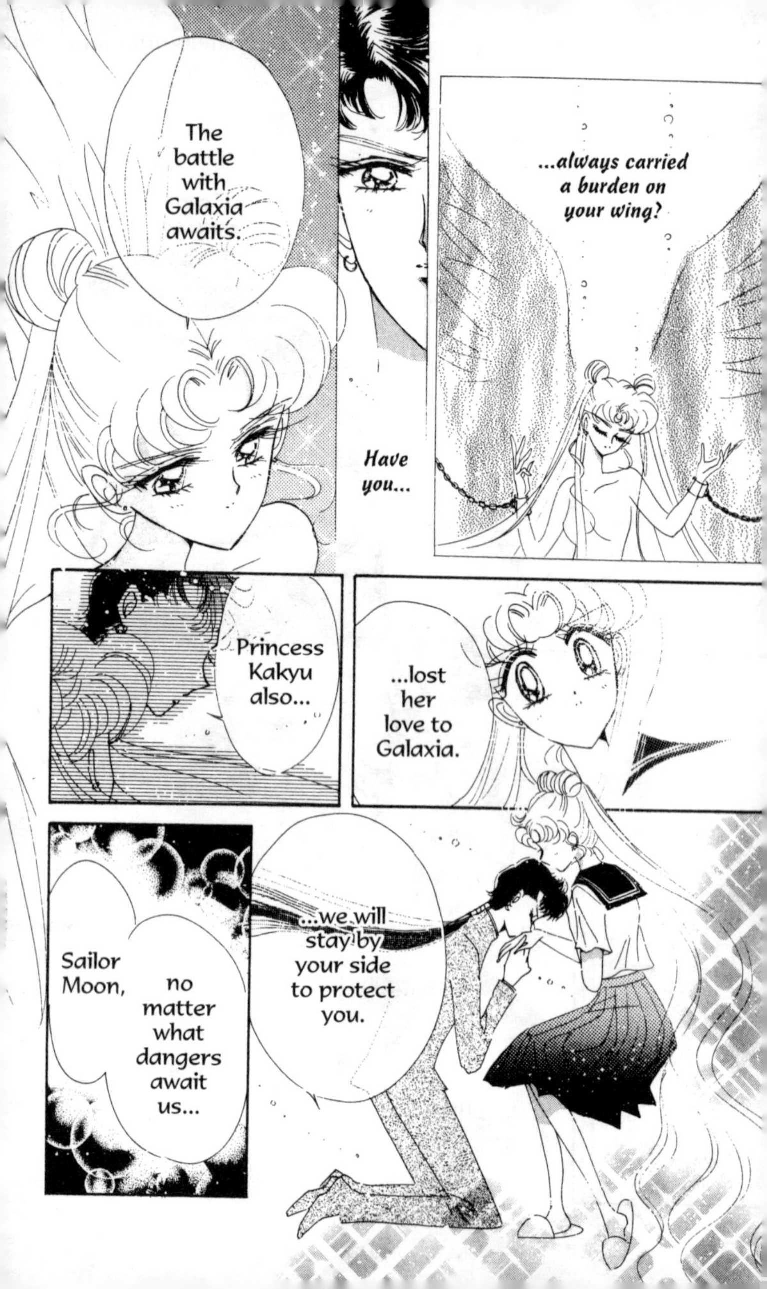
The battle with Galaxia awaits.
Have you...
...always carried a burden on your wing?
Princess Kakyu also...
...lost her love to Galaxia.
Sailor Moon,
no matter what dangers await us...
...we will stay by your side to protect you.

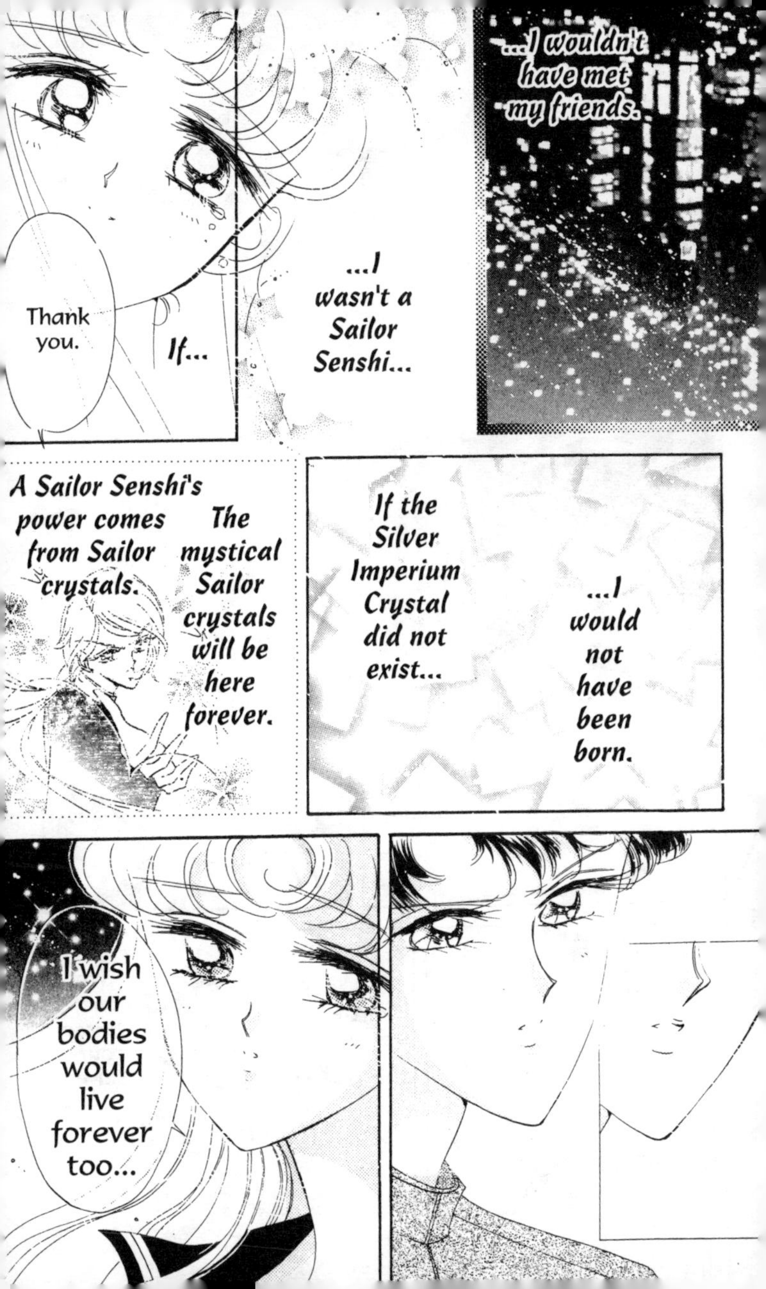
Thank you.
If...
...I wasn't a Sailor Senshi...
...I wouldn't have met my friends.
A Sailor Senshi's power comes from Sailor crystals.
The mystical Sailor crystals will be here forever.
If the Silver Imperium Crystal did not exist...
...I would not have been born.
I wish our bodies would live forever too...

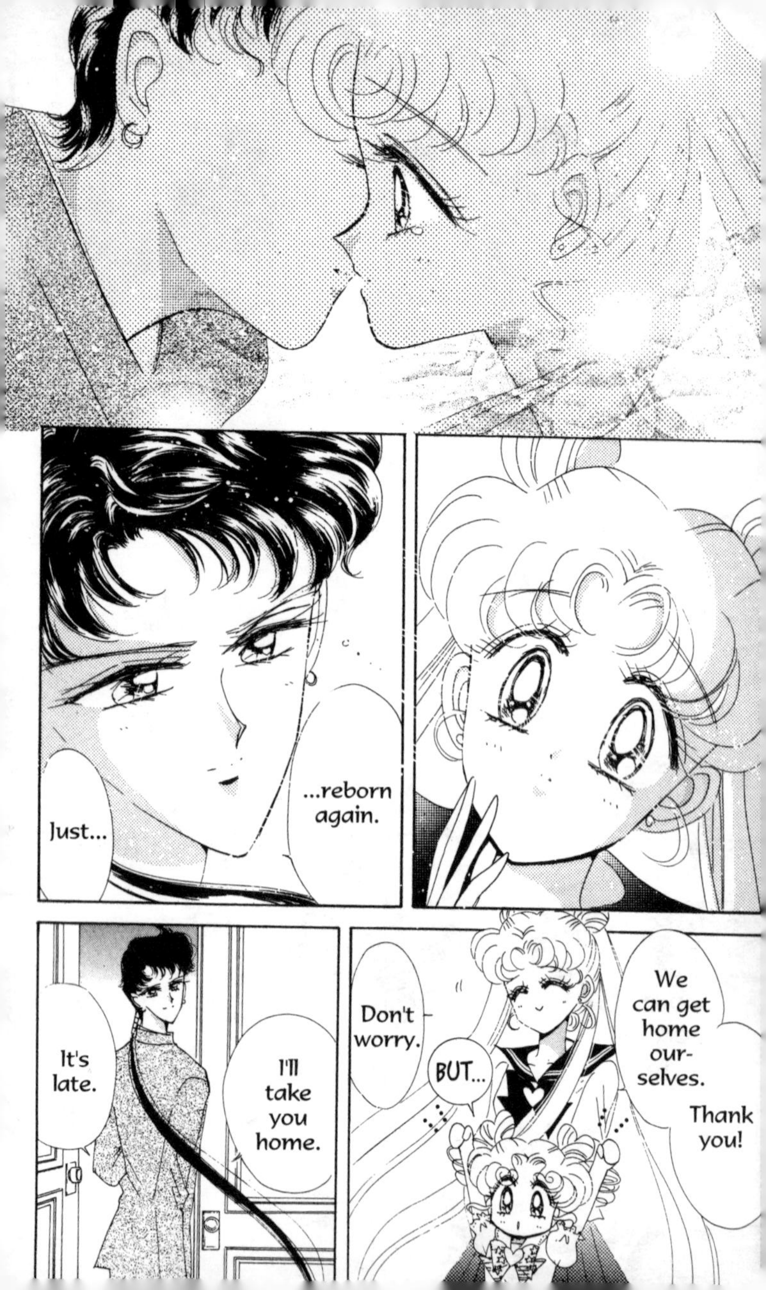
Just...
...reborn again.
It's late.
I'll take you home.
Don't worry.
BUT...
We can get home our-selves.
Thank you!

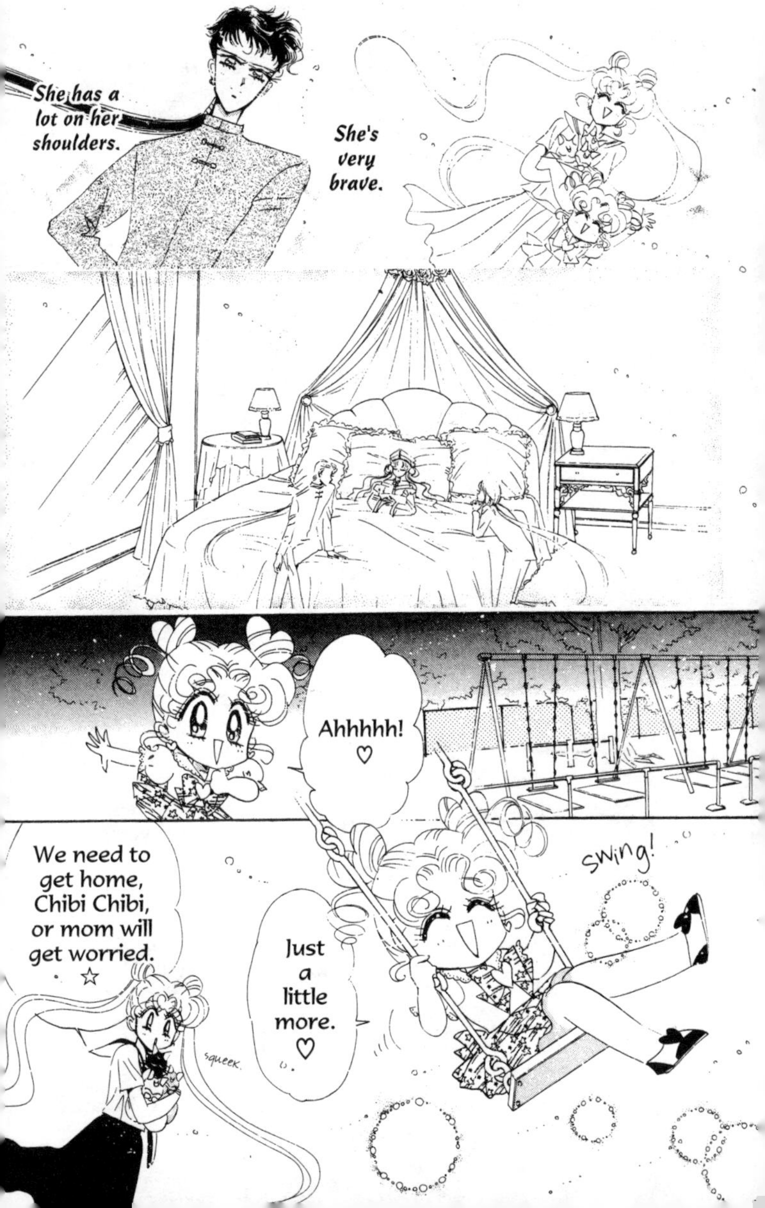
She has a lot on her shoulders.
She's very brave.
Ahhhhh! ♡
We need to get home, Chibi Chibi, or mom will get worried. ☆
squeek.
Just a little more. ♡
swing!

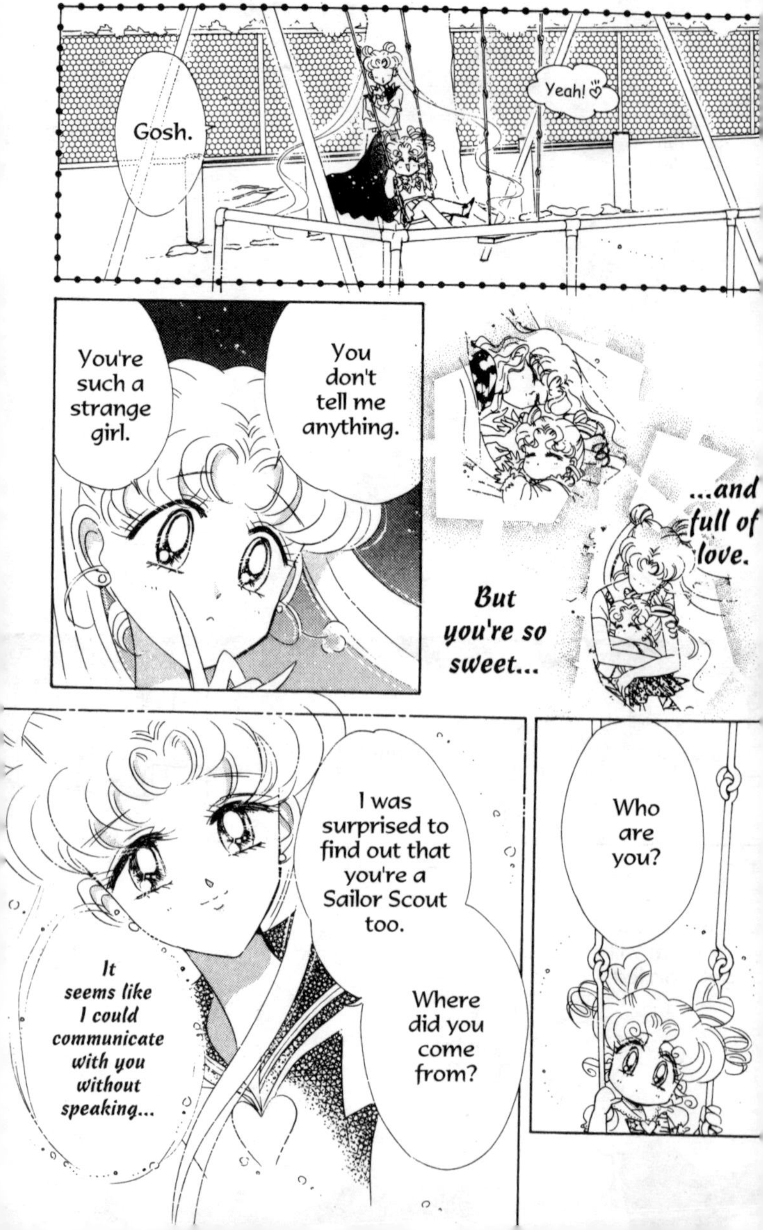
Gosh.
Yeah! ♡
You're such a strange girl.
You don't tell me anything.
But you're so sweet...
...and full of love.
It seems like I could communicate with you without speaking...
I was surprised to find out that you're a Sailor Scout too.
Where did you come from?
Who are you?

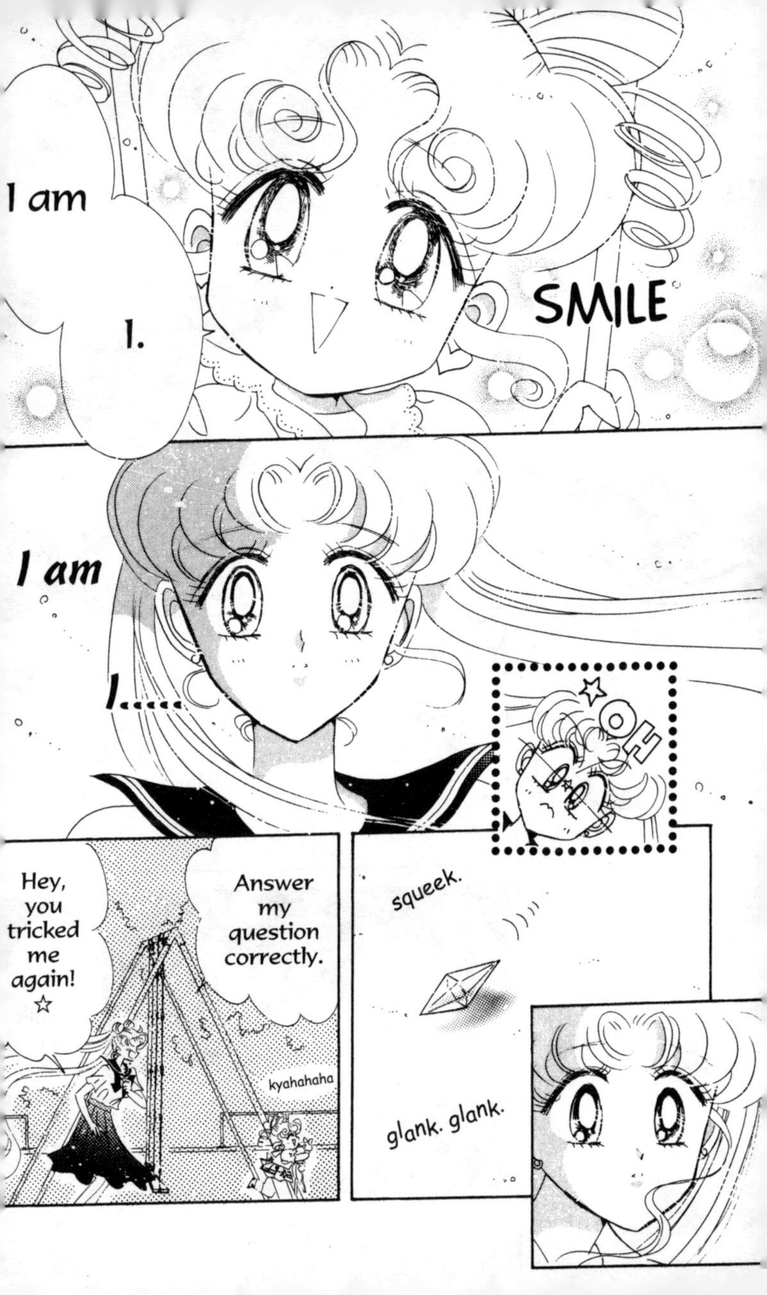

I am
I.
SMILE
I am
I.....
OH
Hey, you tricked me again! ☆
Answer my question correctly.
kyahahaha
squeek.
glank. glank.

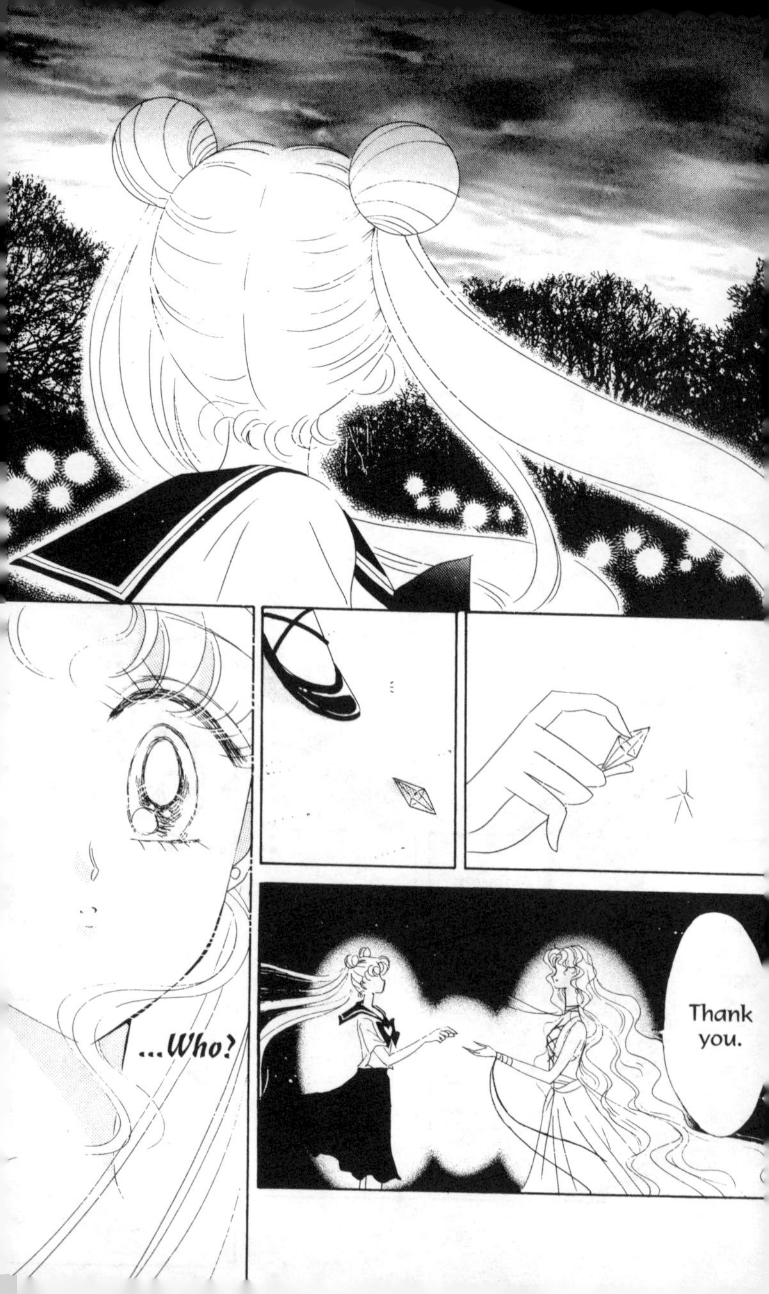
...Who?
Thank you.

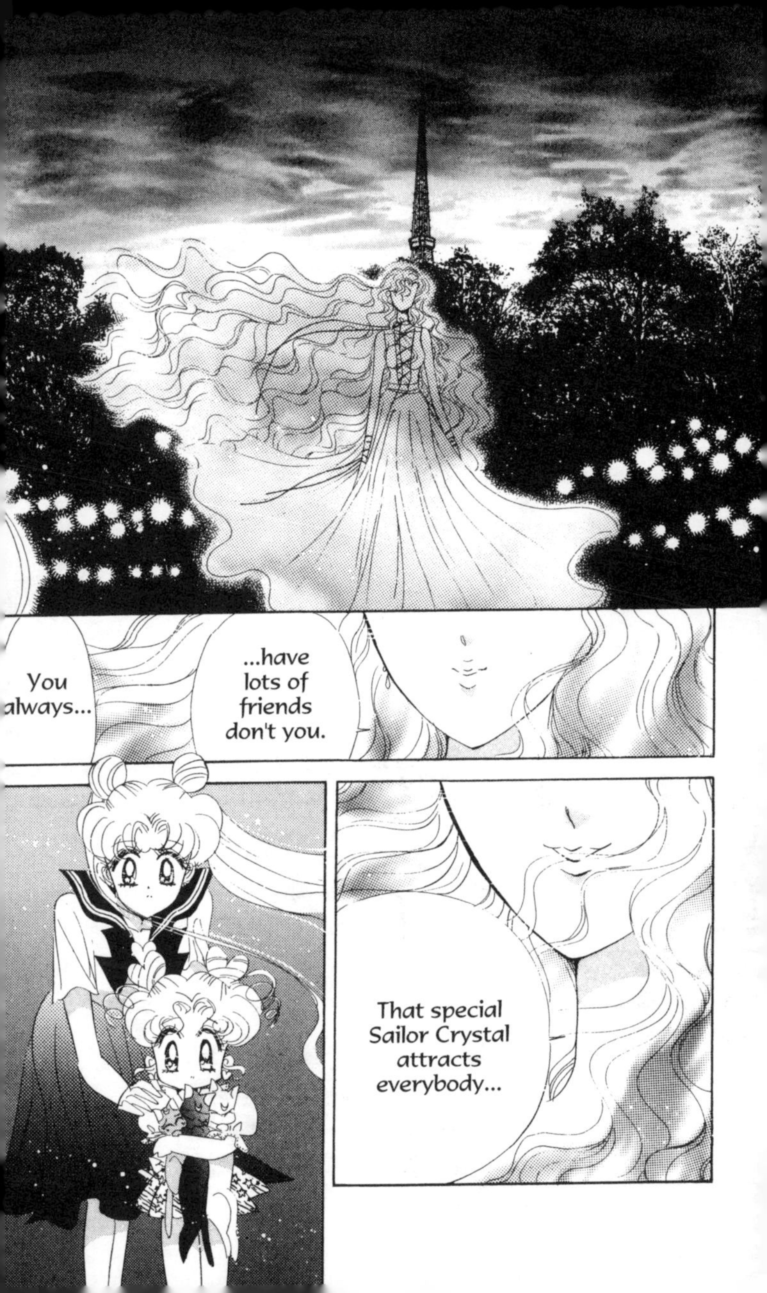
You always...
...have lots of friends don't you.
That special Sailor Crystal attracts everybody...

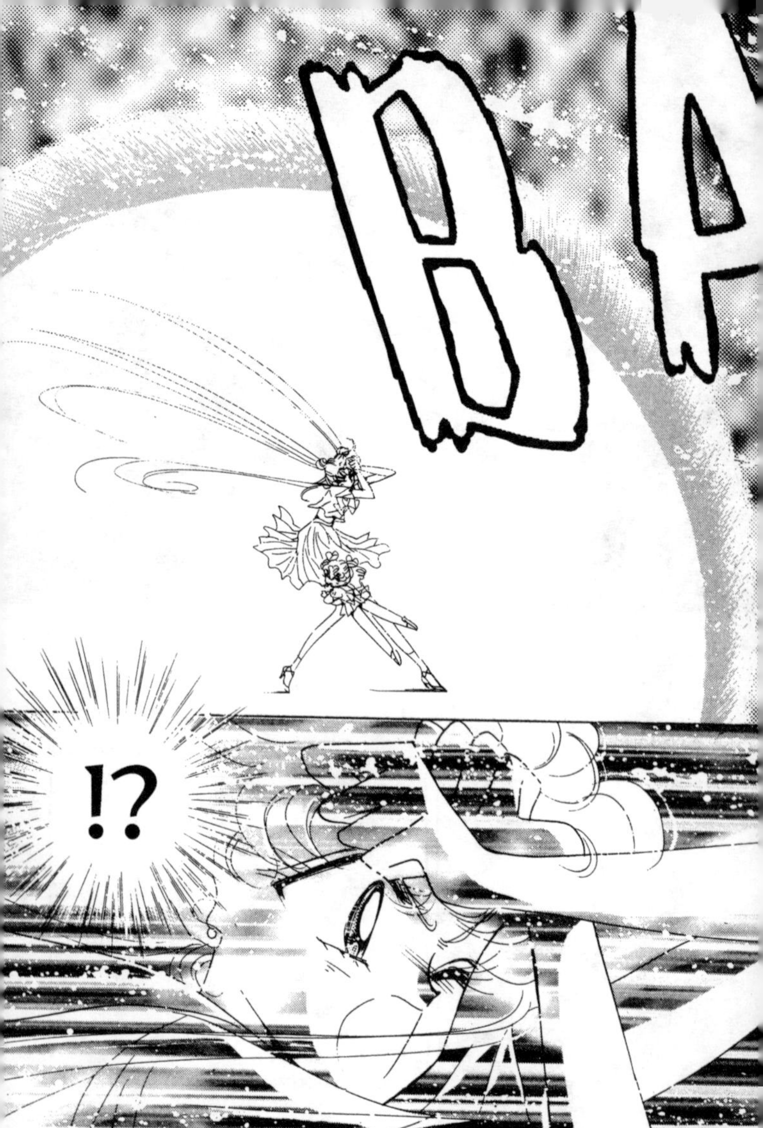
BA
!?

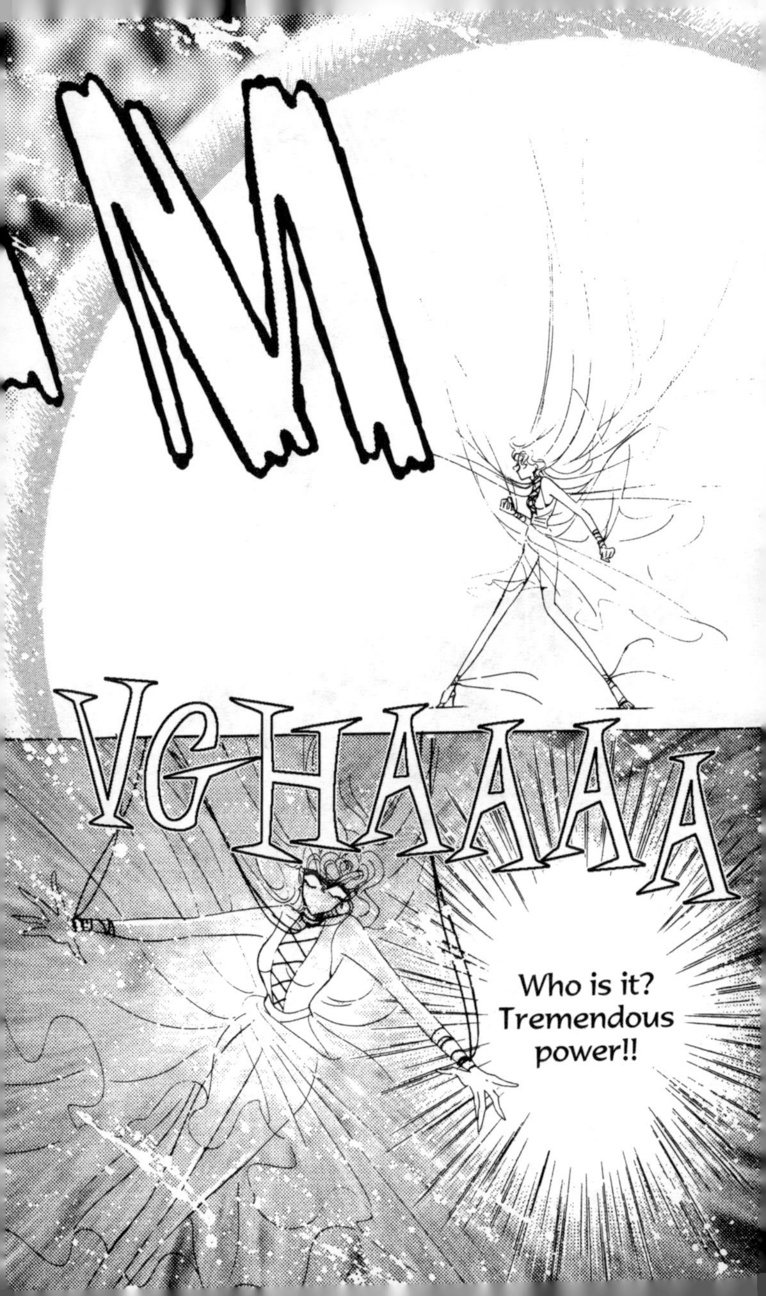
M
VGHAAAA
Who is it? Tremendous power!!

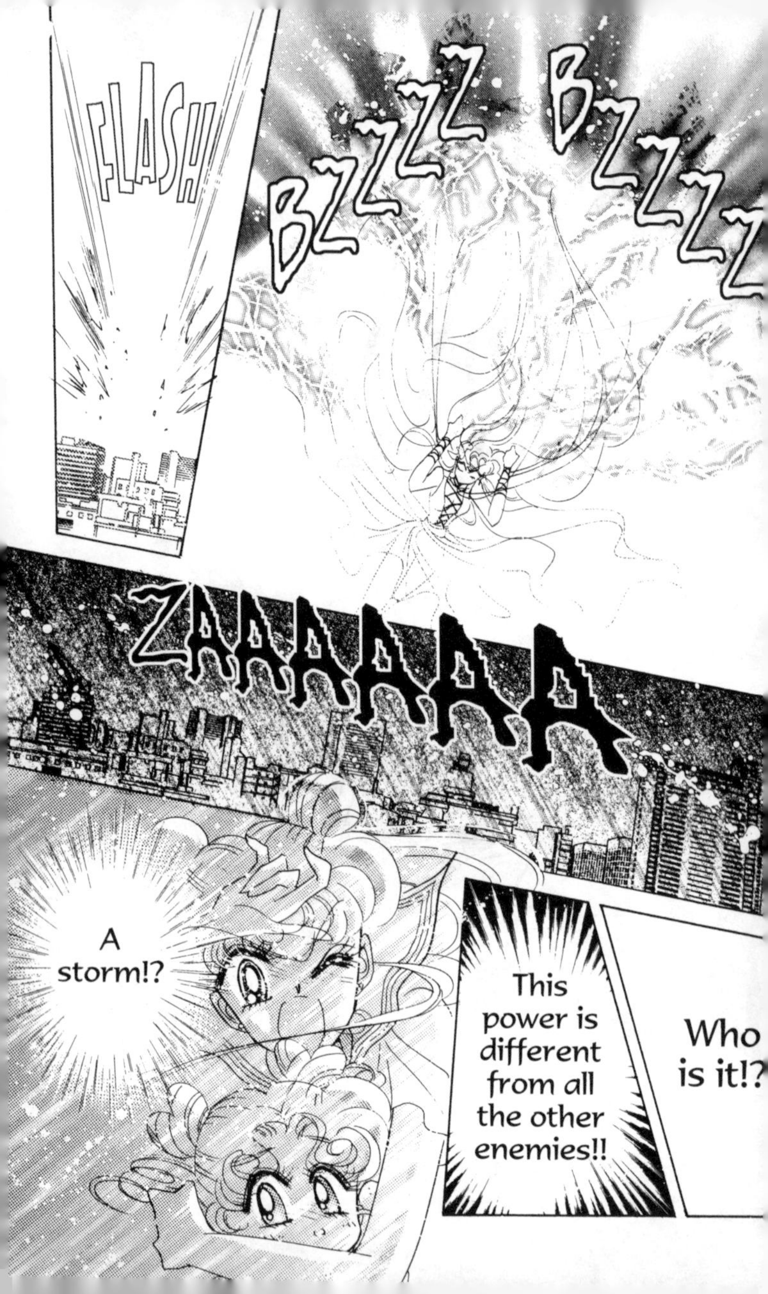
FLASH
BZZZZZ BZZZZZ
ZAAAAAA
A storm!?
This power is different from all the other enemies!!
Who is it!?

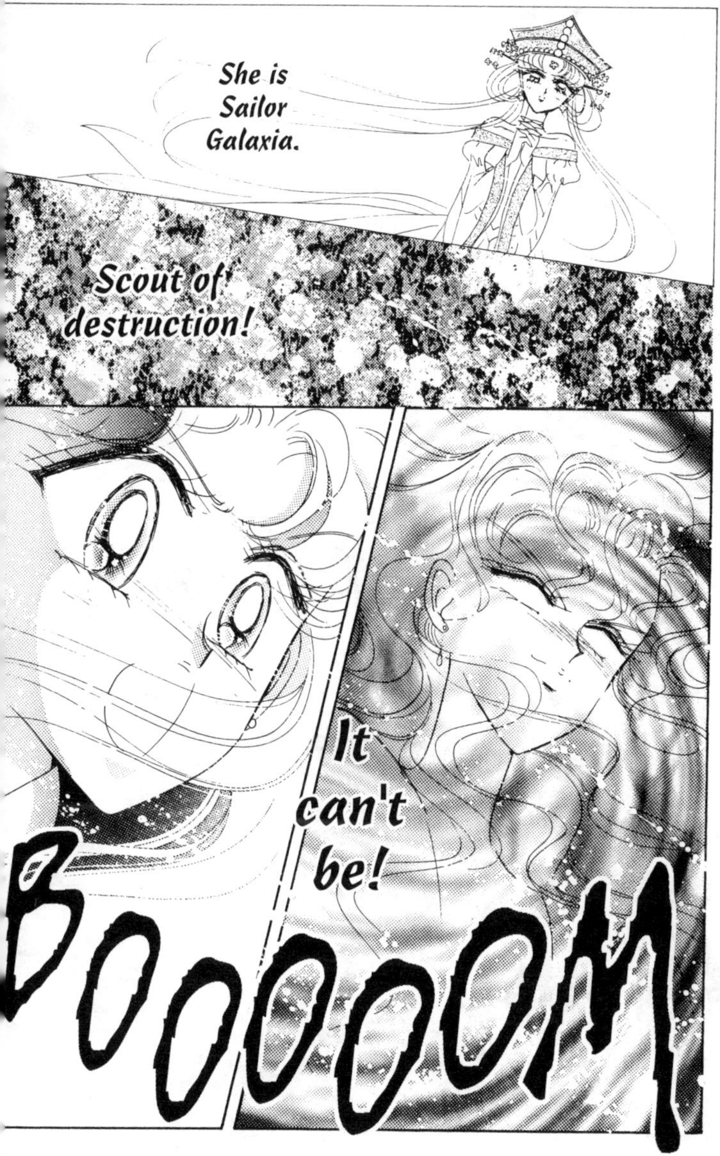
She is Sailor Galaxia.
Scout of destruction!
It can't be!
BOOOOOM

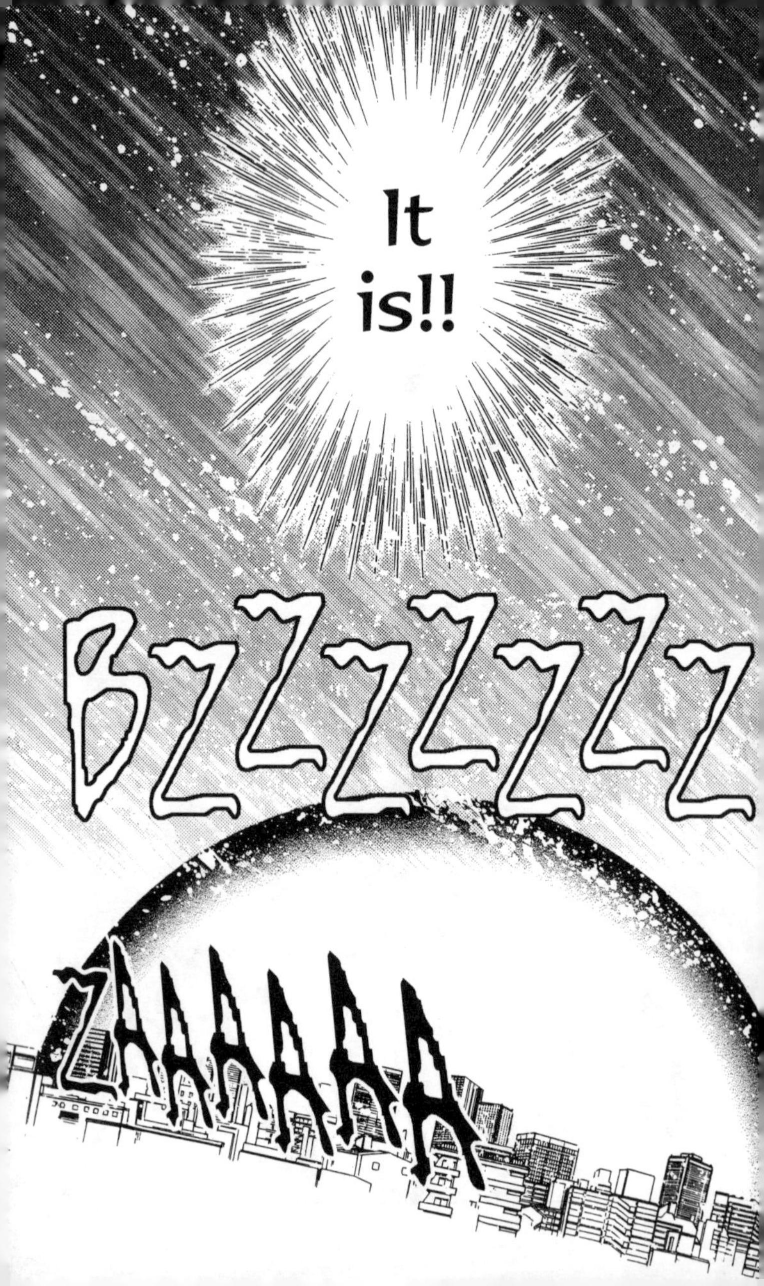
It is!!
BZZZZZZ
ZAAAAAA

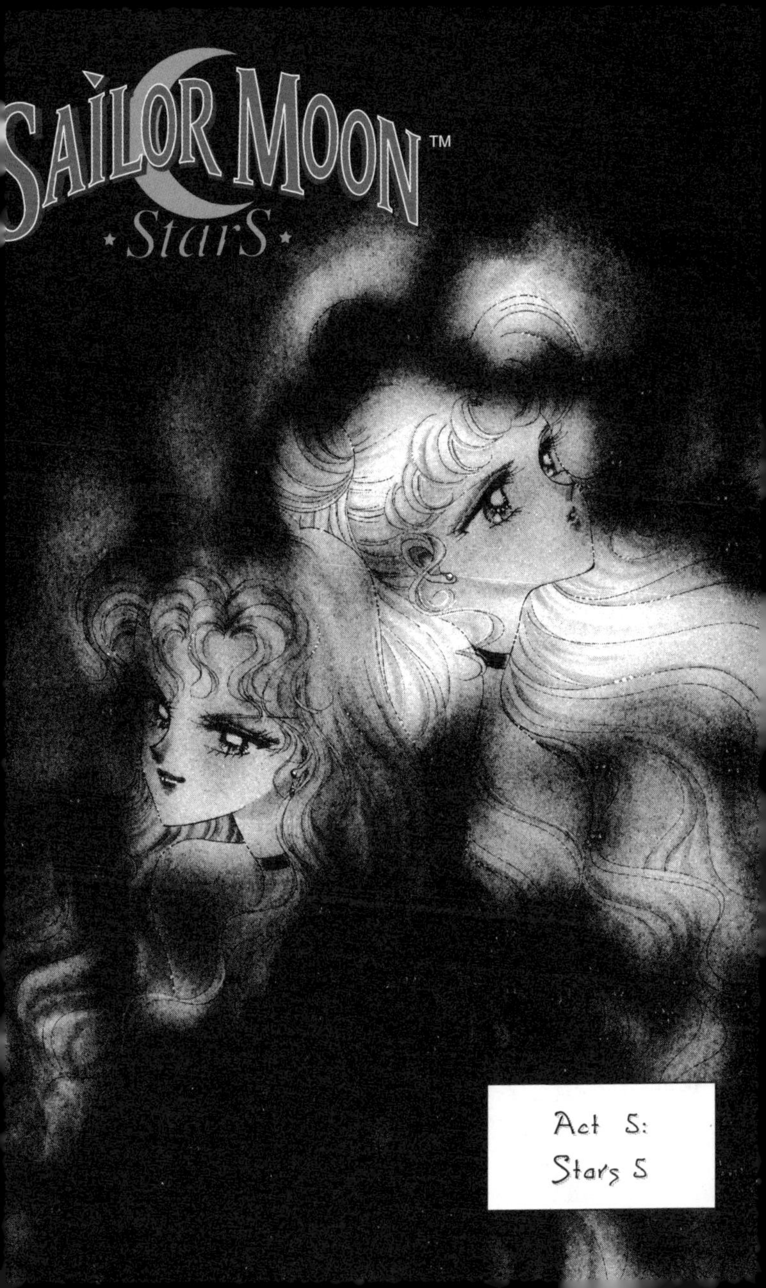
Sailor Moon™
Stars
Act 5:
Stars 5

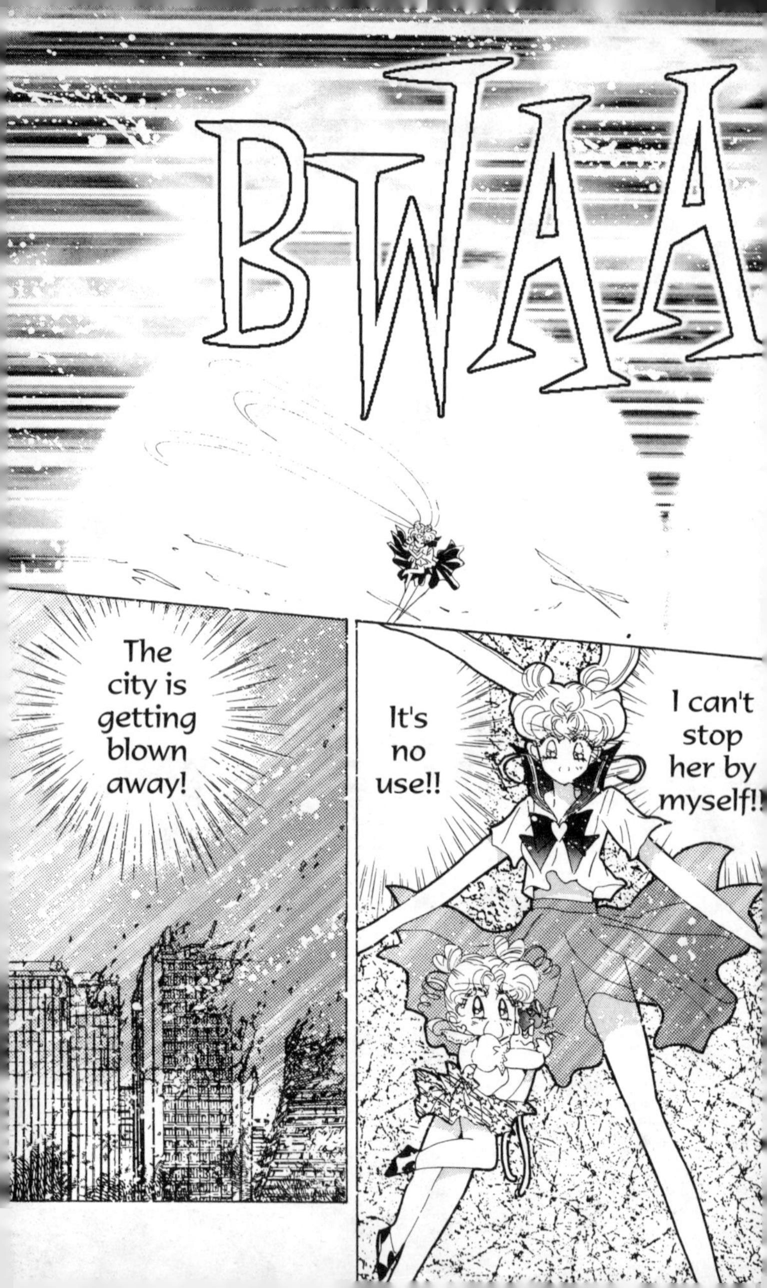
BWAA
The city is getting blown away!
It's no use!!
I can't stop her by myself!!

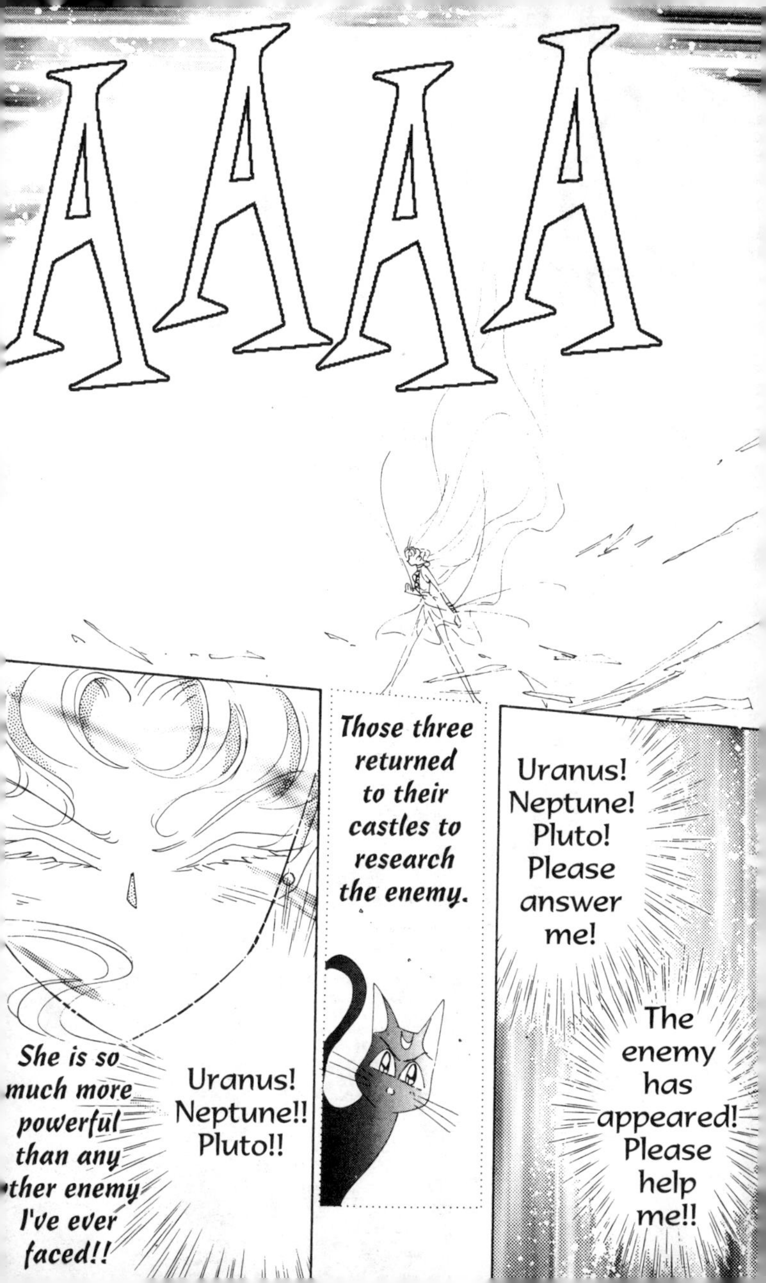
AAAA
She is so much more powerful than any ther enemy I've ever faced!!
Uranus! Neptune!! Pluto!!
Those three returned to their castles to research the enemy.
Uranus! Neptune! Pluto! Please answer me!
The enemy has appeared! Please help me!!

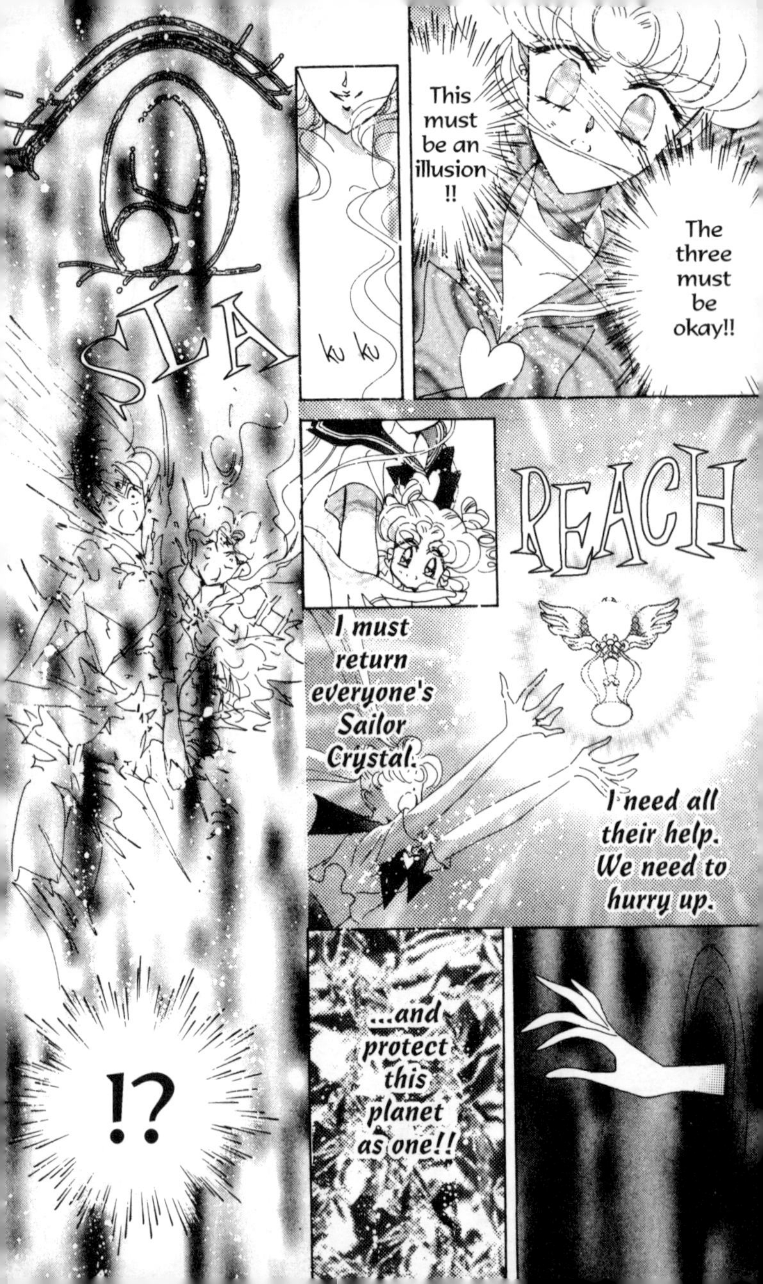
SLA
!?
ku ku
This must be an illusion!!
The three must be okay!!
REACH
I must return everyone's Sailor Crystal.
I need all their help. We need to hurry up.
...and protect this planet as one!!

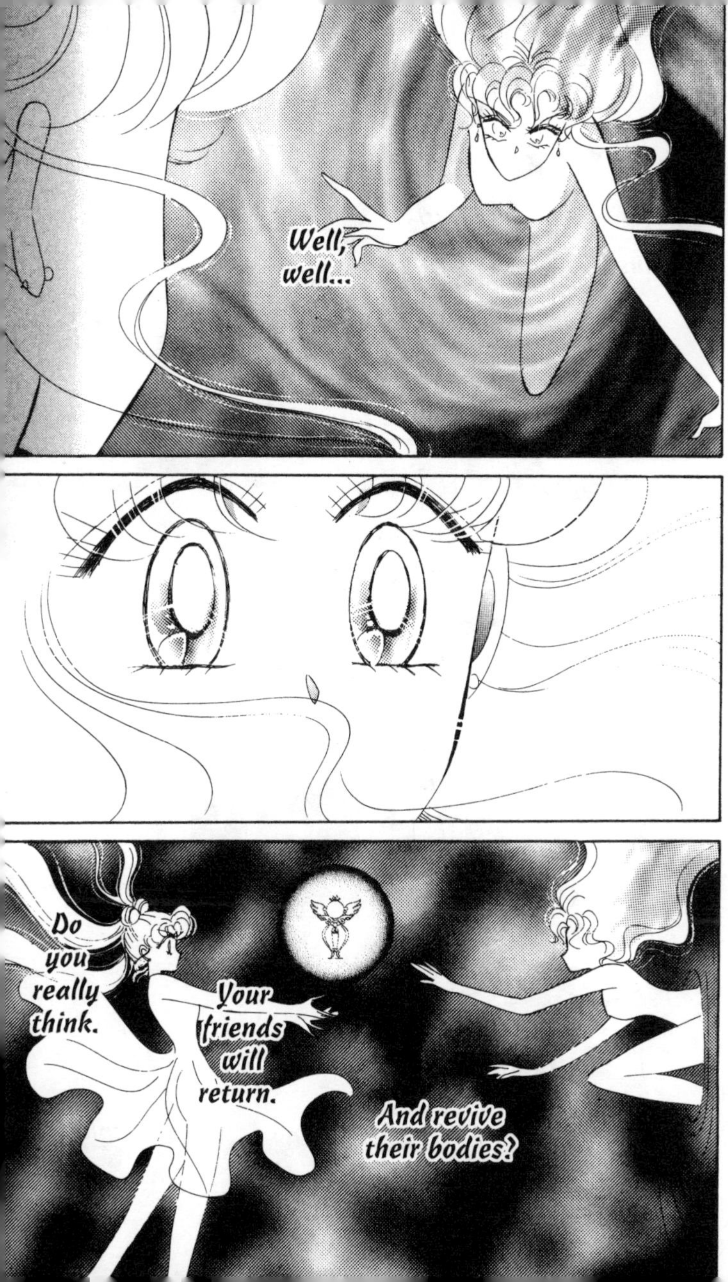
Well, well...
Do you really think.
Your friends will return.
And revive their bodies?

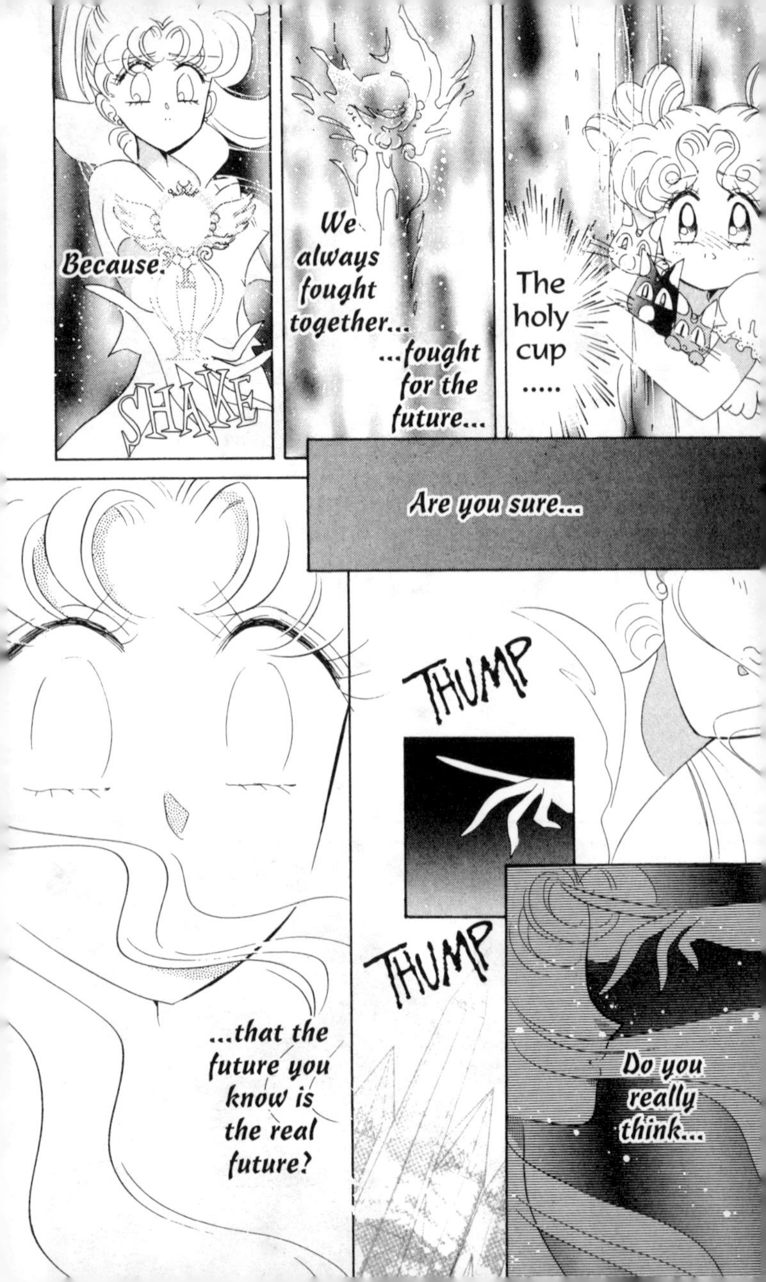

Because.
SHAKE
We always fought together...
...fought for the future...
The holy cup .....
Are you sure...
...that the future you know is the real future?
THUMP
THUMP
Do you really think...

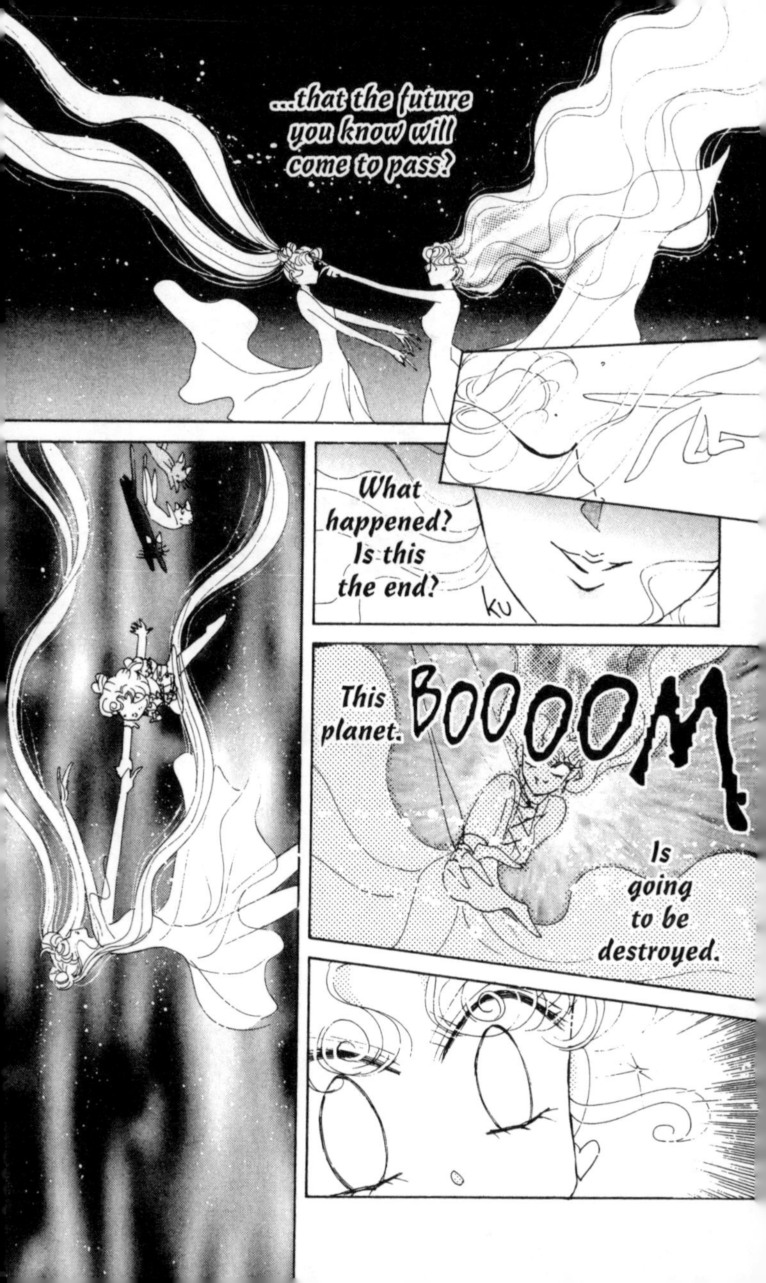
...that the future you know will come to pass?
What happened? Is this the end?
KU
This planet.
BOOOOM
Is going to be destroyed.

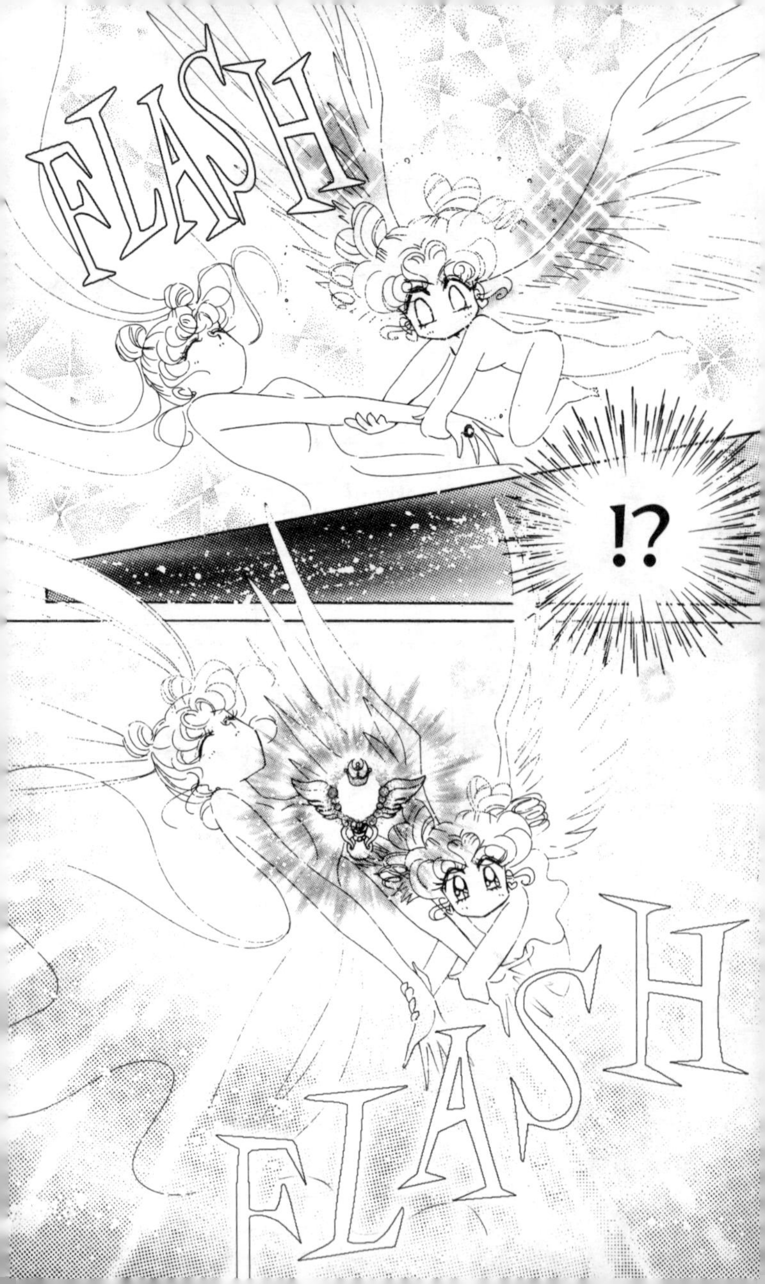
FLASH
!?
FLASH

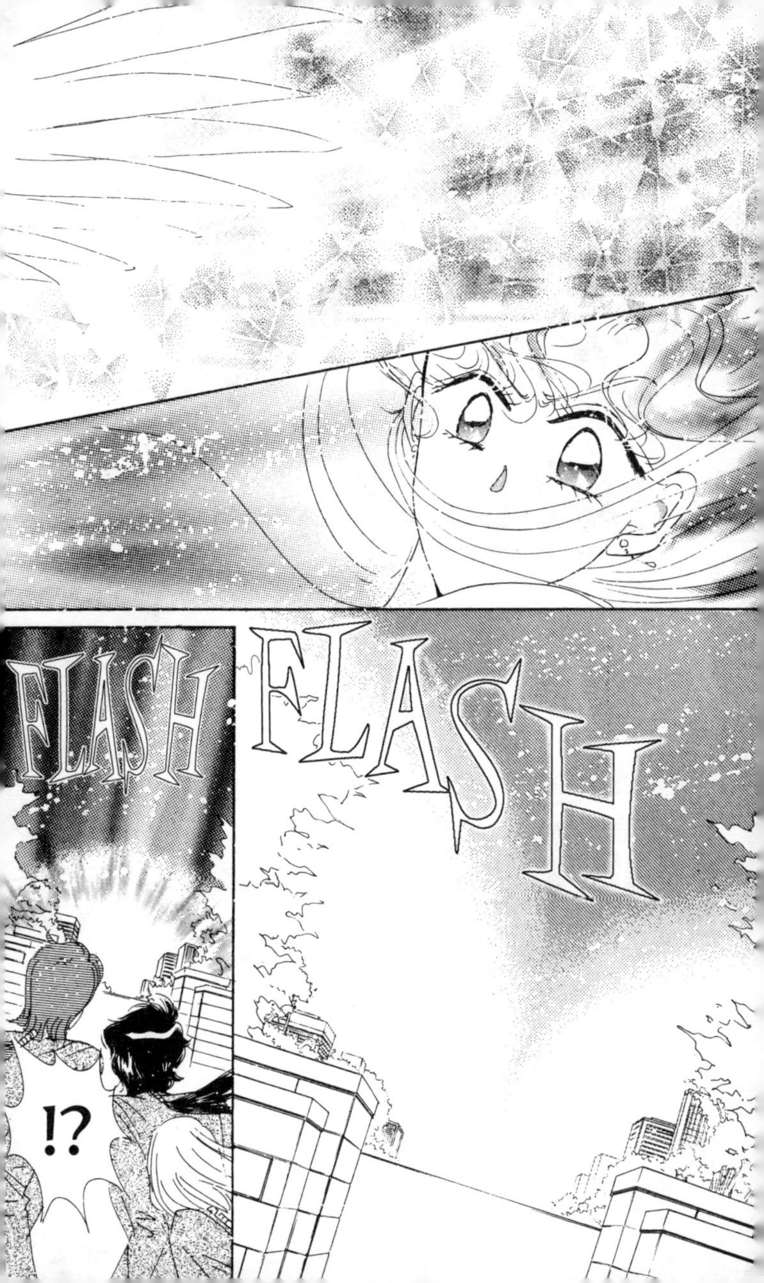
FLASH
!?
FLASH

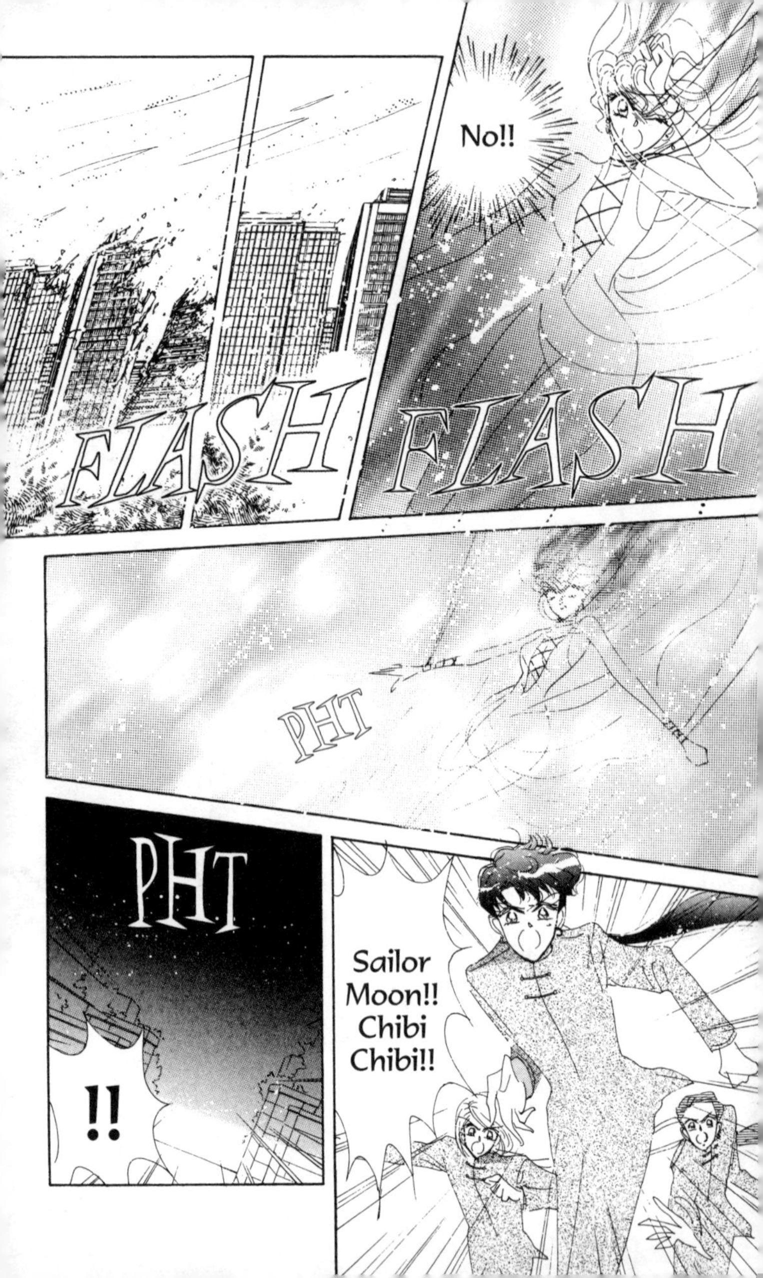
FLASH
No!!
FLASH
PHT
PHT
!!
Sailor Moon!! Chibi Chibi!!

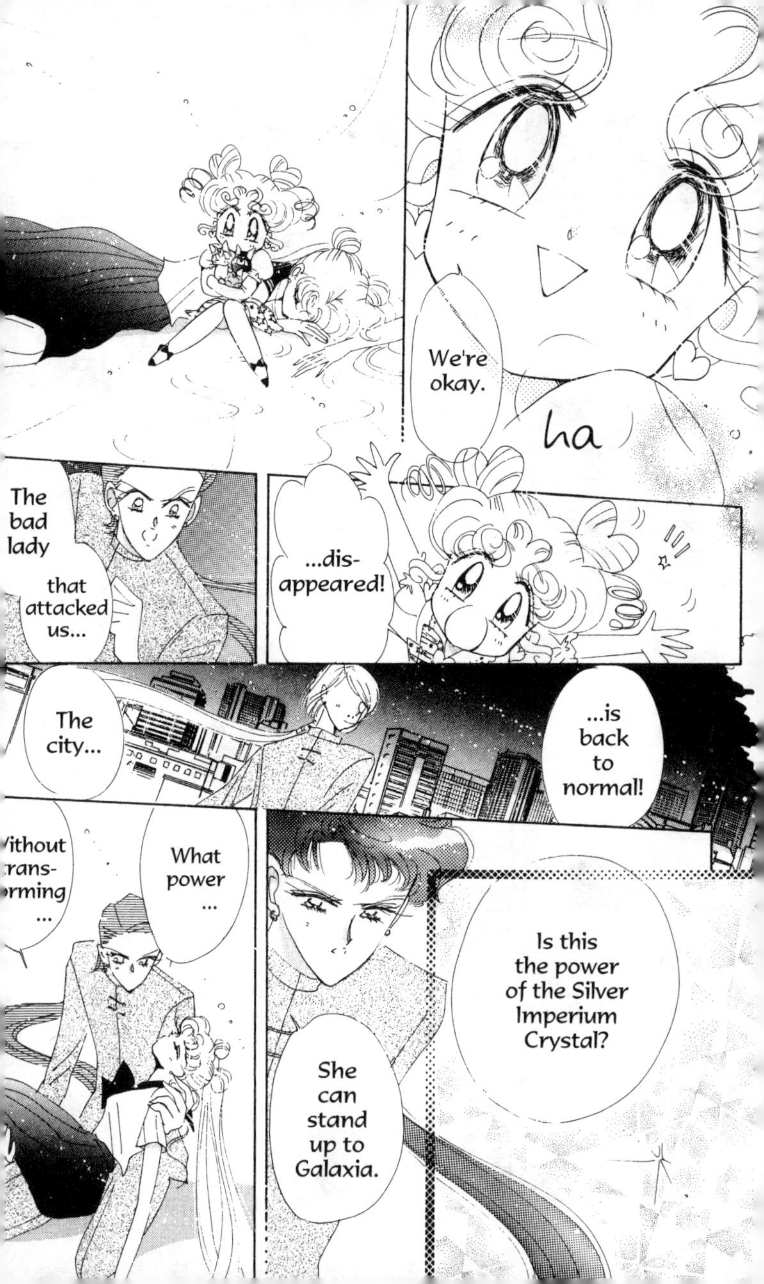

We're okay.
ha
The bad lady that attacked us...
...dis-appeared!
The city...
...is back to normal!
ithout rans-rming ...
What power ...
Is this the power of the Silver Imperium Crystal?
She can stand up to Galaxia.

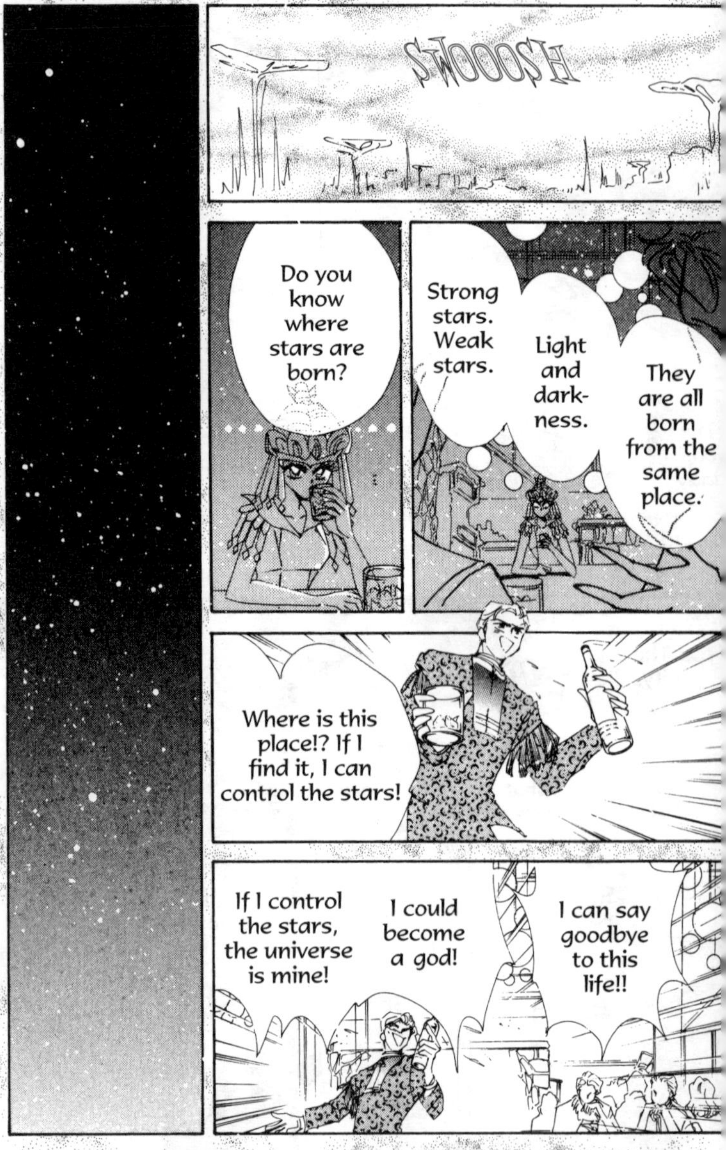
SWOOOSH
Do you know where stars are born?
Strong stars. Weak stars.
Light and dark-ness.
They are all born from the same place.
Where is this place!? If I find it, I can control the stars!
If I control the stars, the universe is mine!
I could become a god!
I can say goodbye to this life!!

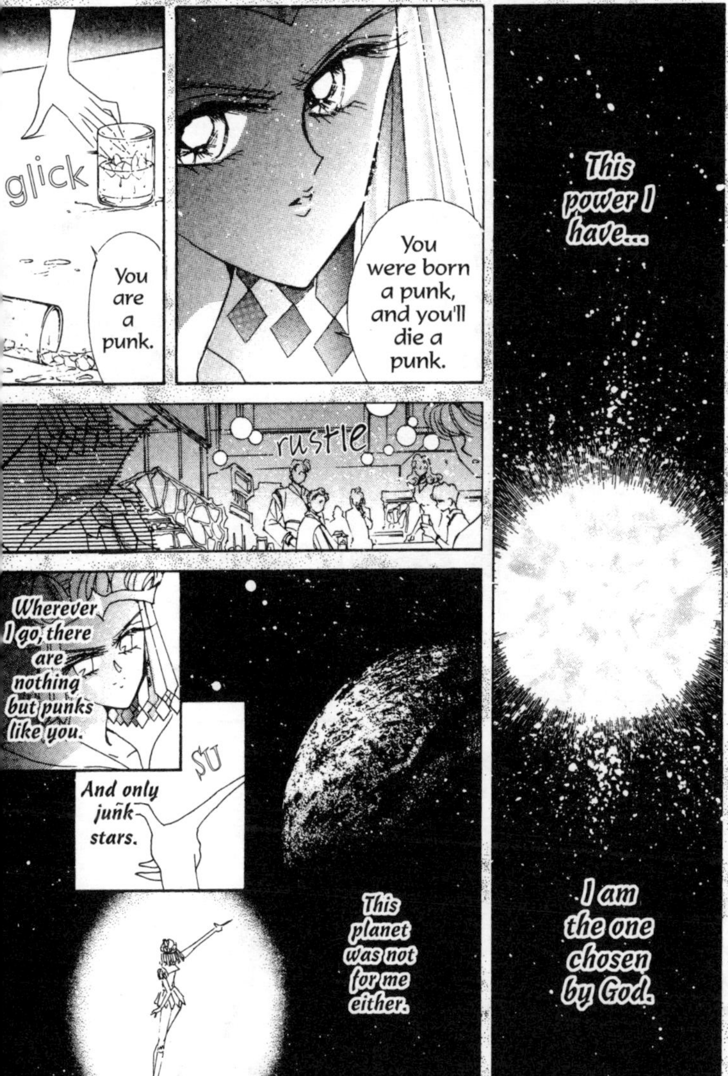
glick
You are a punk.
You were born a punk, and you'll die a punk.
rustle
Wherever I go, there are nothing but punks like you.
SU
And only junk stars.
This planet was not for me either.
This power I have...
I am the one chosen by God.

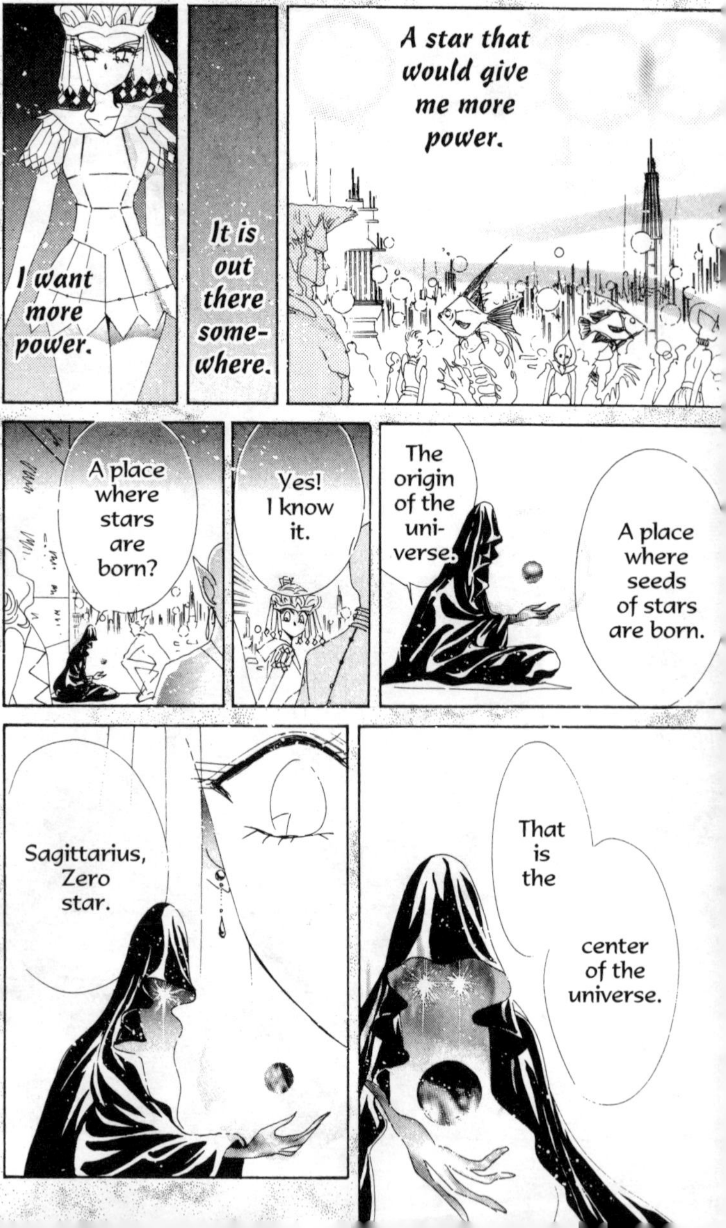
I want more power.
It is out there some-where.
A star that would give me more power.
A place where stars are born?
Yes! I know it.
The origin of the uni-verse.
A place where seeds of stars are born.
Sagittarius, Zero star.
That is the
center of the universe.

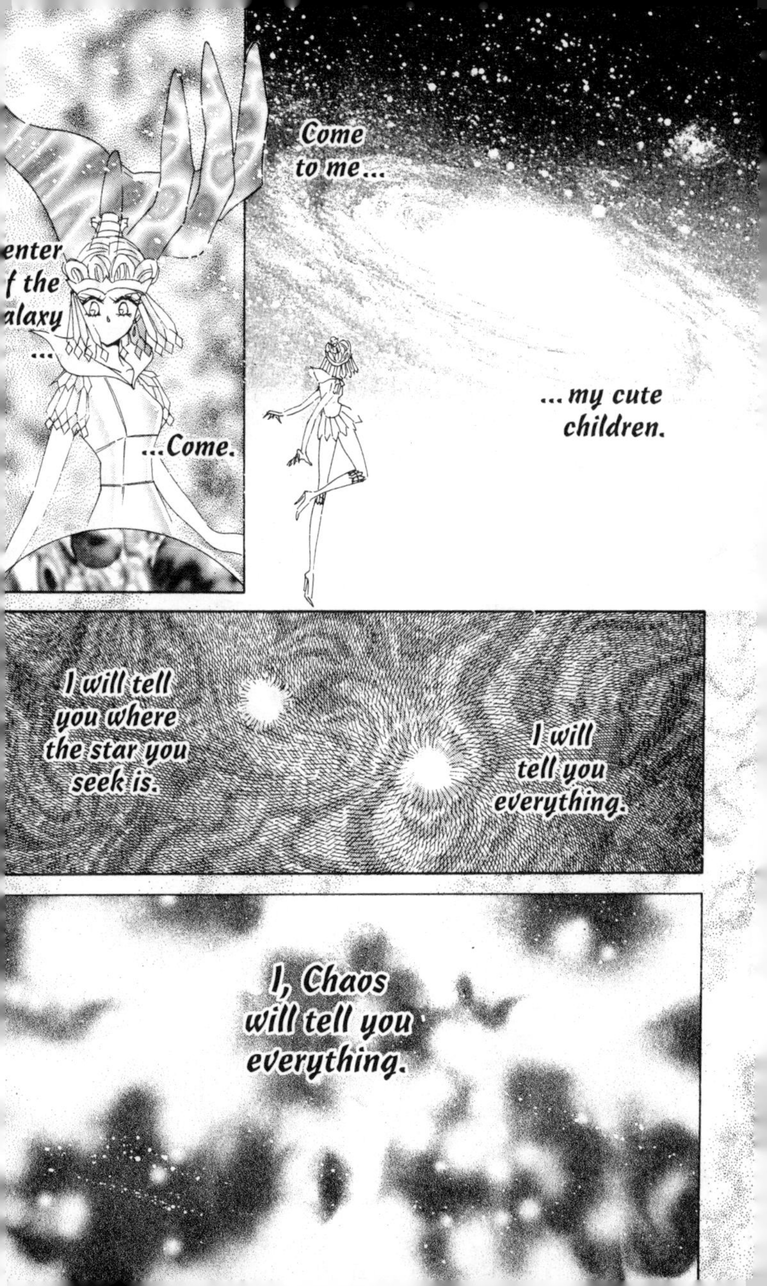
enter
f the
alaxy
...
...Come.
Come to me...
...my cute children.
I will tell you where the star you seek is.
I will tell you everything.
I, Chaos will tell you everything.

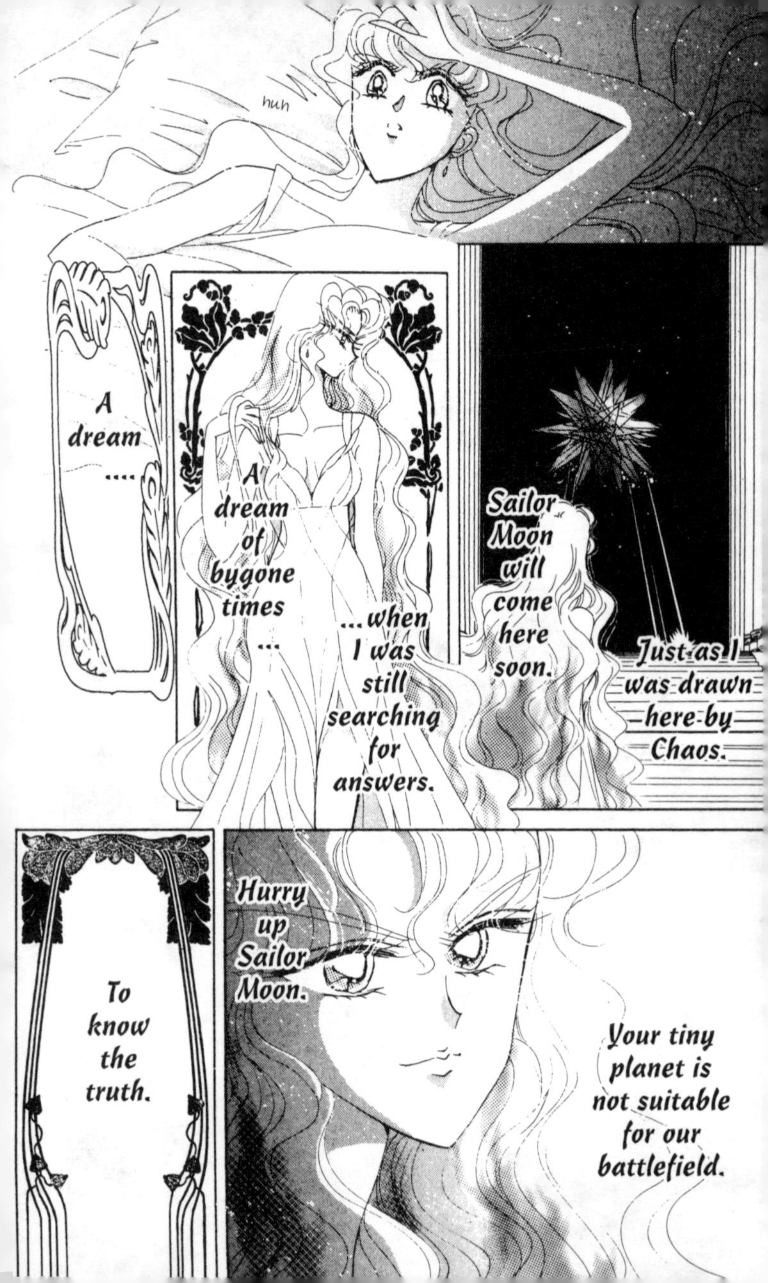
huh
A dream ....
A dream of bygone times ...
...when I was still searching for answers.
Sailor Moon will come here soon.
Just as I was drawn here by Chaos.
To know the truth.
Hurry up Sailor Moon.
Your tiny planet is not suitable for our battlefield.

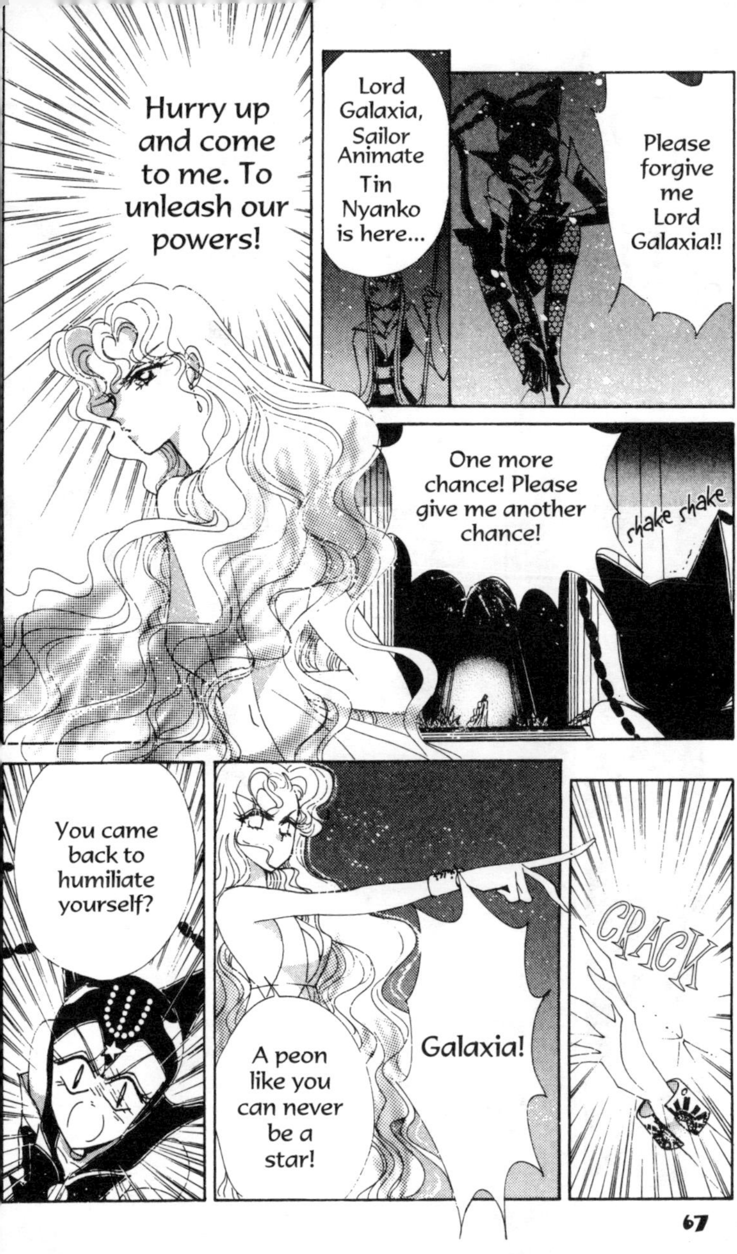

Hurry up and come to me. To unleash our powers!
Lord Galaxia, Sailor Animate Tin Nyanko is here...
Please forgive me Lord Galaxia!!
One more chance! Please give me another chance!
shake shake
You came back to humiliate yourself?
A peon like you can never be a star!
Galaxia!
CRACK

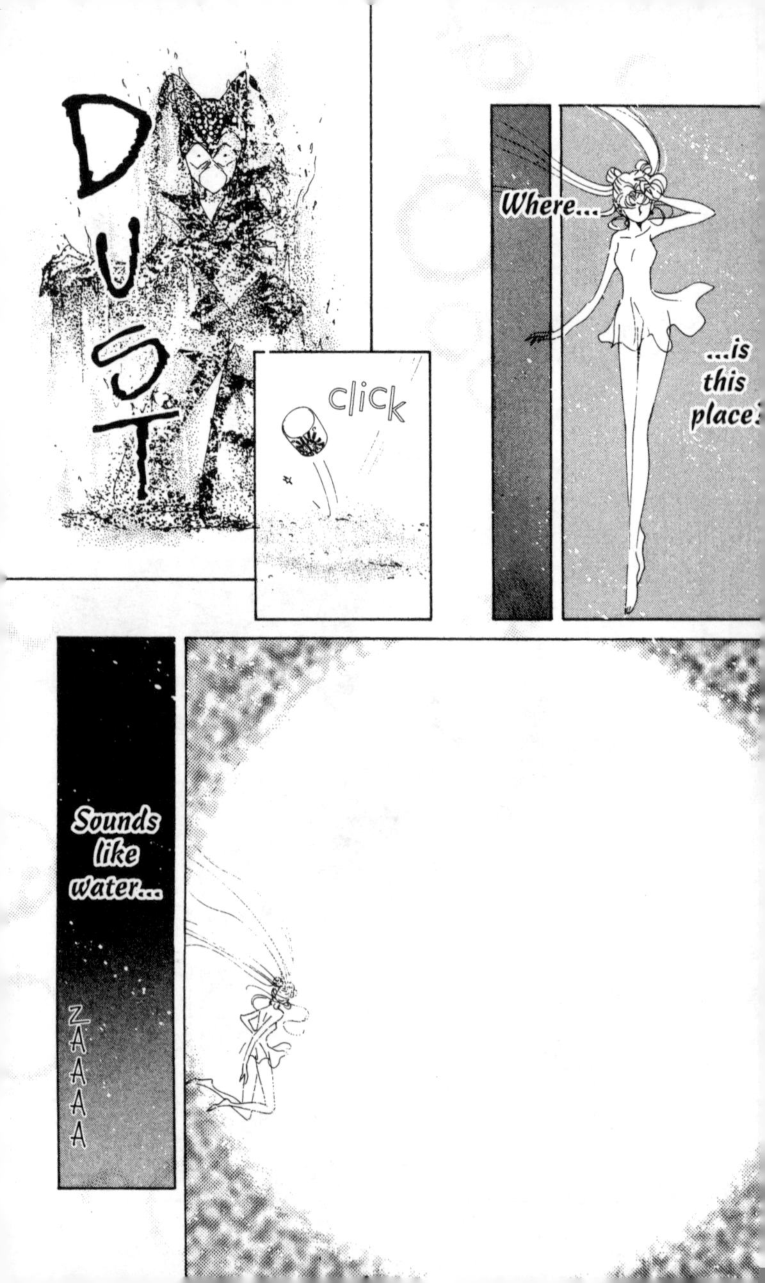
DUST
click
Where...
...is this place?
Sounds like water...
ZAAAAA

Where am I?

Sagittarius... Zero Star.

The Galaxy Cauldron.

Your final resting place!

69

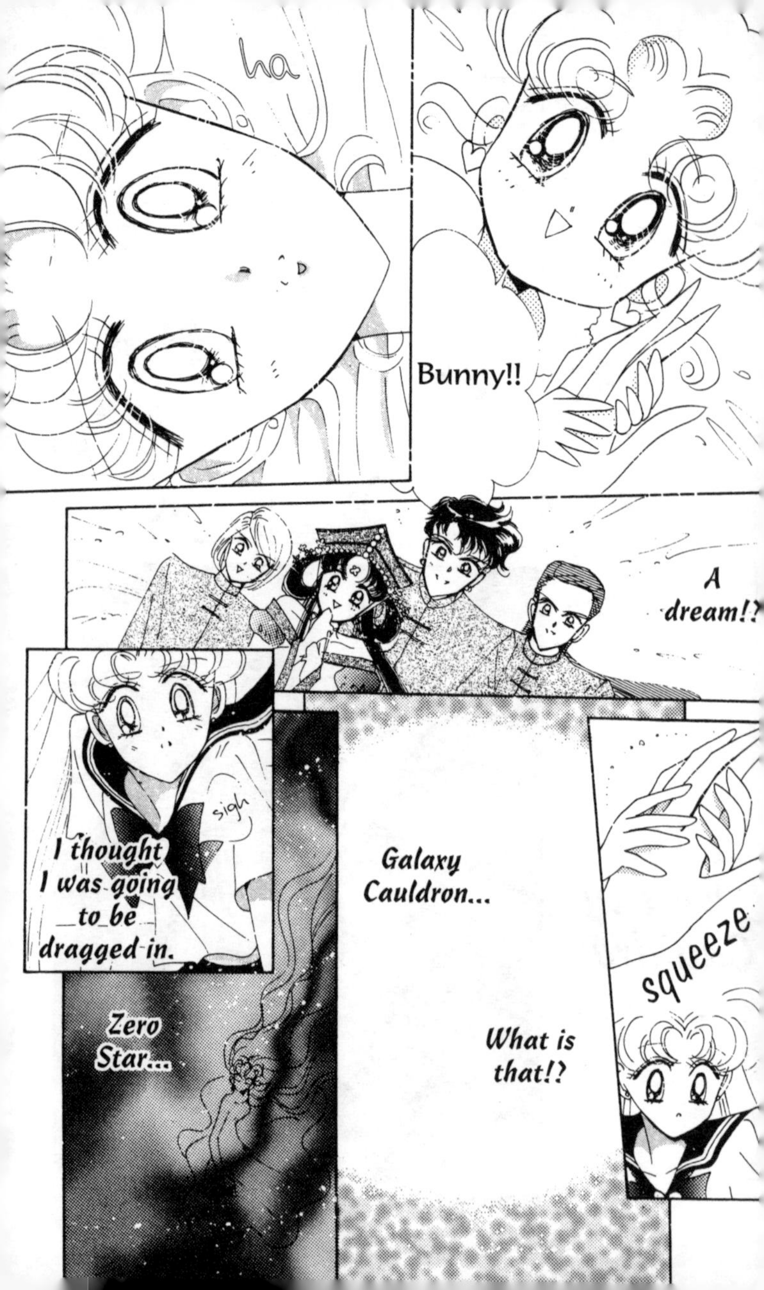
ha
Bunny!!
A dream!?
I thought I was going to be dragged in.
sigh
Galaxy Cauldron...
Zero Star...
What is that!?
squeeze

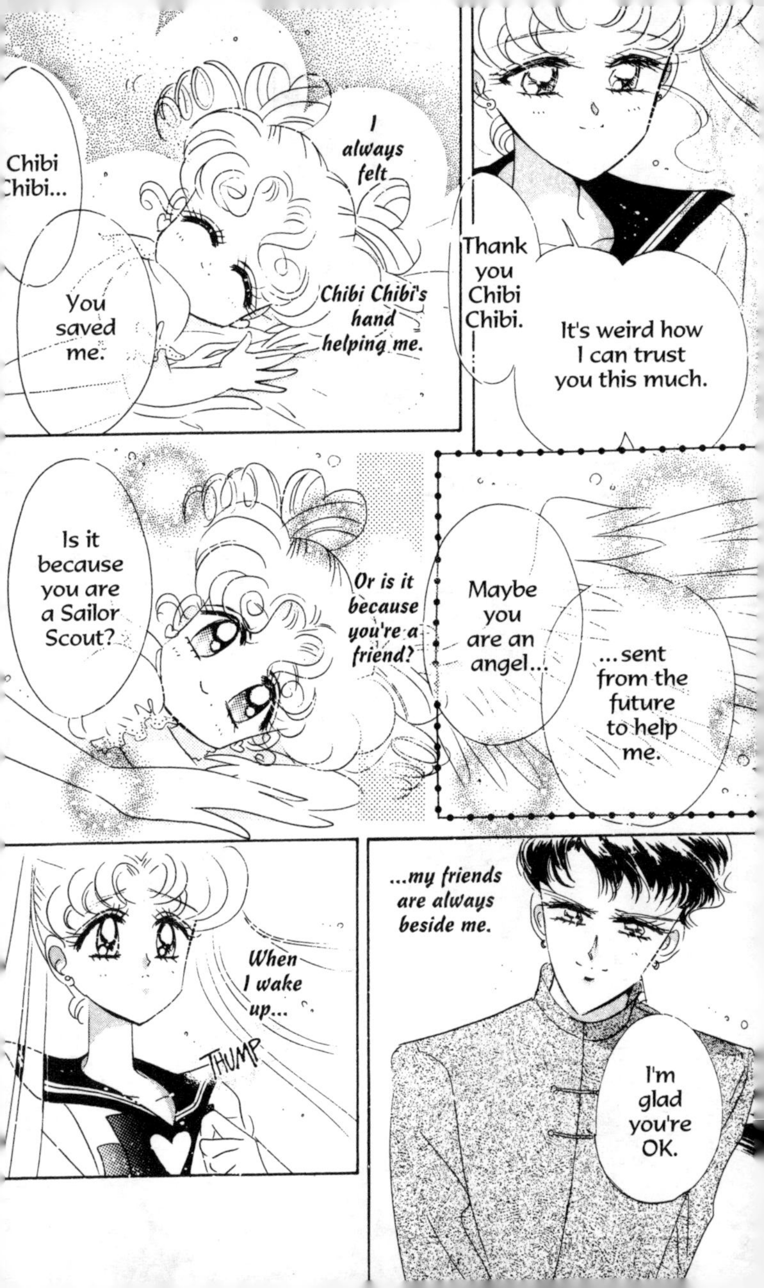
Chibi Chibi...
You saved me.
I always felt
Chibi Chibi's hand helping me.
Thank you Chibi Chibi.
It's weird how I can trust you this much.
Is it because you are a Sailor Scout?
Or is it because you're a friend?
Maybe you are an angel...
...sent from the future to help me.
When I wake up...
THUMP
...my friends are always beside me.
I'm glad you're OK.

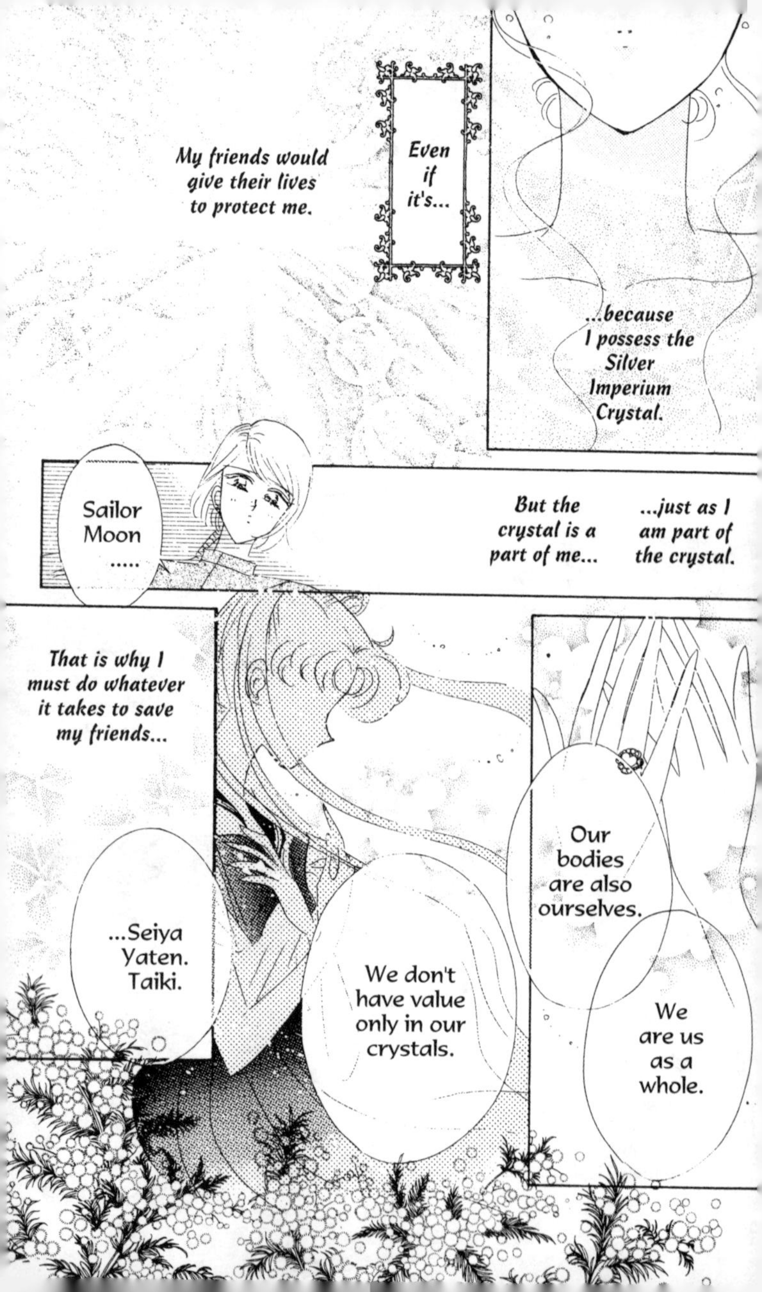
My friends would give their lives to protect me.
Even if it's...
...because I possess the Silver Imperium Crystal.
Sailor Moon .....
But the crystal is a part of me...
...just as I am part of the crystal.
That is why I must do whatever it takes to save my friends...
...Seiya Yaten. Taiki.
We don't have value only in our crystals.
Our bodies are also ourselves.
We are us as a whole.

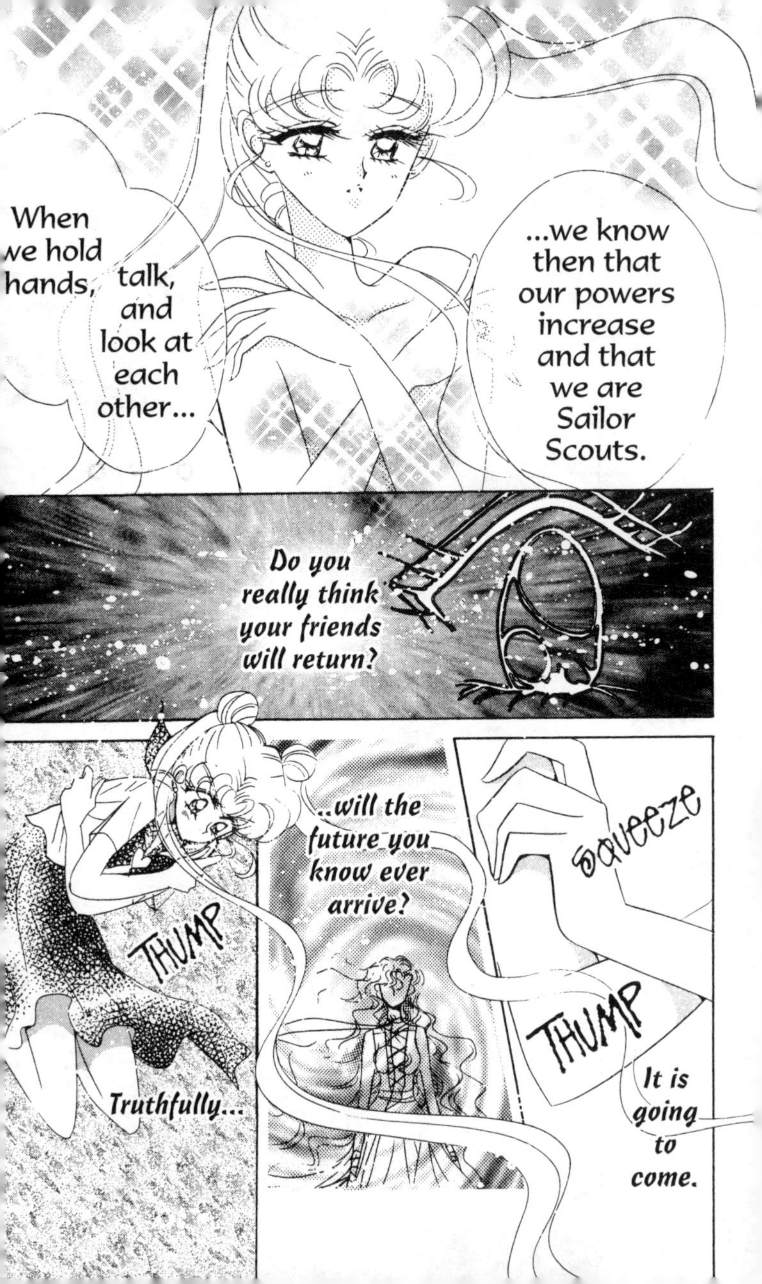
When we hold hands,
talk, and look at each other...
...we know then that our powers increase and that we are Sailor Scouts.
Do you really think your friends will return?
Truthfully...
THUMP
..will the future you know ever arrive?
squeeze
THUMP
It is going to come.

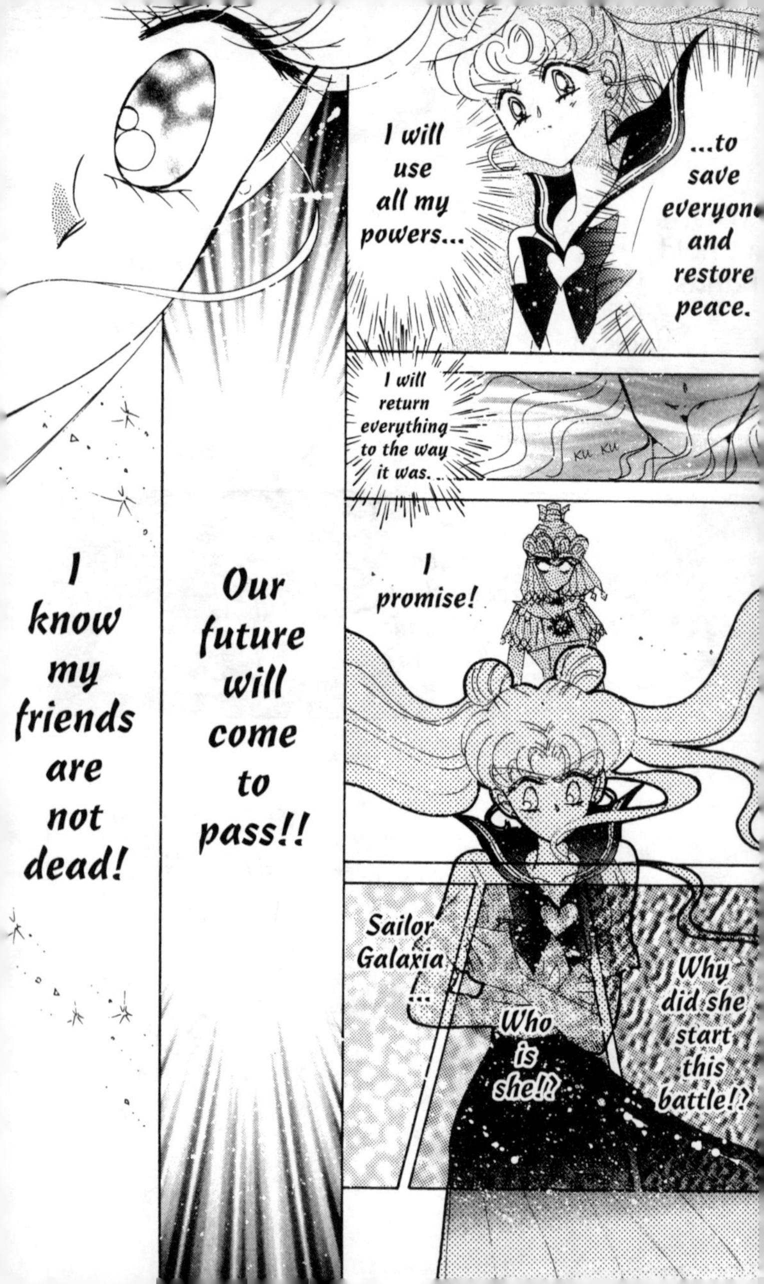
I know my friends are not dead!
Our future will come to pass!!
I will use all my powers...
...to save everyon
and restore peace.
I will return everything to the way it was.
KU KU
I promise!
Sailor Galaxia ...
Who is she!?
Why did she start this battle!?

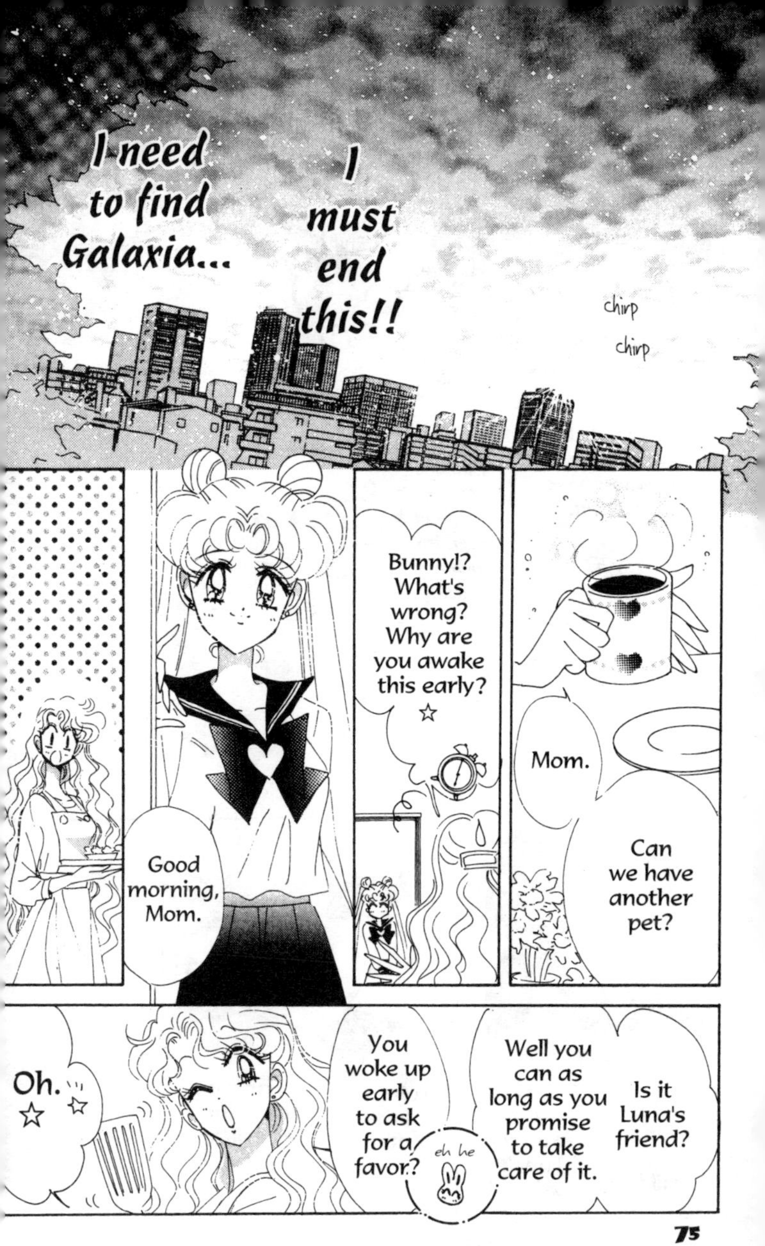
I need to find Galaxia...
I must end this!!
chirp
chirp
Good morning, Mom.
Bunny!? What's wrong? Why are you awake this early? ☆
Mom.
Can we have another pet?
Oh. ☆ ☆
You woke up early to ask for a favor?
eh he
Well you can as long as you promise to take care of it.
Is it Luna's friend?

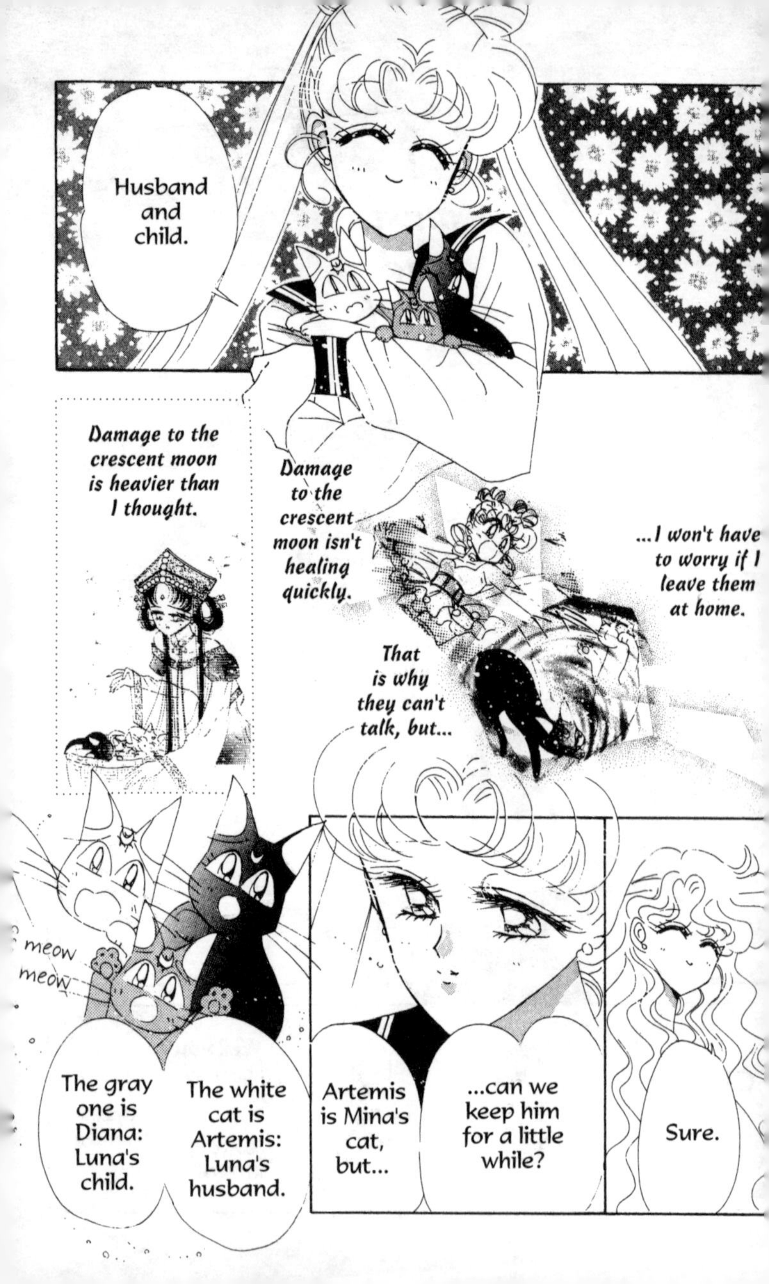
Husband and child.
Damage to the crescent moon is heavier than I thought.
Damage to the crescent moon isn't healing quickly.
That is why they can't talk, but...
...I won't have to worry if I leave them at home.
meow
meow
The gray one is Diana: Luna's child.
The white cat is Artemis: Luna's husband.
Artemis is Mina's cat, but...
...can we keep him for a little while?
Sure.

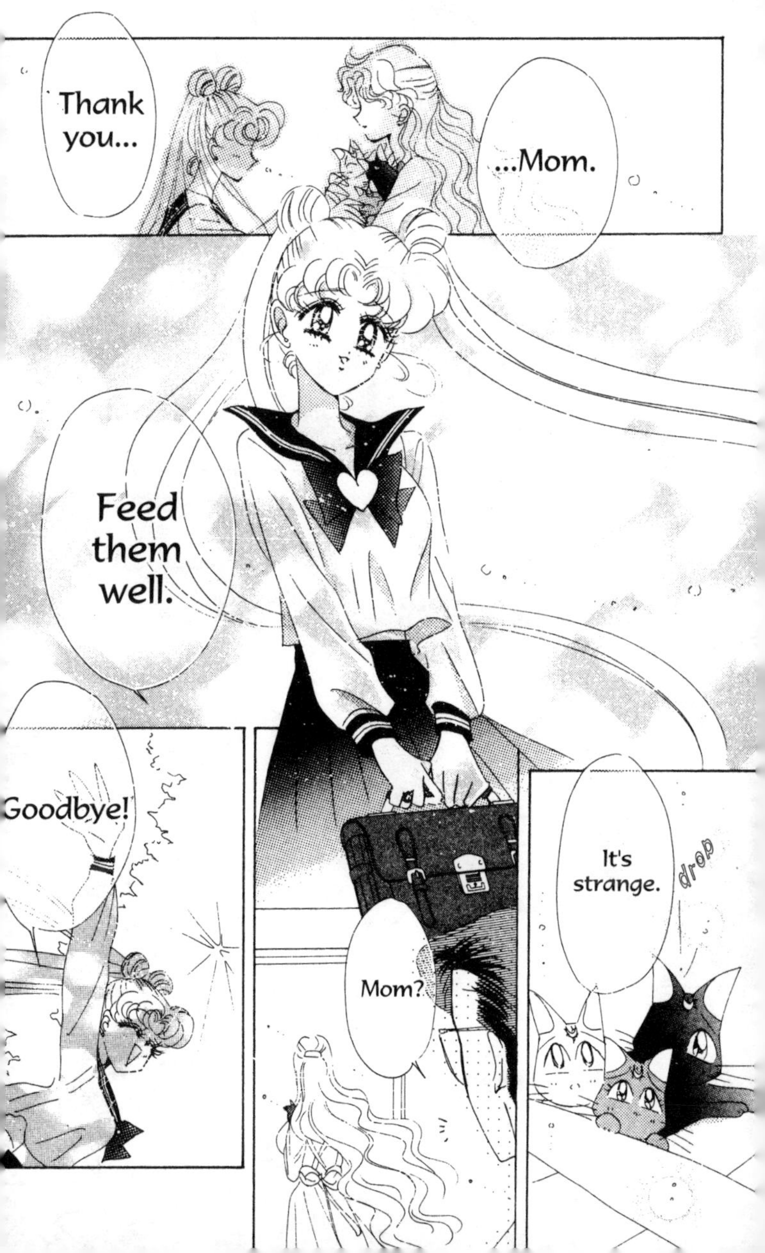
Thank you...
...Mom.
Feed them well.
Goodbye!
Mom?
It's strange.
drop

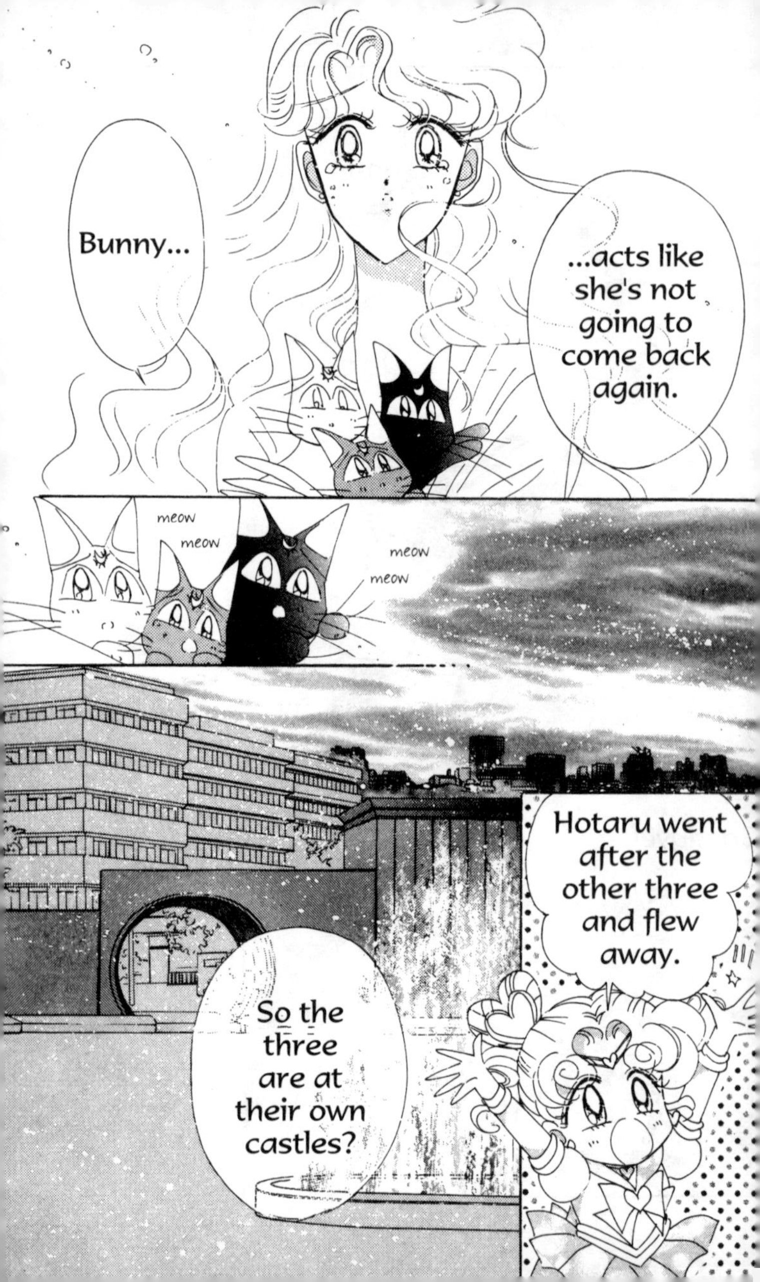
Bunny...
...acts like she's not going to come back again.
meow
meow
meow
meow
Hotaru went after the other three and flew away.
So the three are at their own castles?

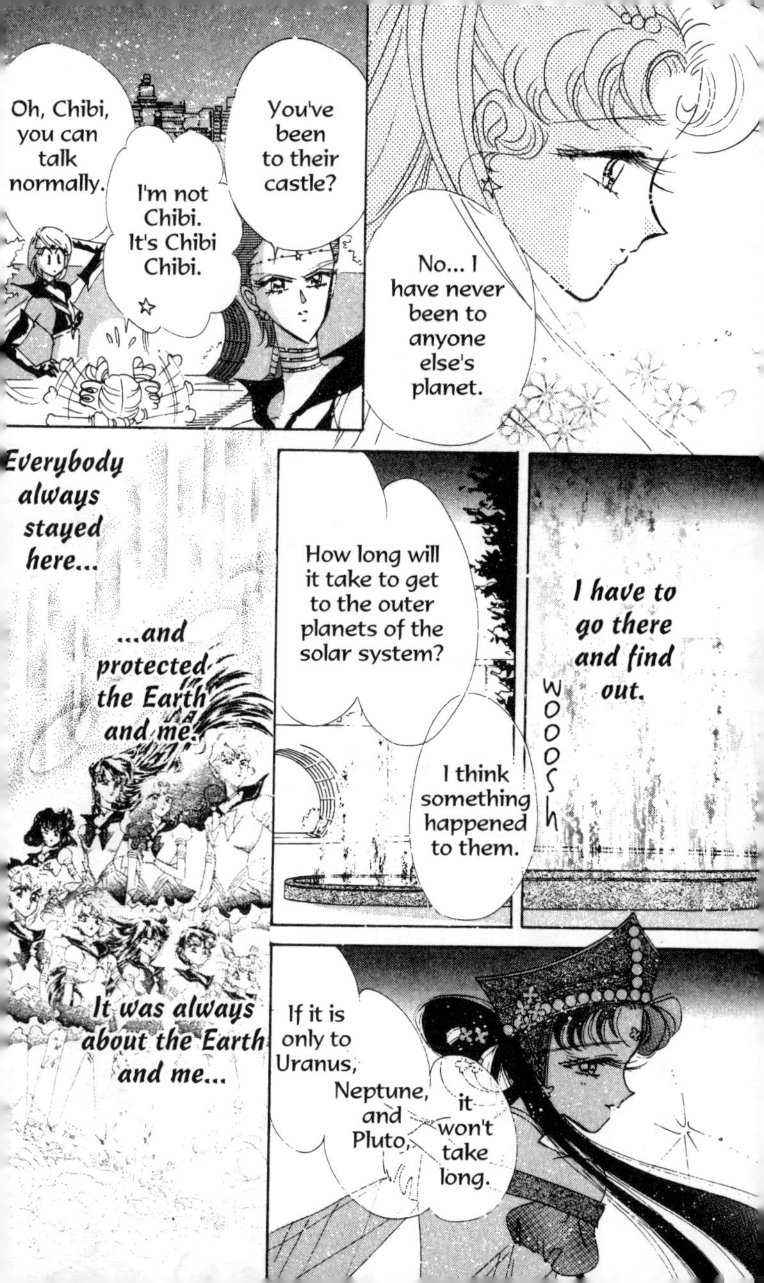
Oh, Chibi, you can talk normally.
I'm not Chibi. It's Chibi Chibi.
You've been to their castle?
No... I have never been to anyone else's planet.
Everybody always stayed here...
...and protected the Earth and me.
It was always about the Earth and me...
How long will it take to get to the outer planets of the solar system?
I think something happened to them.
WOOOSh
I have to go there and find out.
If it is only to Uranus, Neptune, and Pluto, it won't take long.

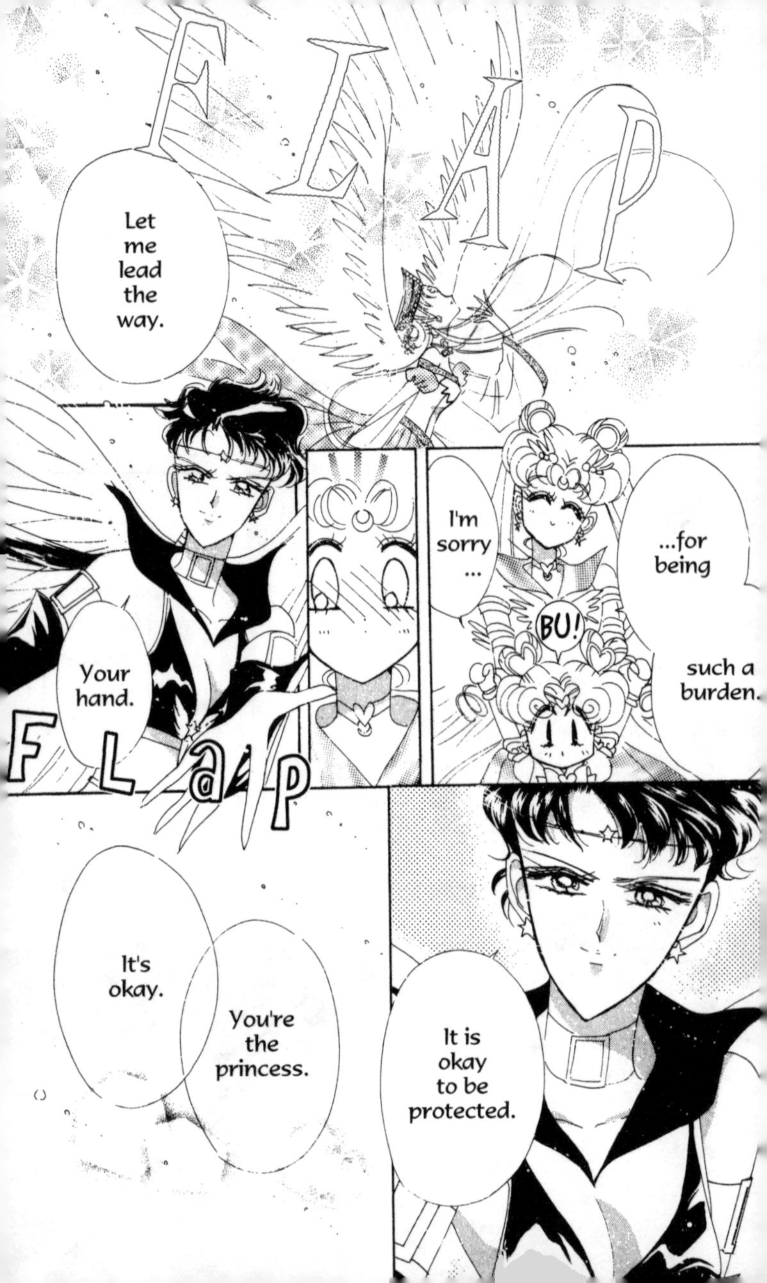

FLAP
Let me lead the way.
Your hand.
FLaP
I'm sorry ...
...for being
BU!
such a burden.
It's okay.
You're the princess.
It is okay to be protected.

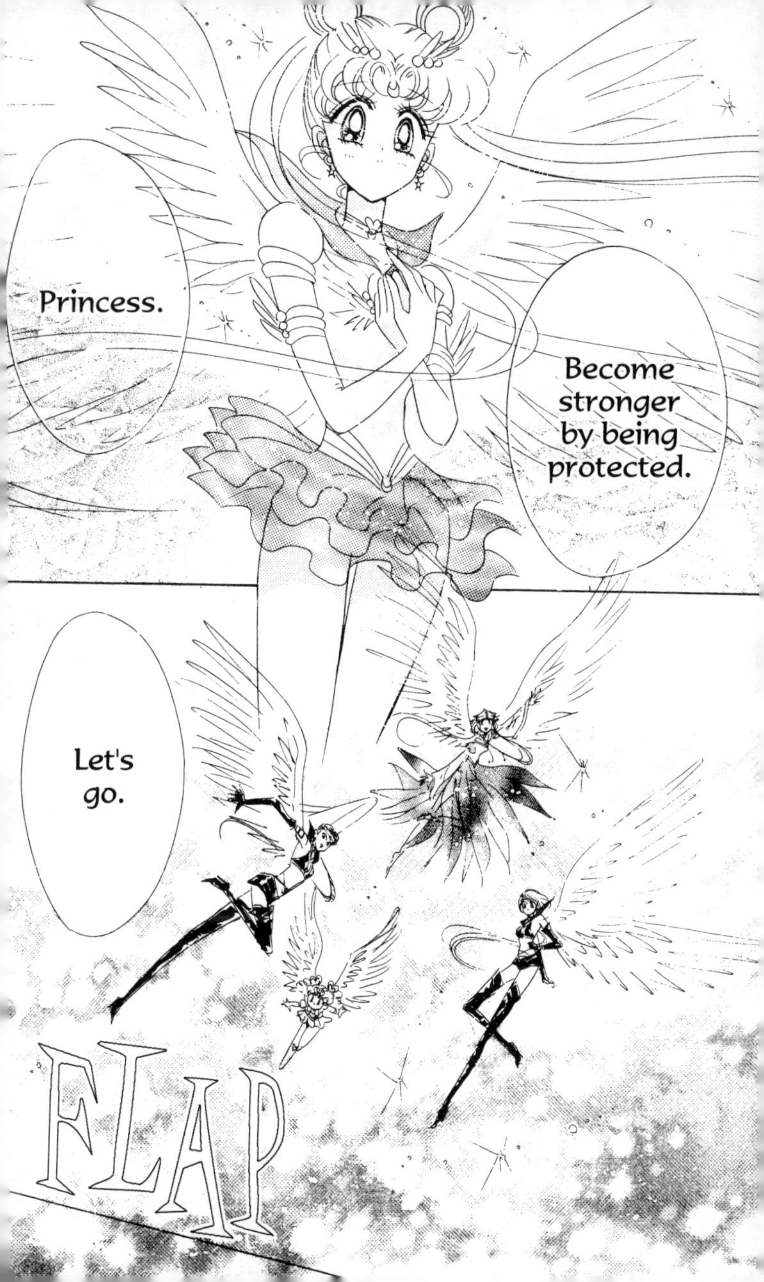
Princess.
Become stronger by being protected.
Let's go.
FLAP

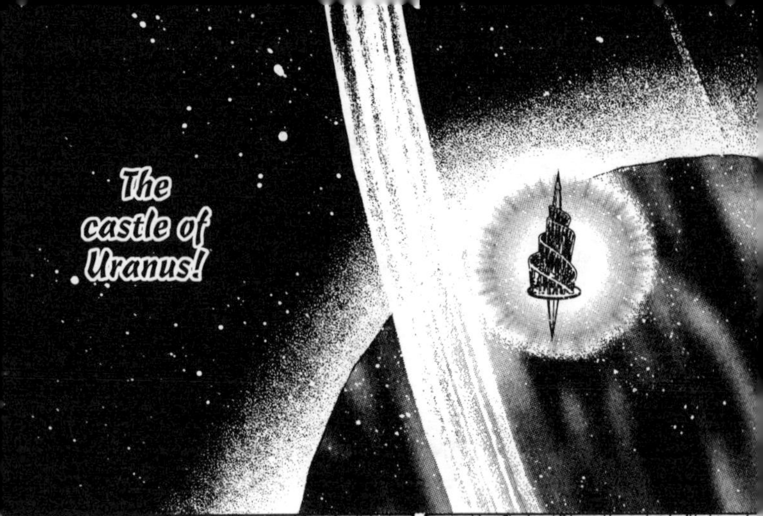
The castle of Uranus!

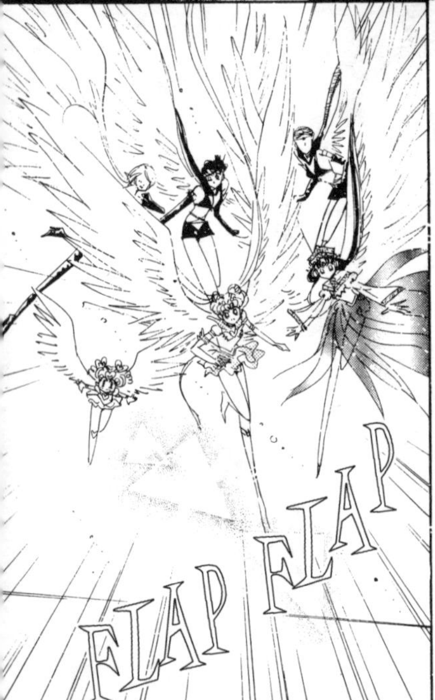
FLAP FLAP

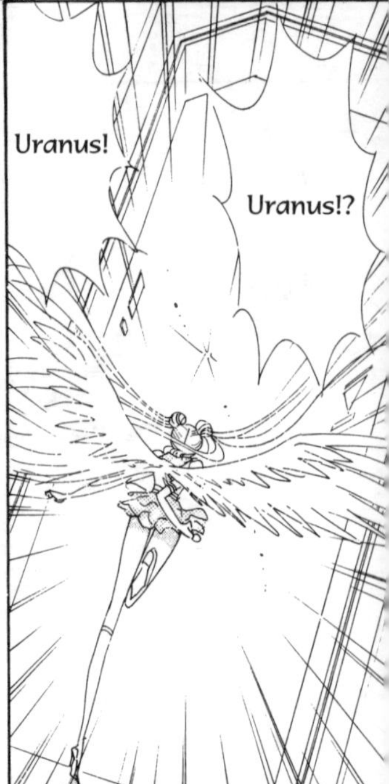
Uranus!
Uranus!?

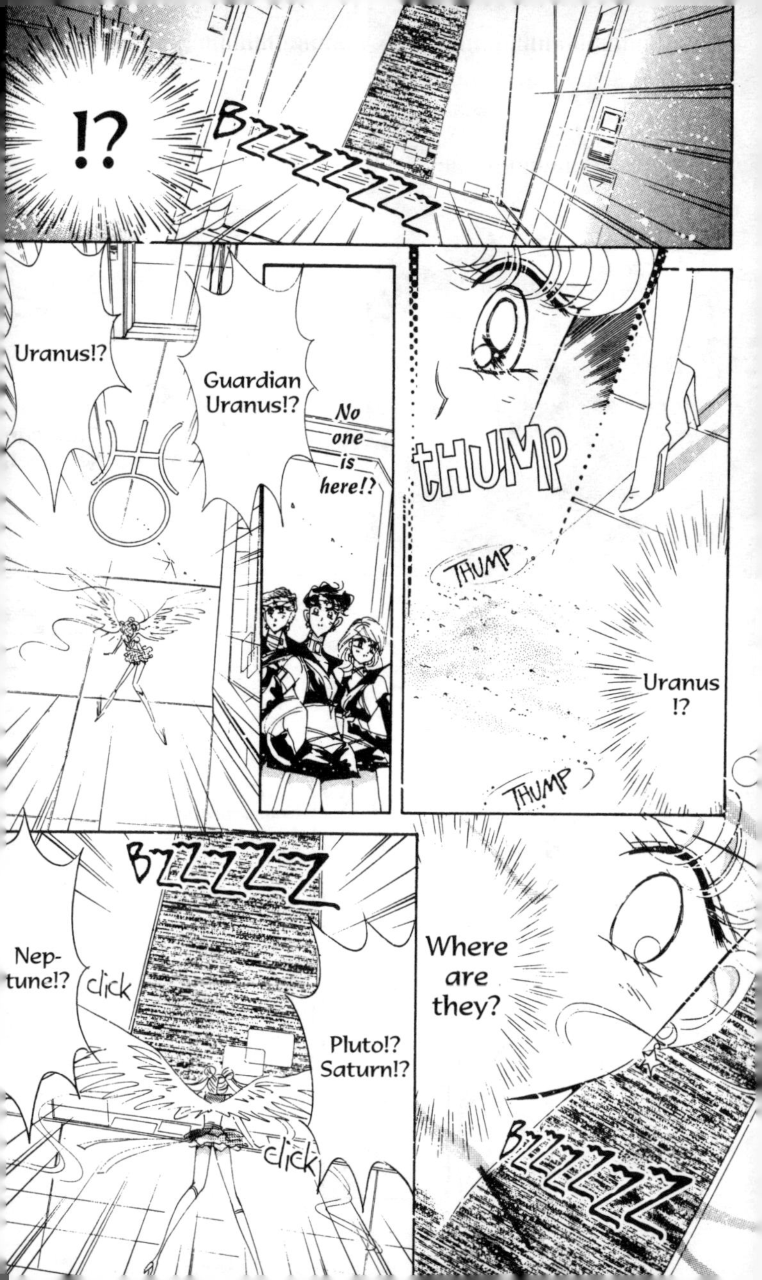

!?
BZZZZZZZZZ
Uranus!?
Guardian Uranus!?
No one is here!?
THUMP
THUMP
Uranus !?
THUMP
BZZZZZ
Nep-tune!?
click
Pluto!? Saturn!?
click
Where are they?
BZZZZZZ

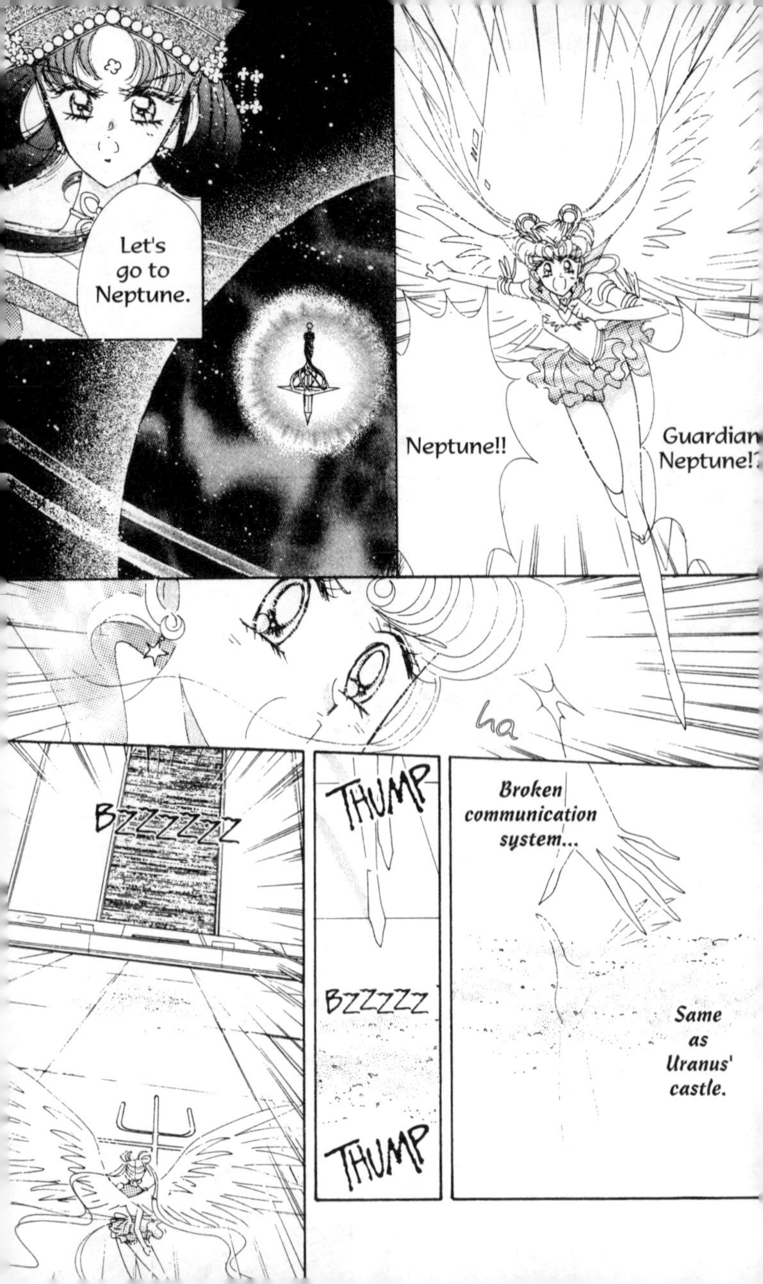

Let's go to Neptune.
Neptune!!
Guardian Neptune!?
ha
BZZZZZZZ
THUMP
BZZZZZ
THUMP
Broken communication system...
Same as Uranus' castle.

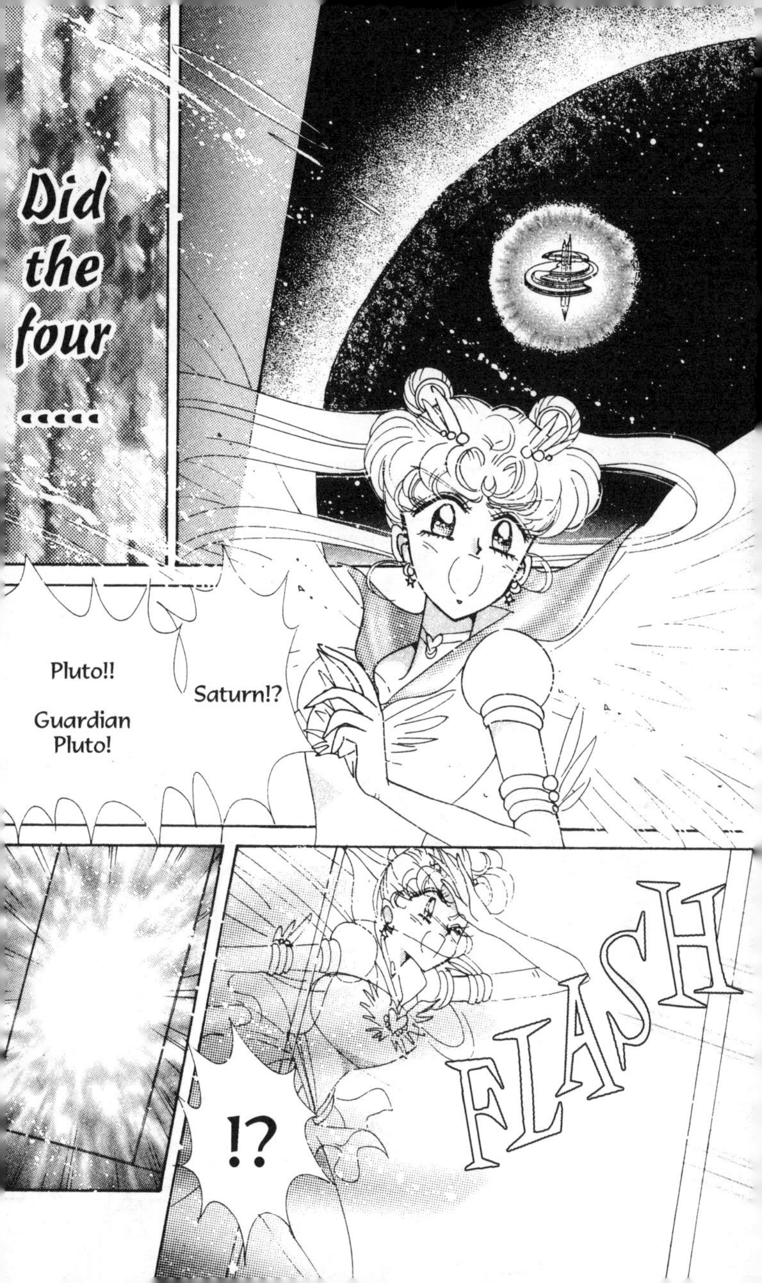
Did the four ......
Pluto!!
Guardian Pluto!
Saturn!?
FLASH
!?

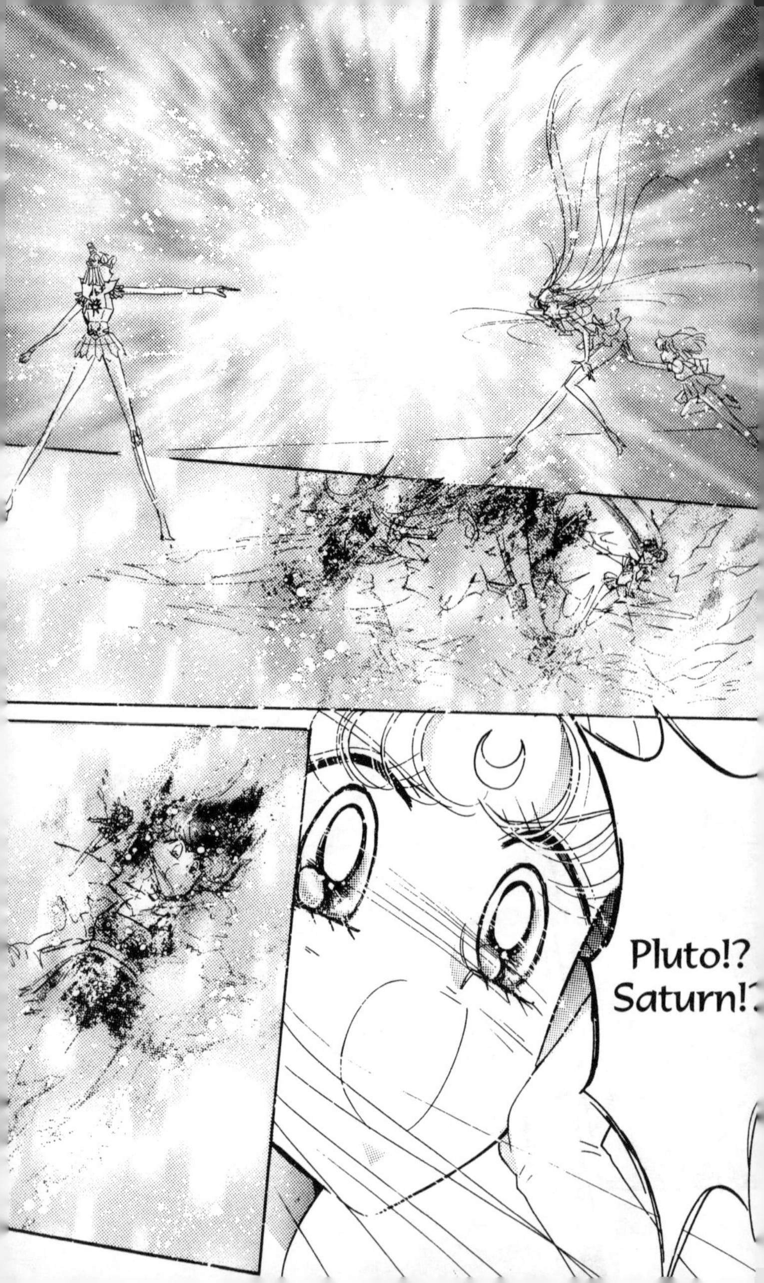
Pluto!? Saturn!?

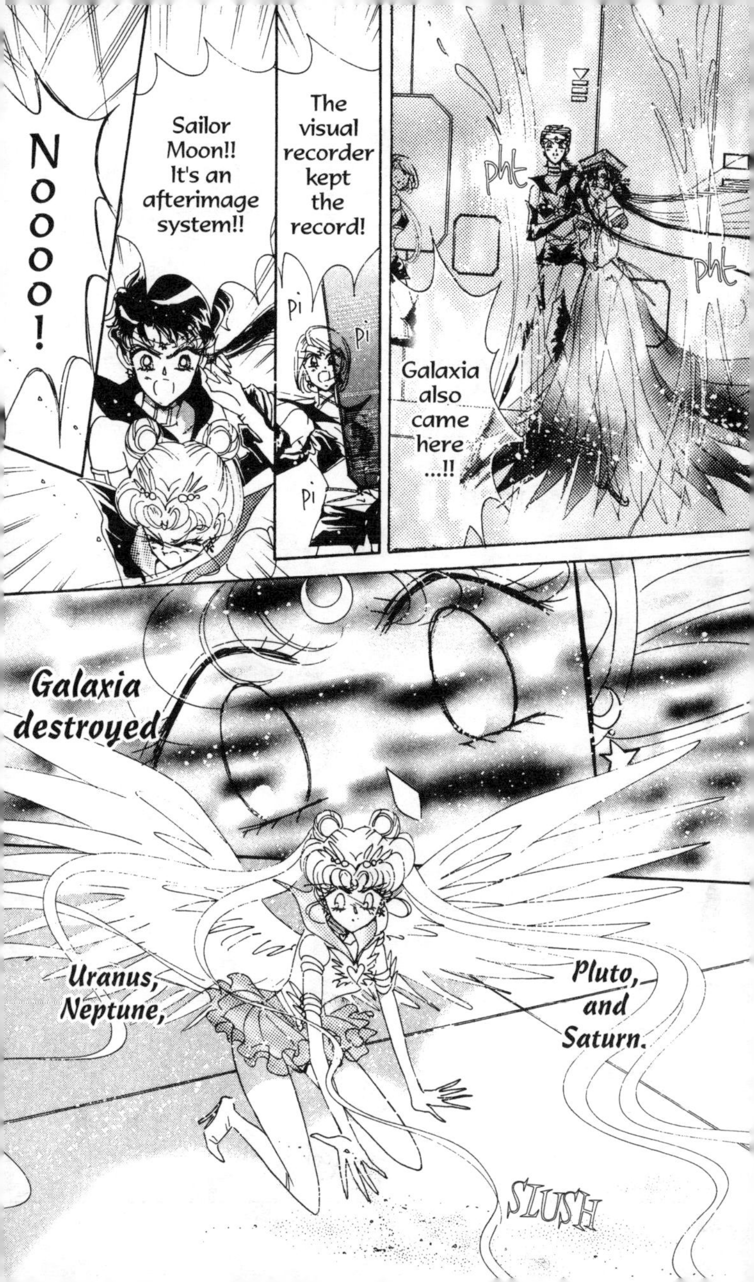
NOOOOO!
Sailor Moon!! It's an afterimage system!!
pi
The visual recorder kept the record!
pi
pi
pht
pht
Galaxia also came here ...!!
Galaxia destroyed
Uranus, Neptune,
Pluto, and Saturn.
SLUSH

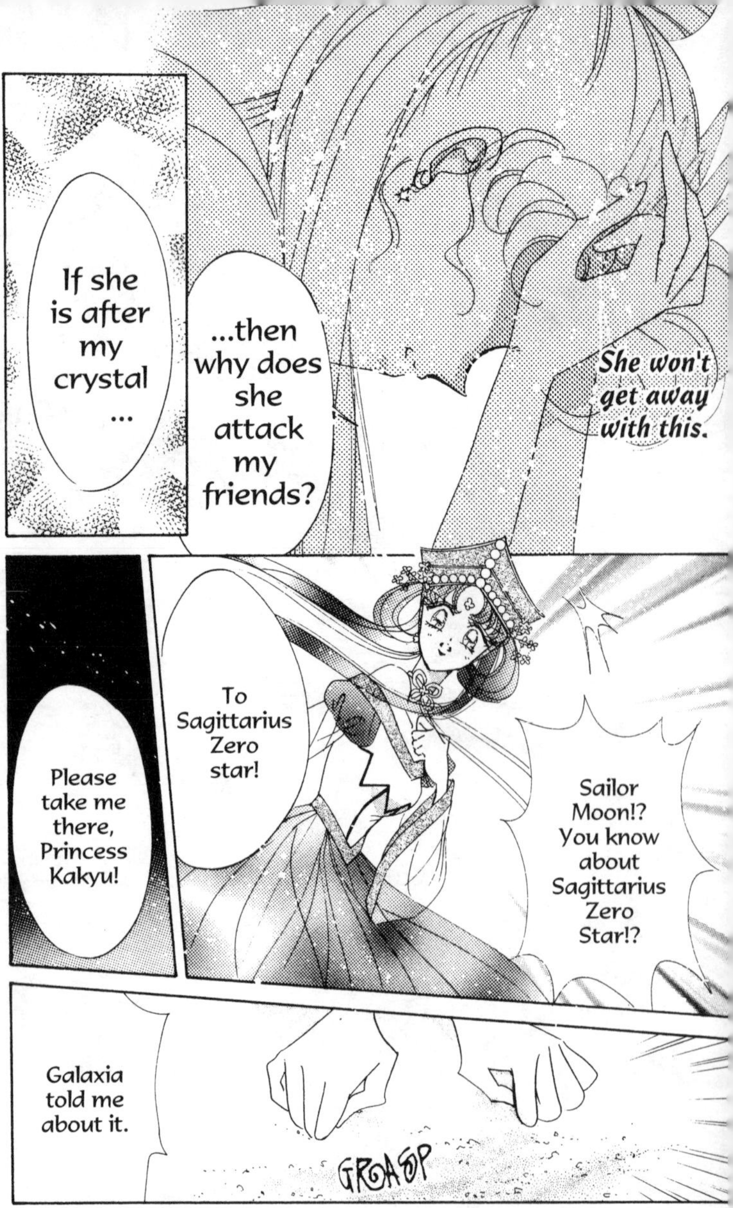
If she is after my crystal ...
...then why does she attack my friends?
She won't get away with this.
Please take me there, Princess Kakyu!
To Sagittarius Zero star!
Sailor Moon!? You know about Sagittarius Zero Star!?
Galaxia told me about it.
GRASP

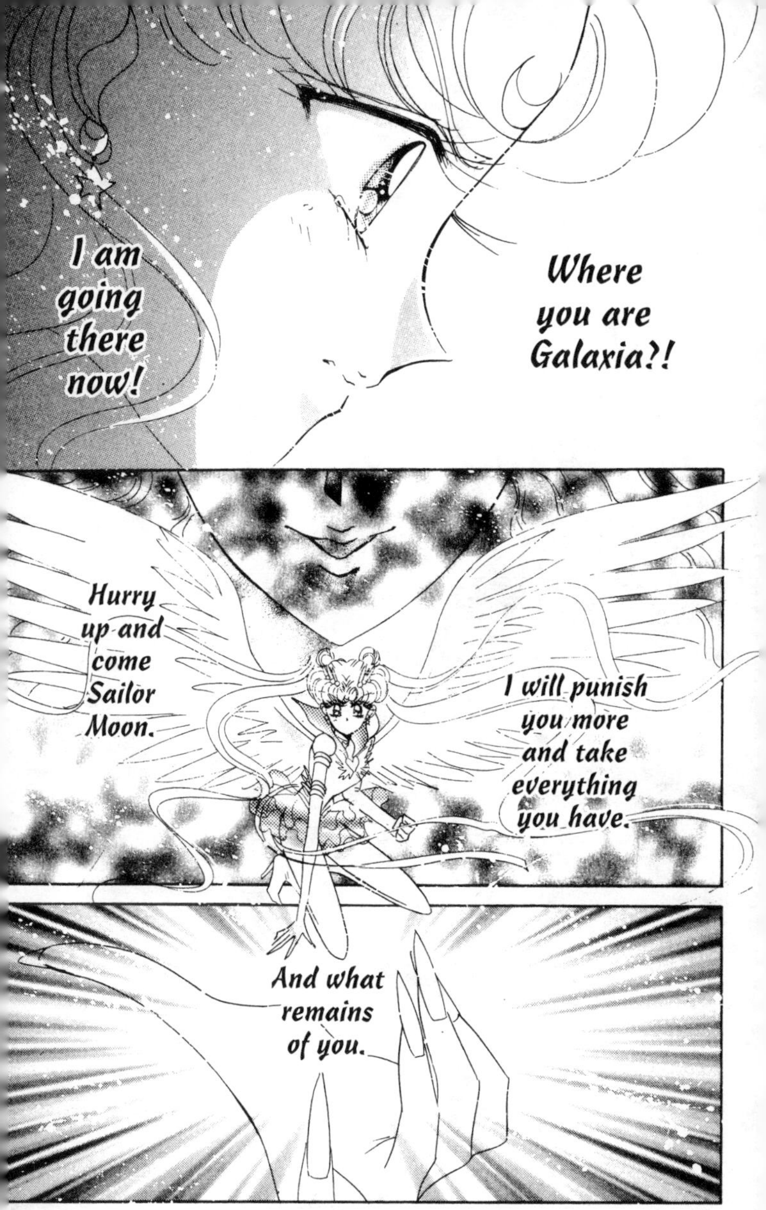
I am going there now!
Where you are Galaxia?!
Hurry up and come Sailor Moon.
I will punish you more and take everything you have.
And what remains of you.

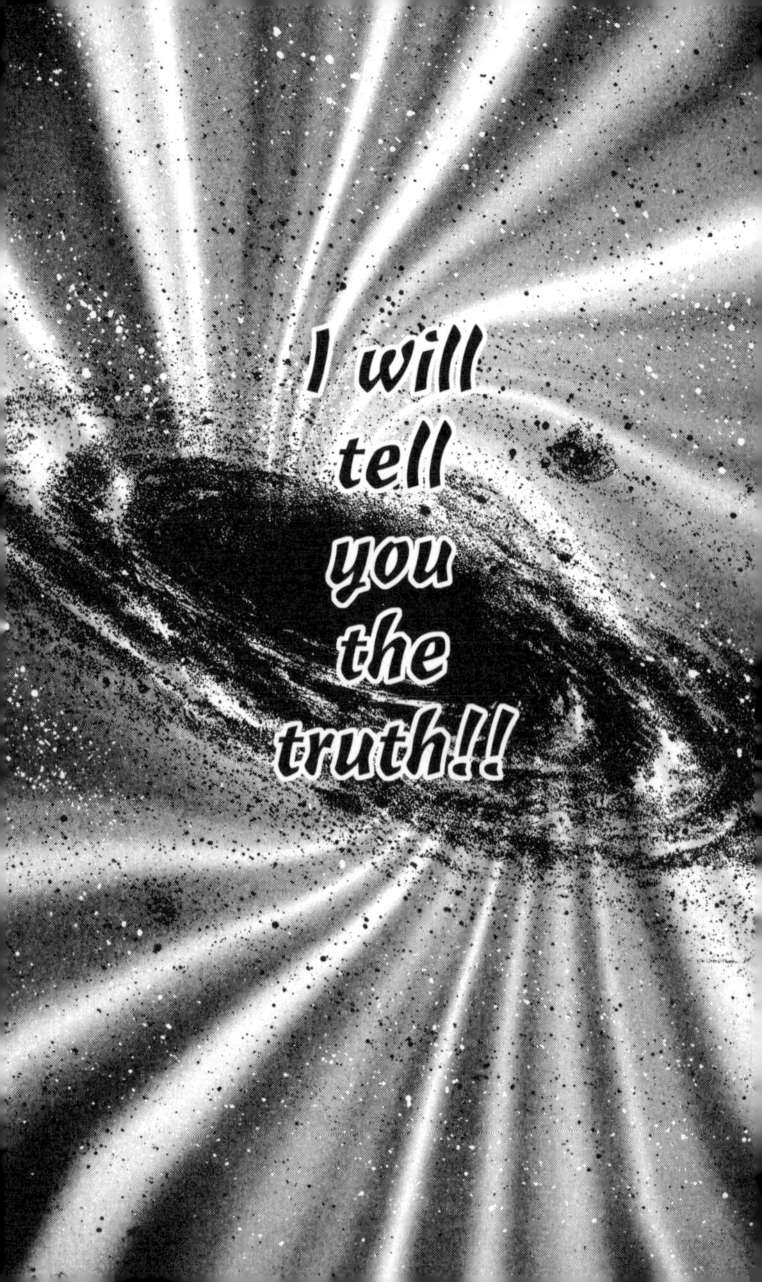
I will tell you the truth!!

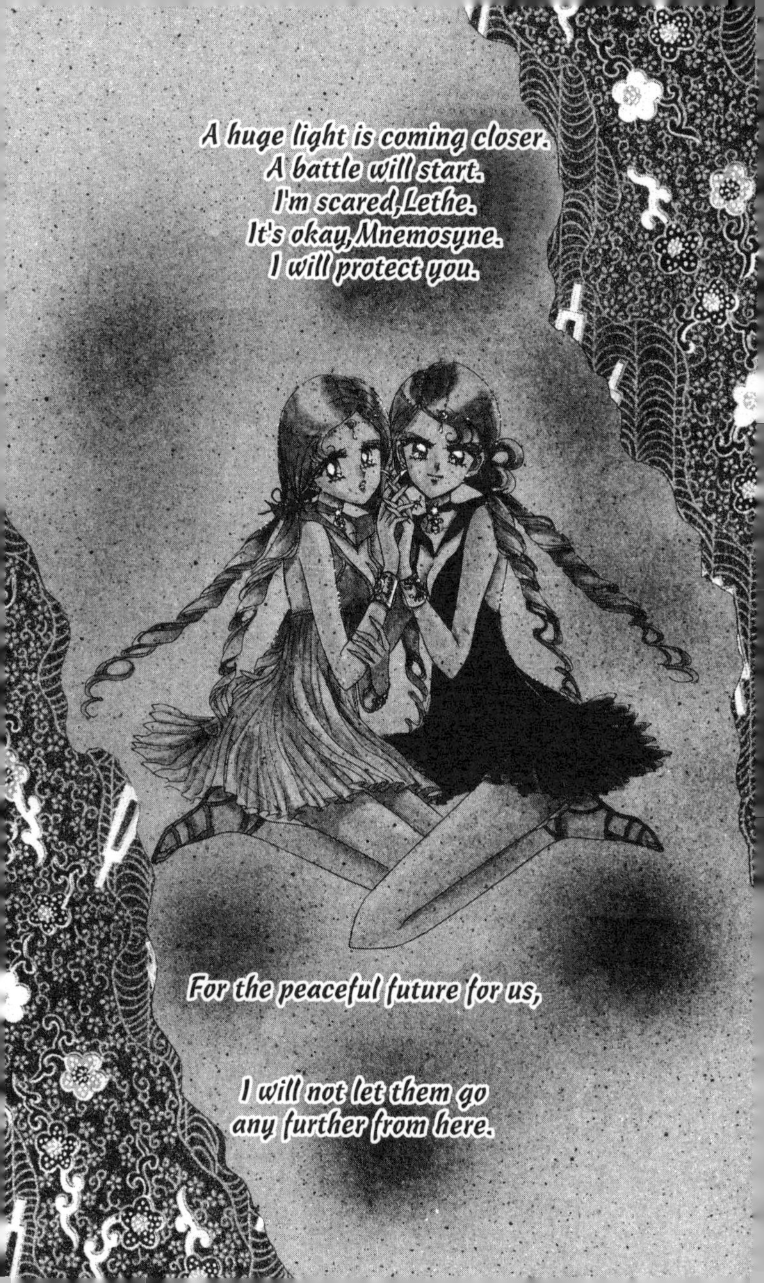
A huge light is coming closer.
A battle will start.
I'm scared,Lethe.
It's okay,Mnemosyne.
I will protect you.
For the peaceful future for us,
I will not let them go
any further from here.

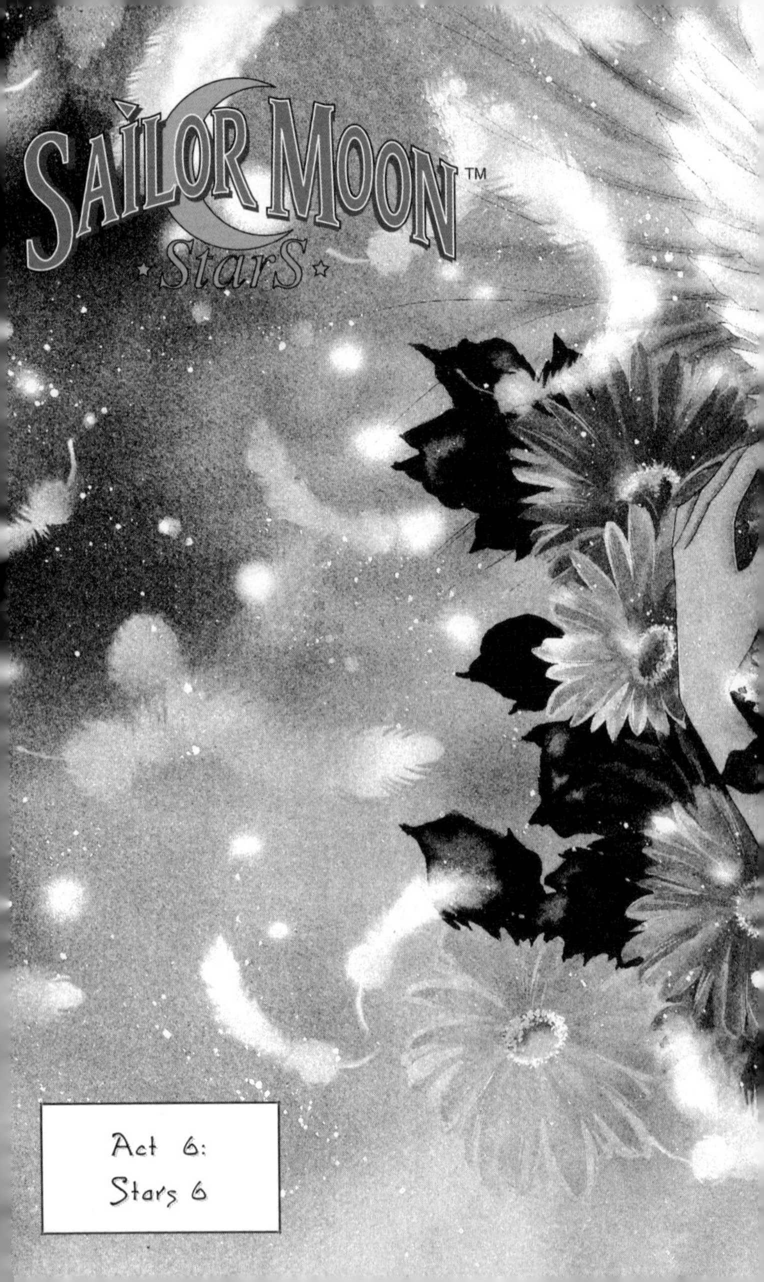
SAILOR MOON™
StarS
Act 6:
Stars 6

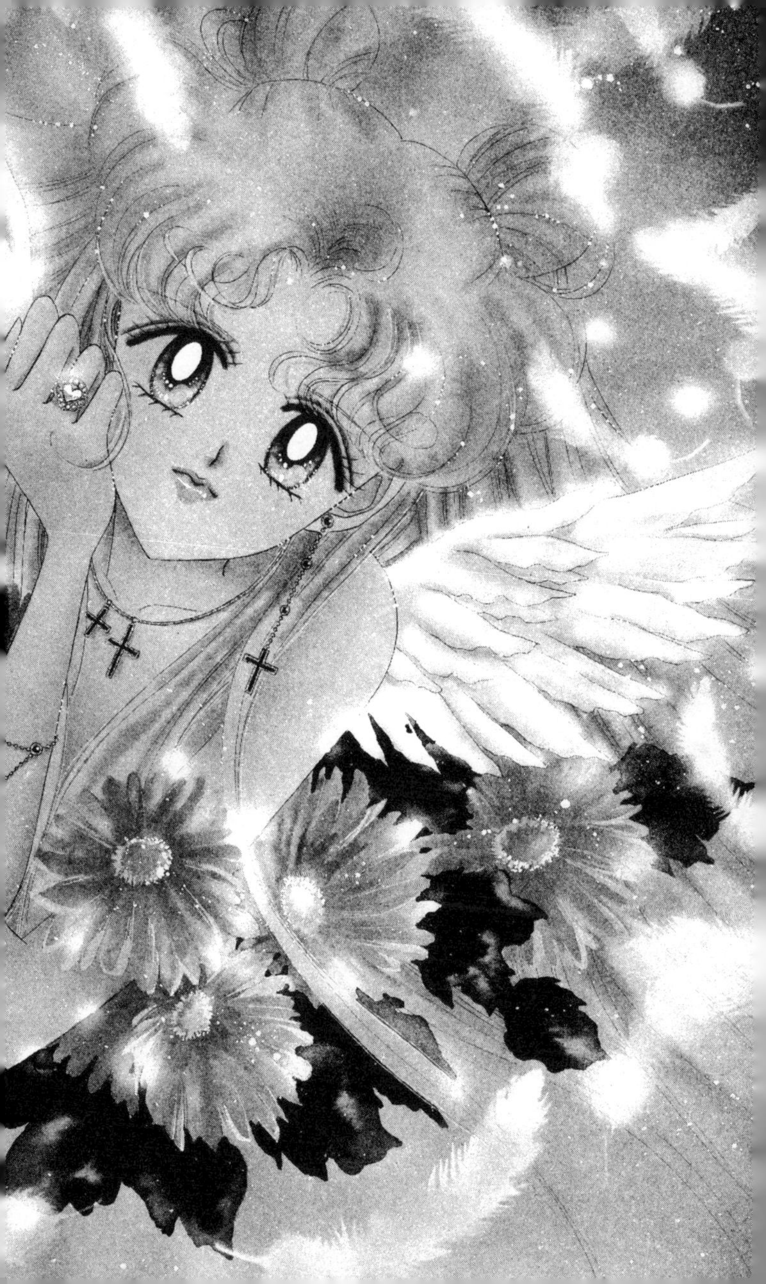

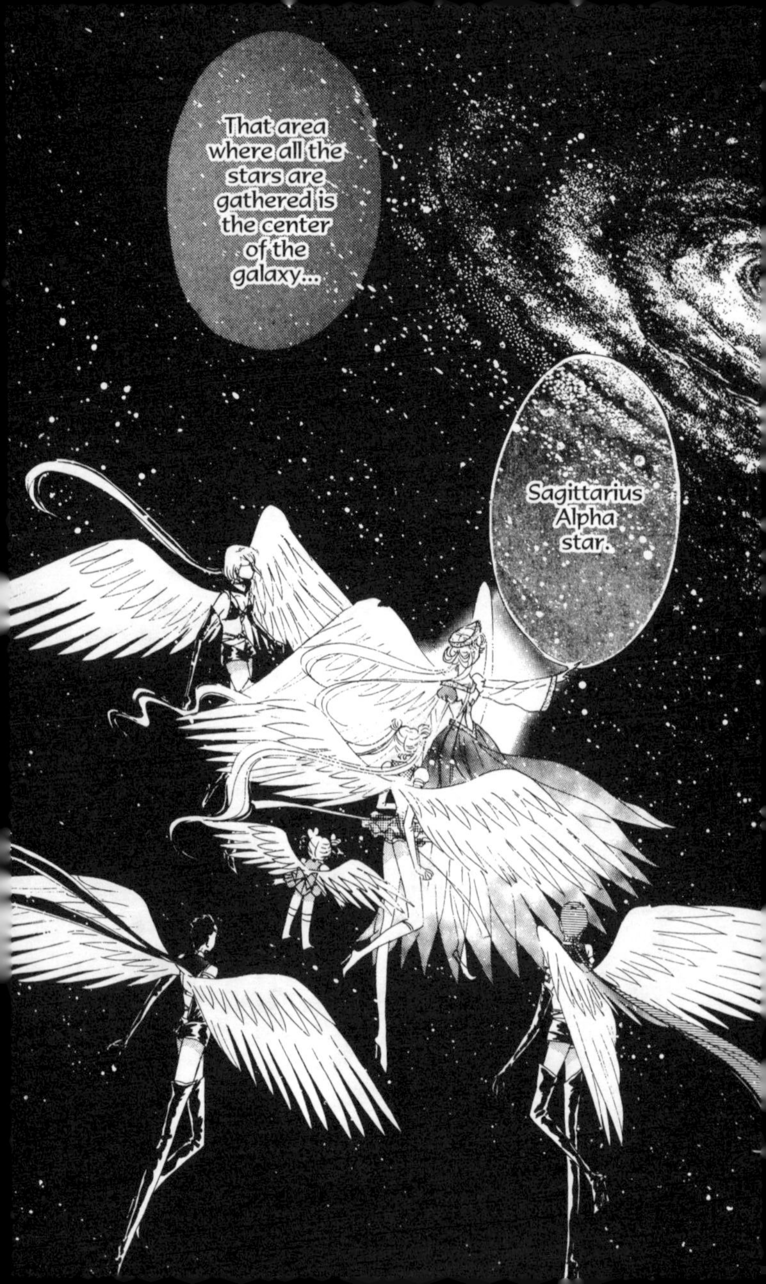
That area where all the stars are gathered is the center of the galaxy...
Sagittarius Alpha star.

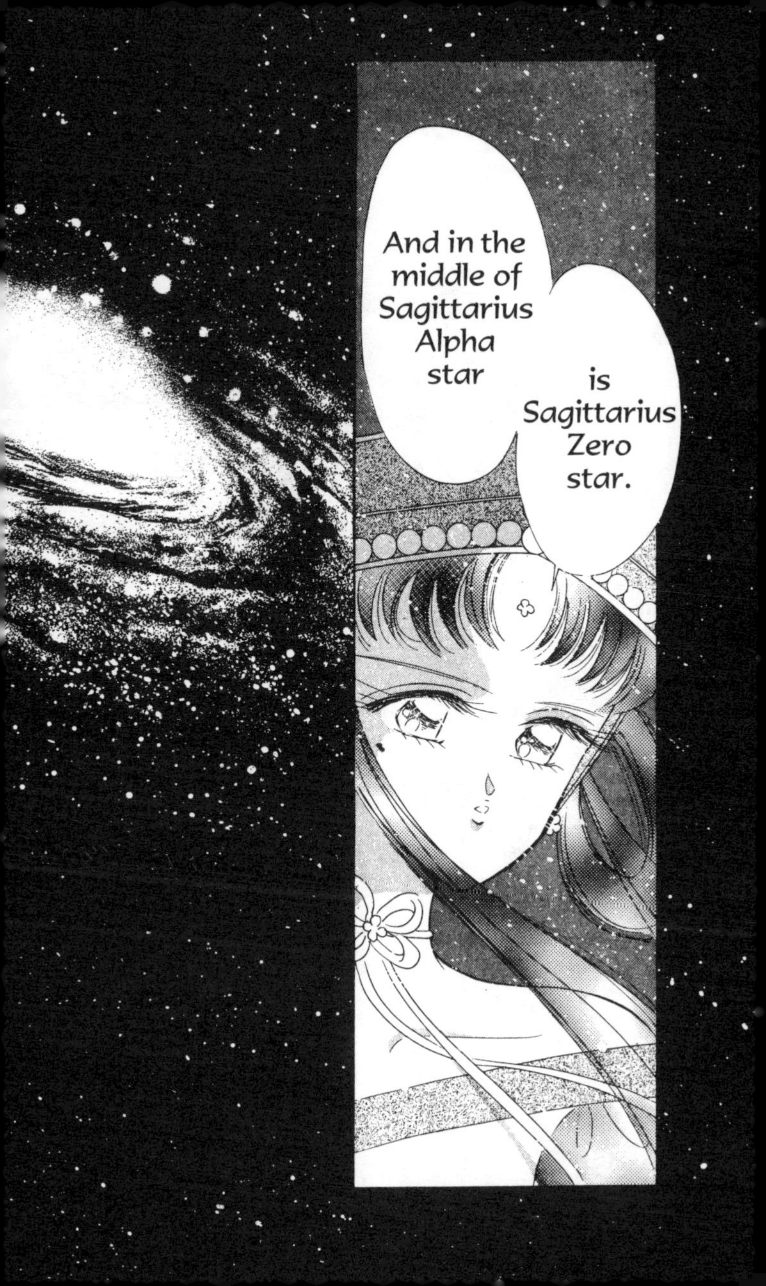
And in the middle of Sagittarius Alpha star
is Sagittarius Zero star.

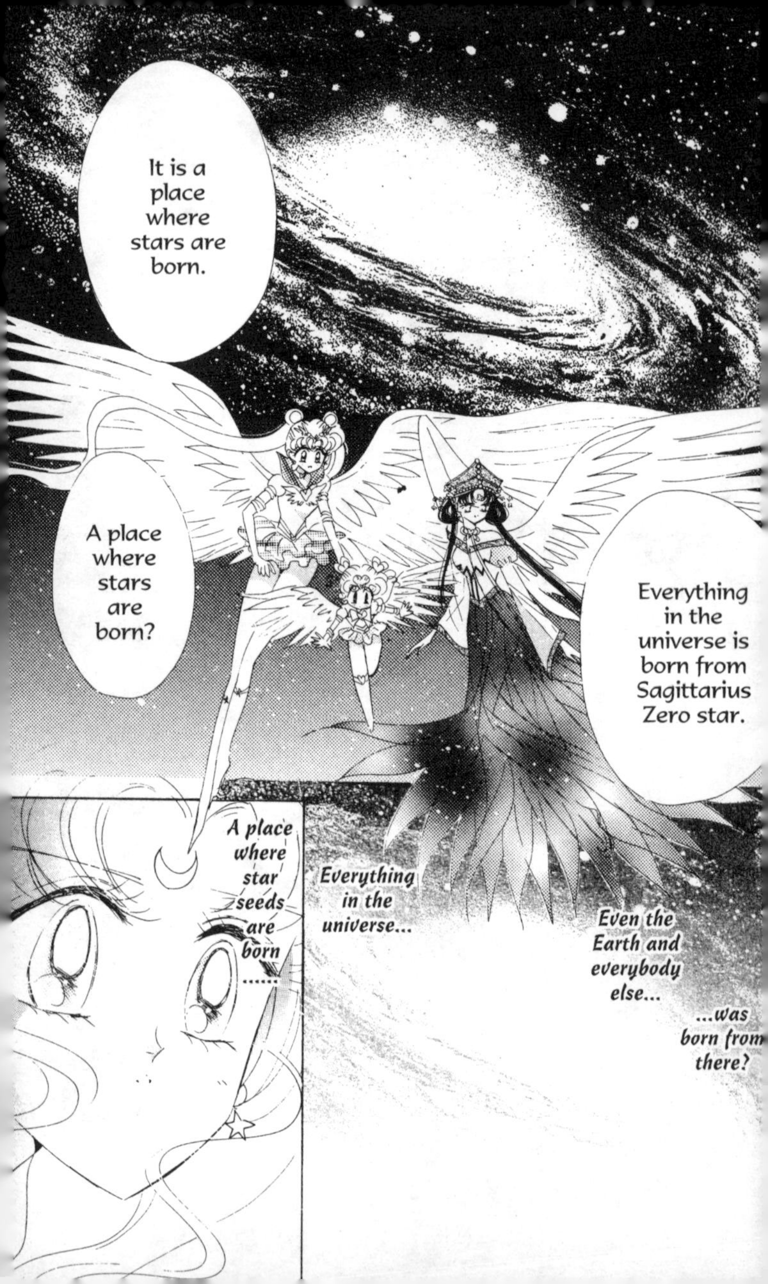
It is a place where stars are born.
A place where stars are born?
Everything in the universe is born from Sagittarius Zero star.
A place where star seeds are born ......
Everything in the universe...
Even the Earth and everybody else...
...was born from there?

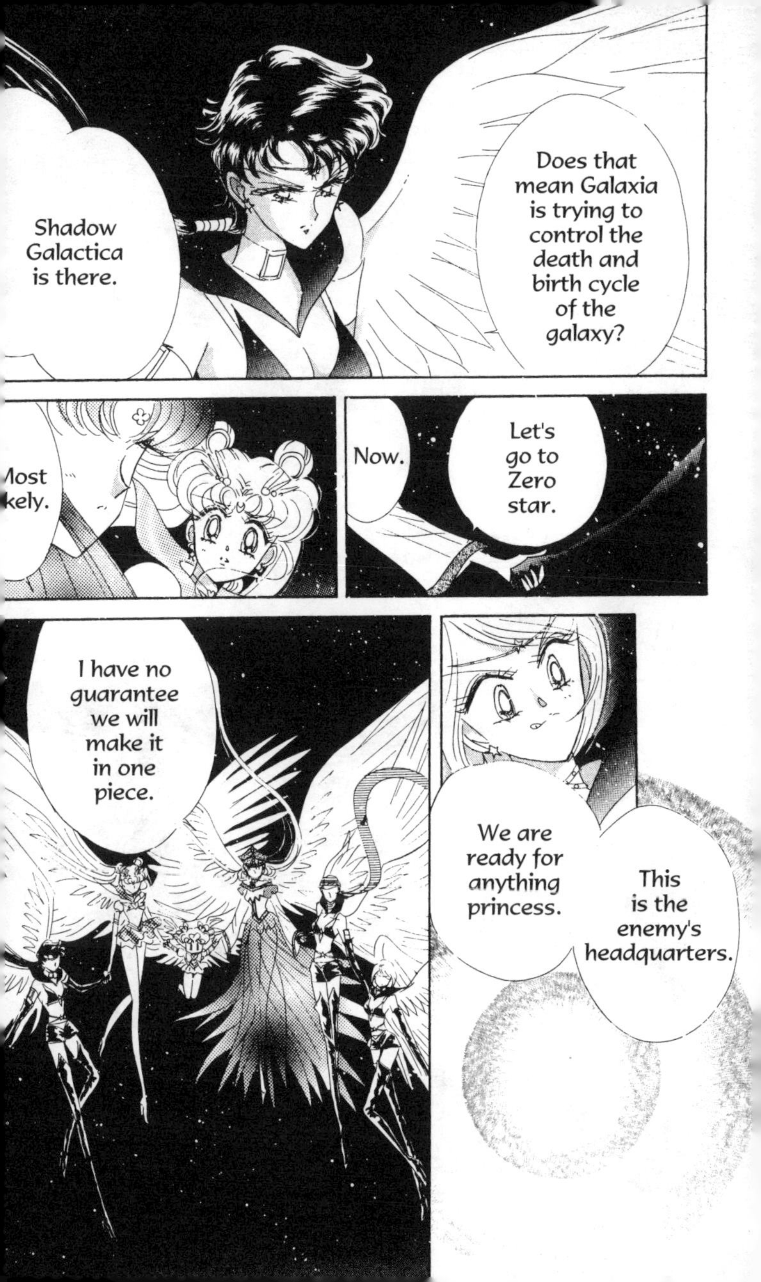
Shadow Galactica is there.
Does that mean Galaxia is trying to control the death and birth cycle of the galaxy?
Most likely.
Now.
Let's go to Zero star.
I have no guarantee we will make it in one piece.
We are ready for anything princess.
This is the enemy's headquarters.

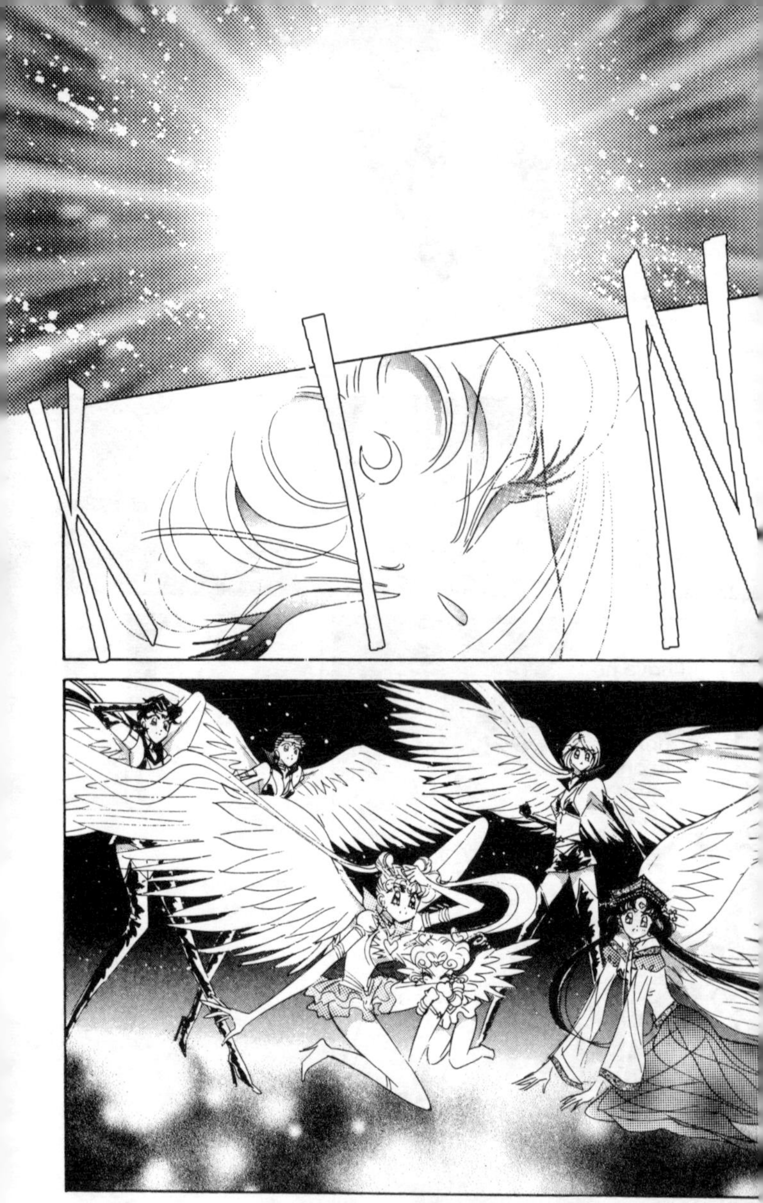
KIN

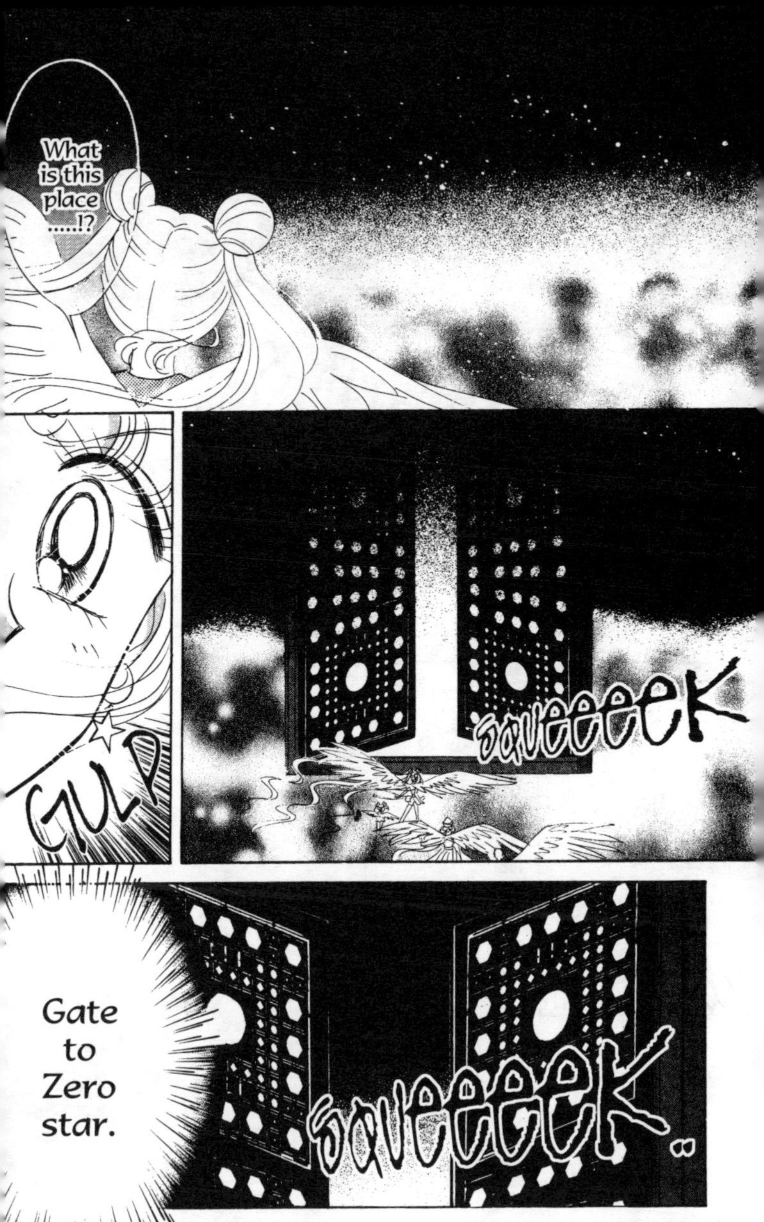
What is this place .....!?
GULP
SQUEEEK
Gate to Zero star.
SQUEEEK..

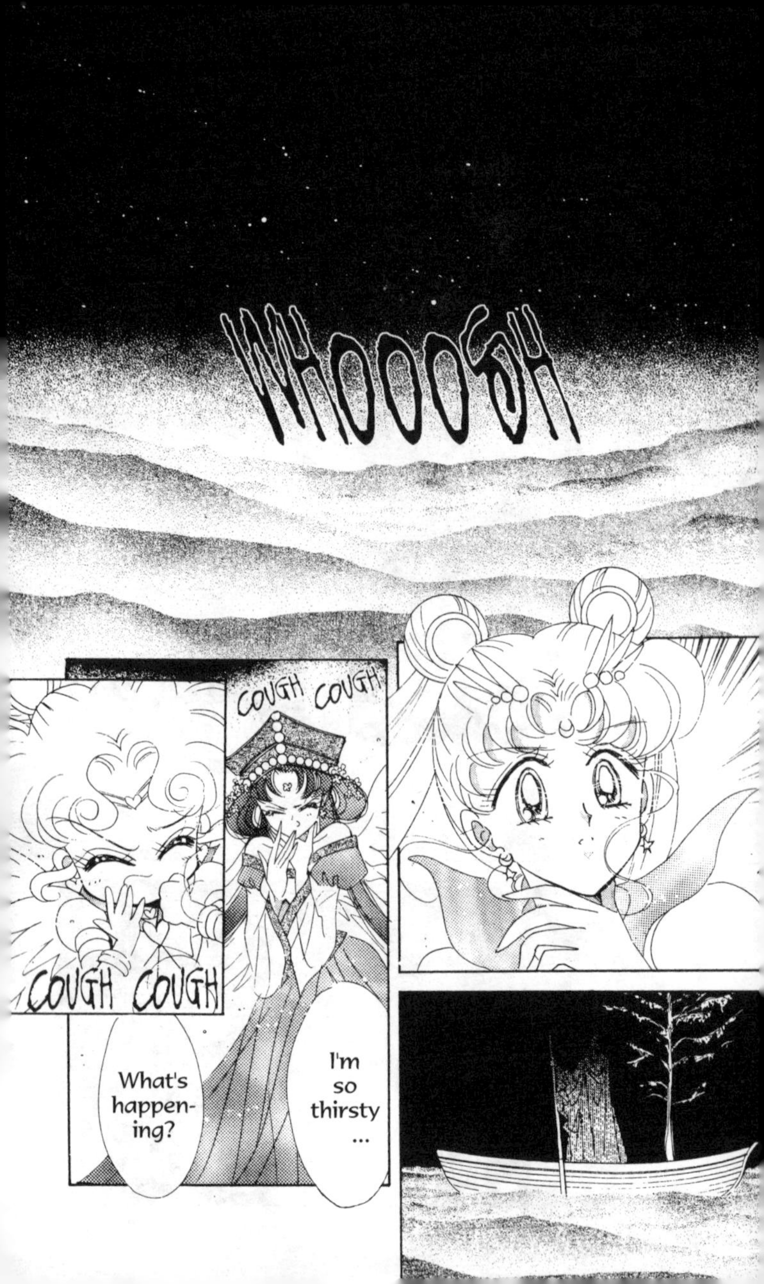
WHOOOSH
COUGH COUGH
COUGH COUGH
What's happening?
I'm so thirsty ...

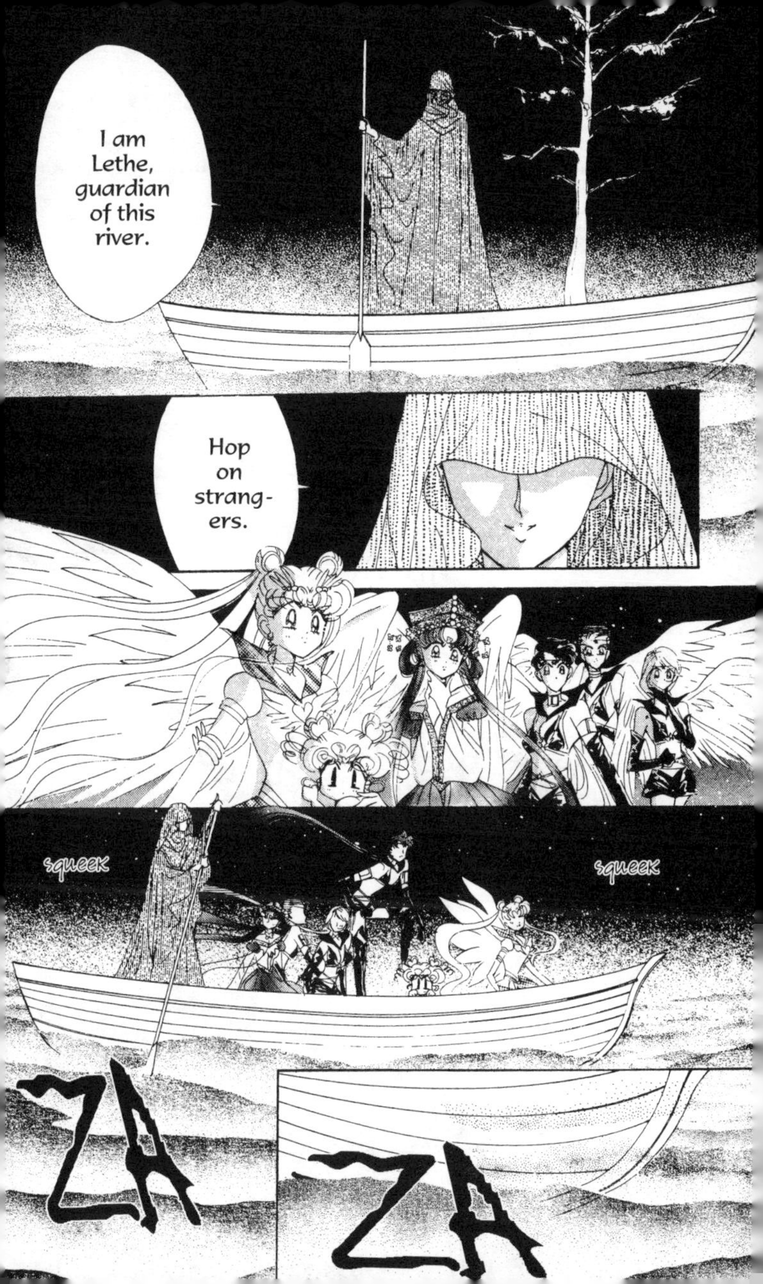

I am Lethe, guardian of this river.
Hop on strang-ers.
squeek
squeek
ZA
ZA

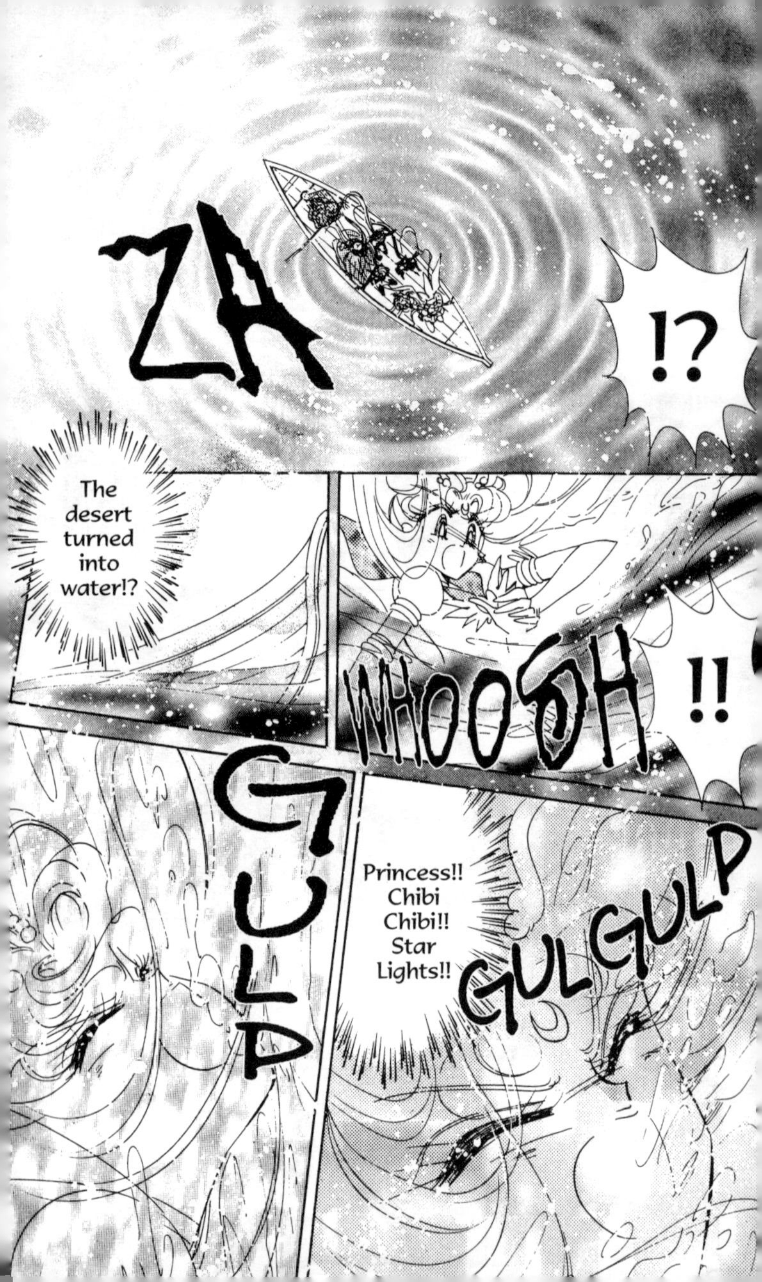
ZA
!?
The desert turned into water!?
WHOOSH
!!
GULP
Princess!! Chibi Chibi!! Star Lights!!
GULGULP

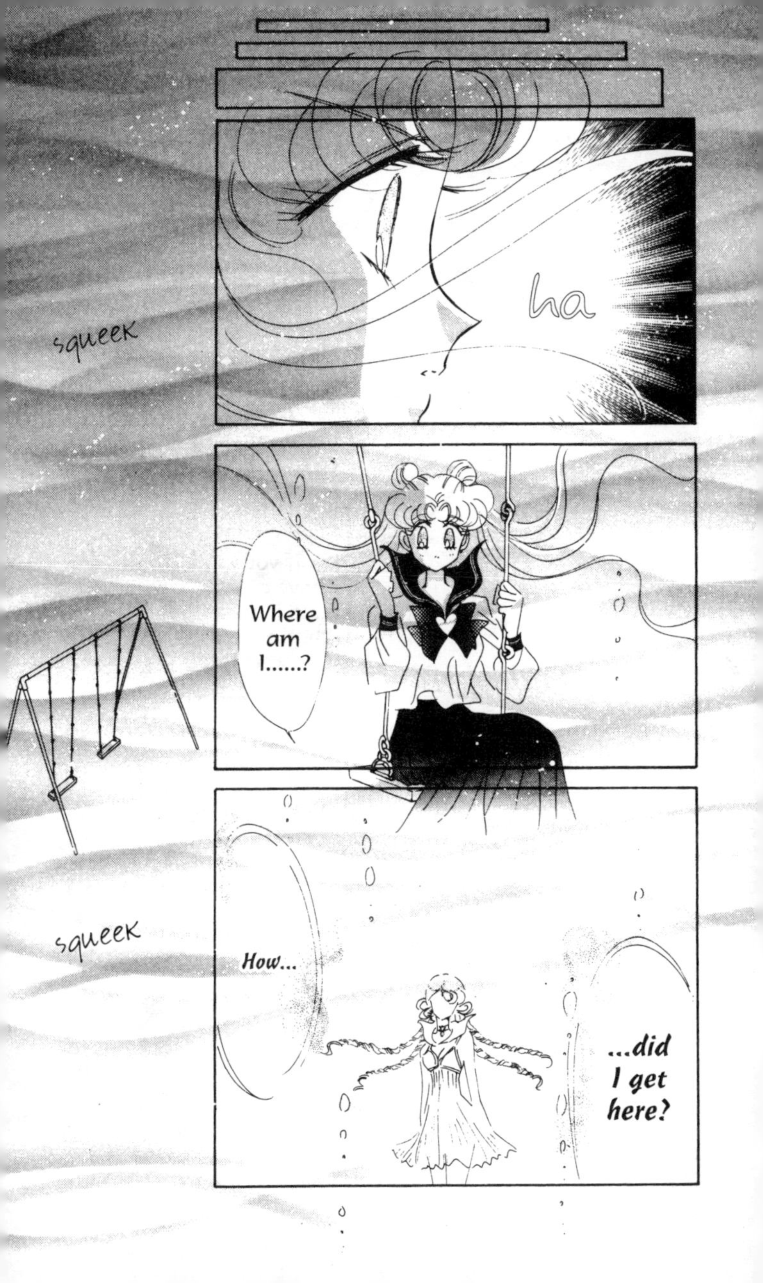

squeek
ha
Where am I......?
squeek
How...
...did I get here?

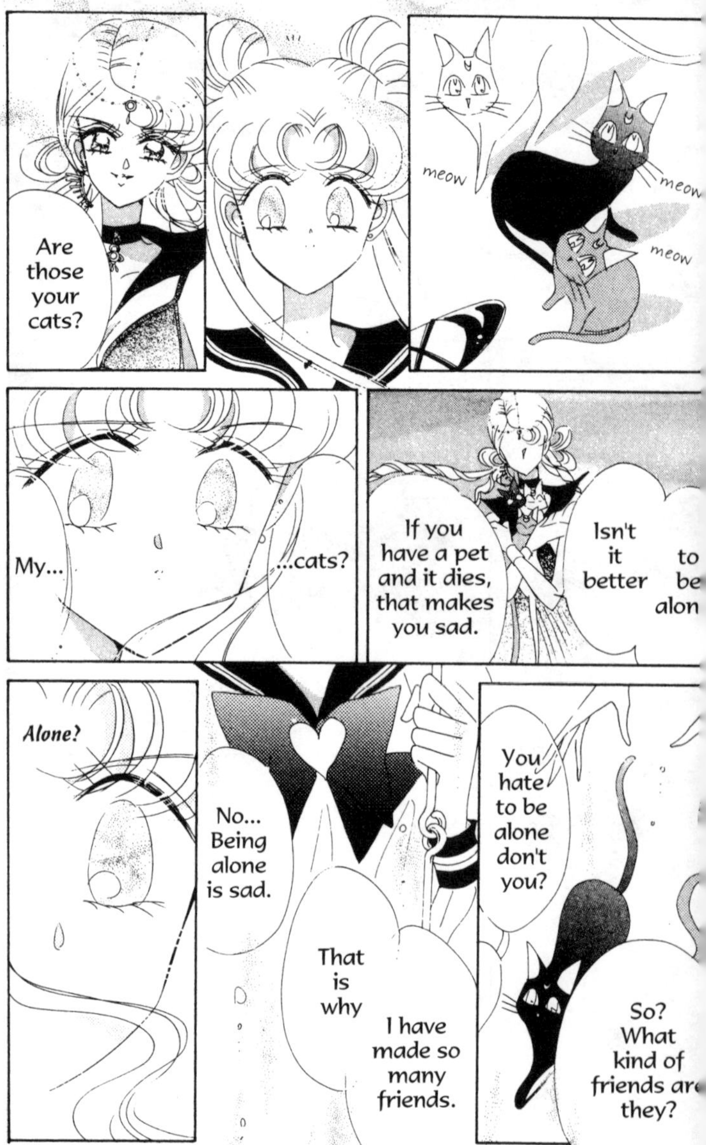

Are those your cats?
meow
meow
meow
My...
...cats?
If you have a pet and it dies, that makes you sad.
Isn't it better to be alon
Alone?
No... Being alone is sad.
That is why
I have made so many friends.
You hate to be alone don't you?
So? What kind of friends ar they?

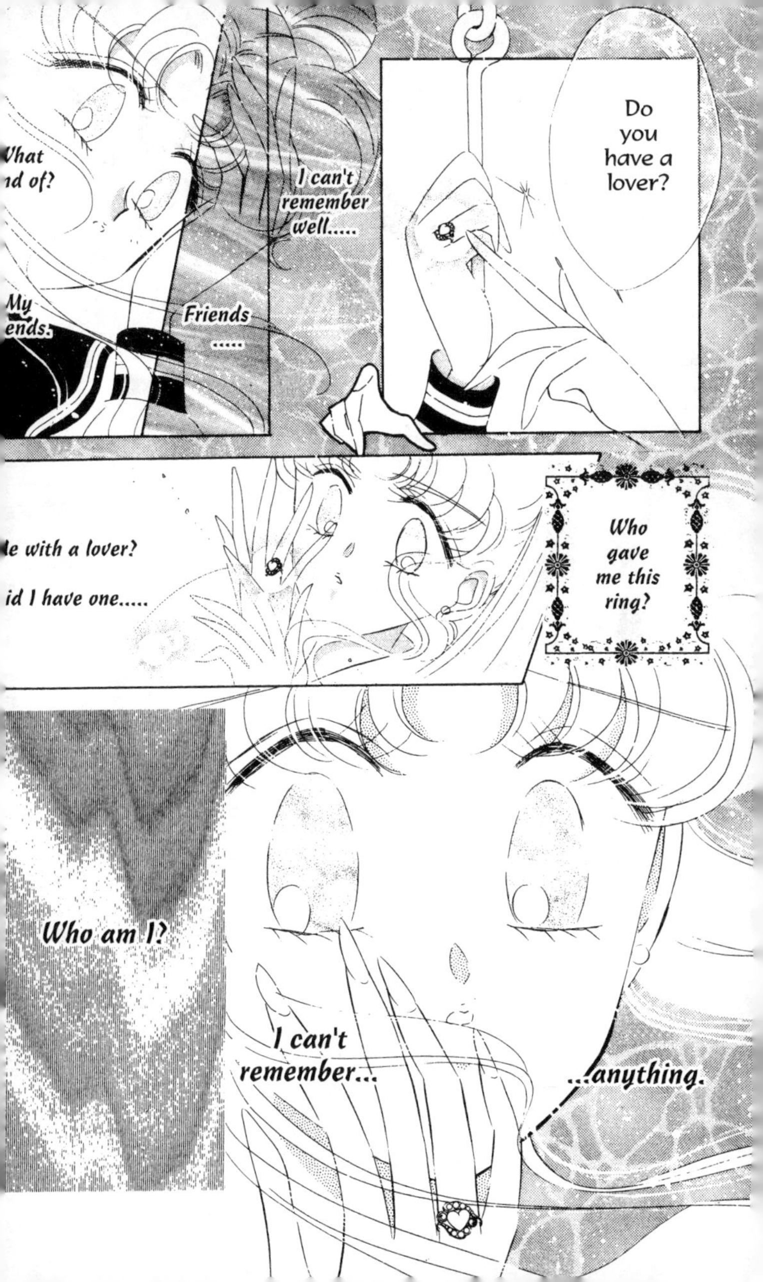

Vhat
ıd of?
My
ends.
I can't remember well.....
Friends
.....
Do you have a lover?
le with a lover?
id I have one.....
Who gave me this ring?
Who am I?
I can't remember...
...anything.

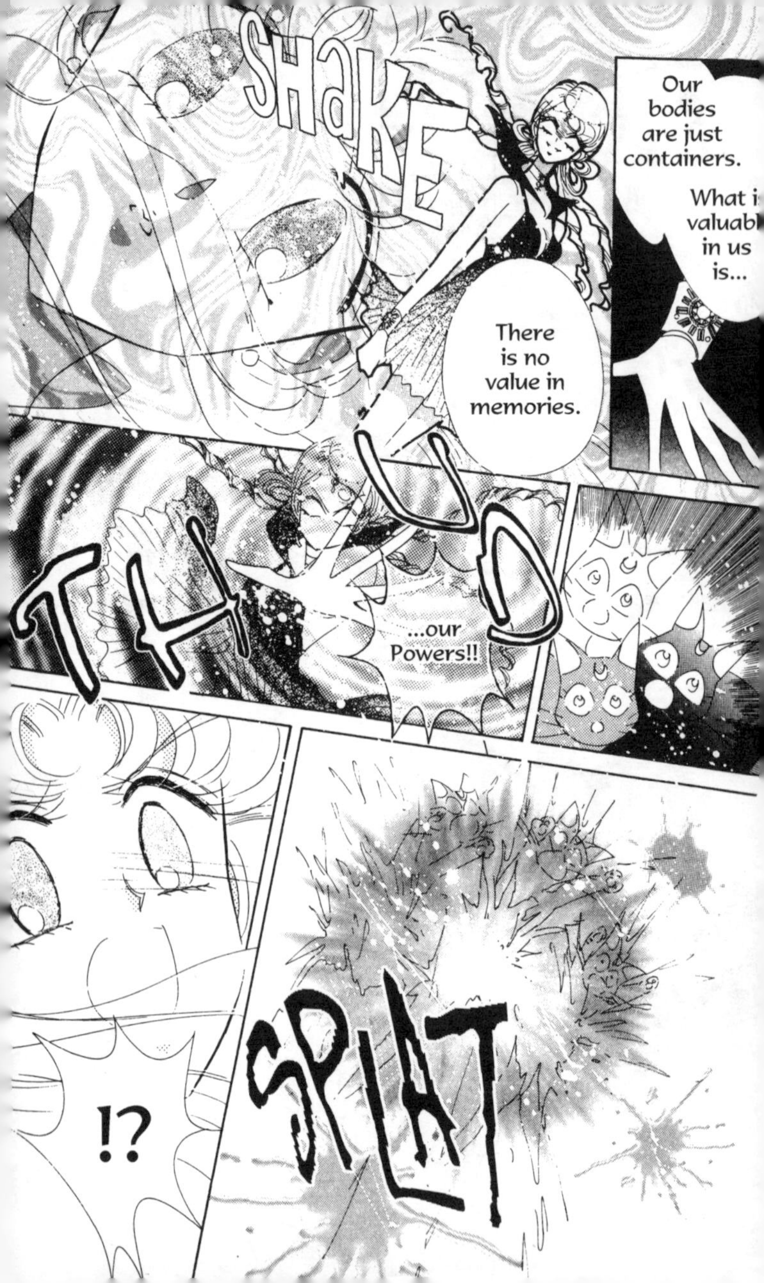
SHAKE
There is no value in memories.
Our bodies are just containers.
What i valuabl in us is...
THUD
...our Powers!!
!?
SPLAT

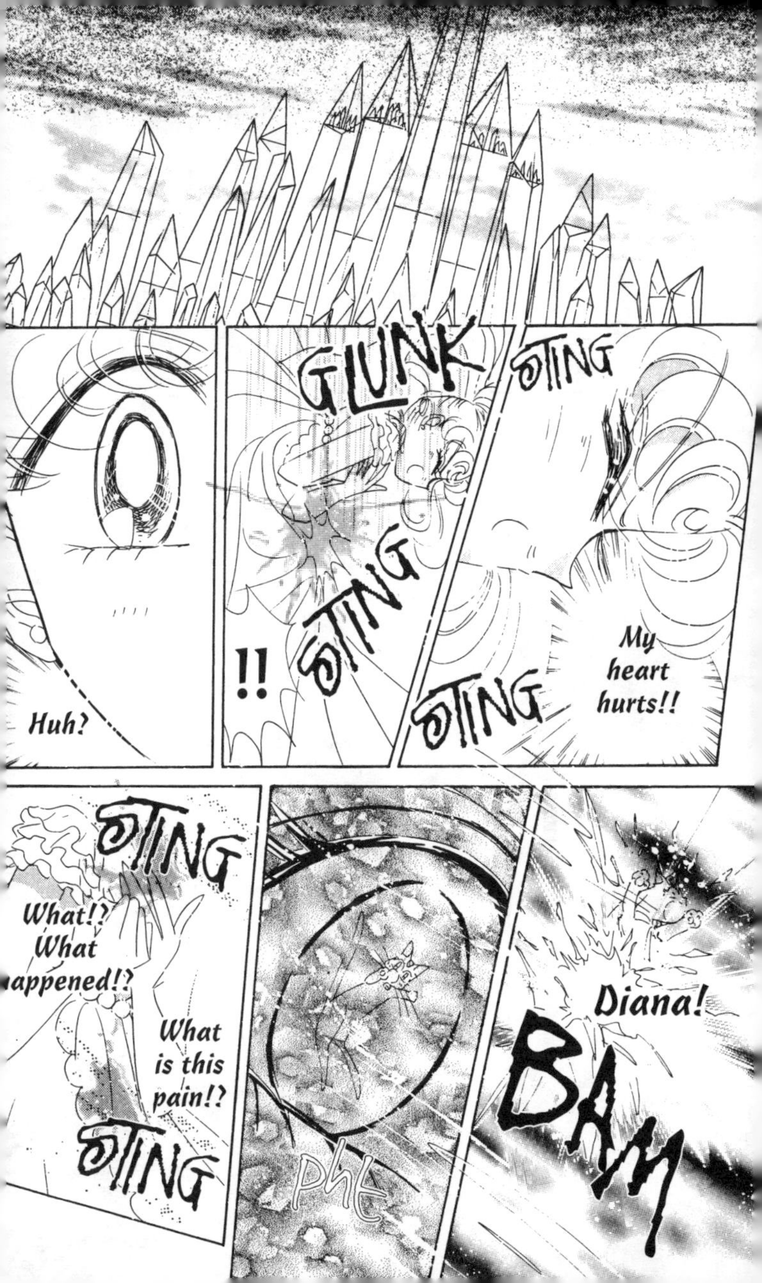
Huh?
GLUNK
!!
STING
STING
My heart hurts!!
STING
STING
What!? What happened!?
What is this pain!?
STING
phe
Diana!
BAM

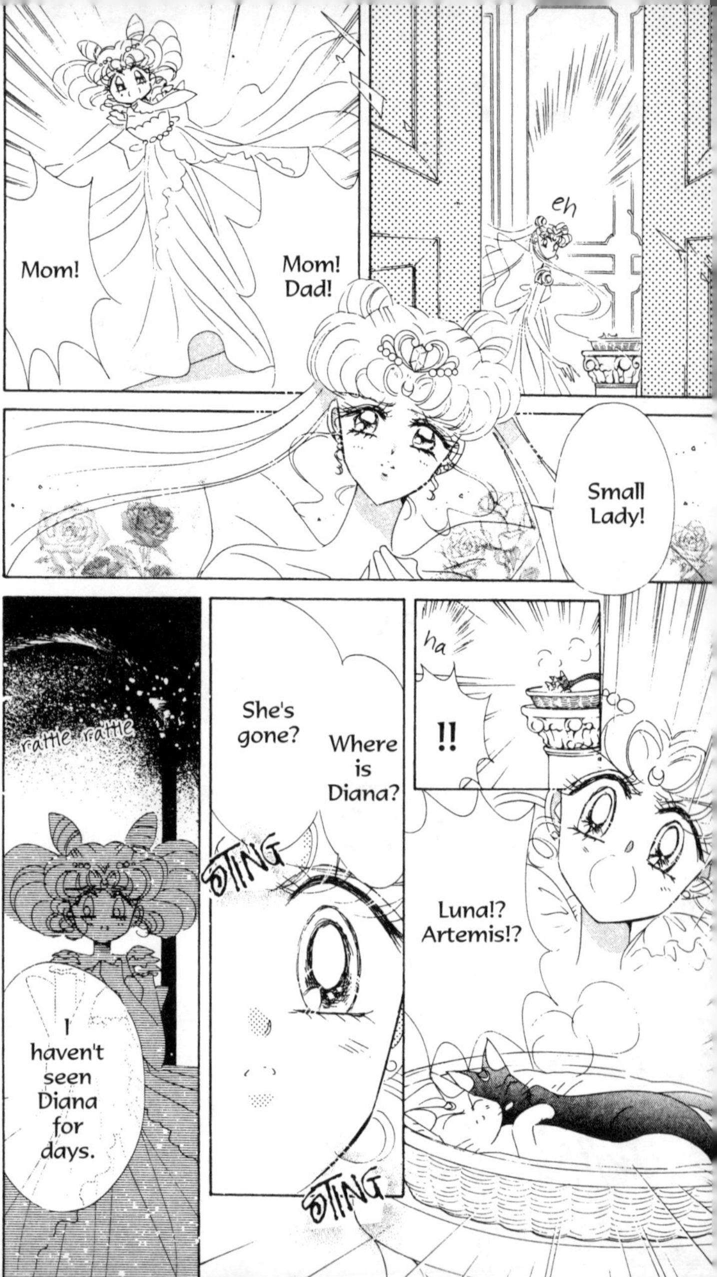
eh
Mom! Dad!
Mom!
Small Lady!
ha
!!
Luna!? Artemis!?
She's gone?
Where is Diana?
STING
STING
rattle rattle
I haven't seen Diana for days.

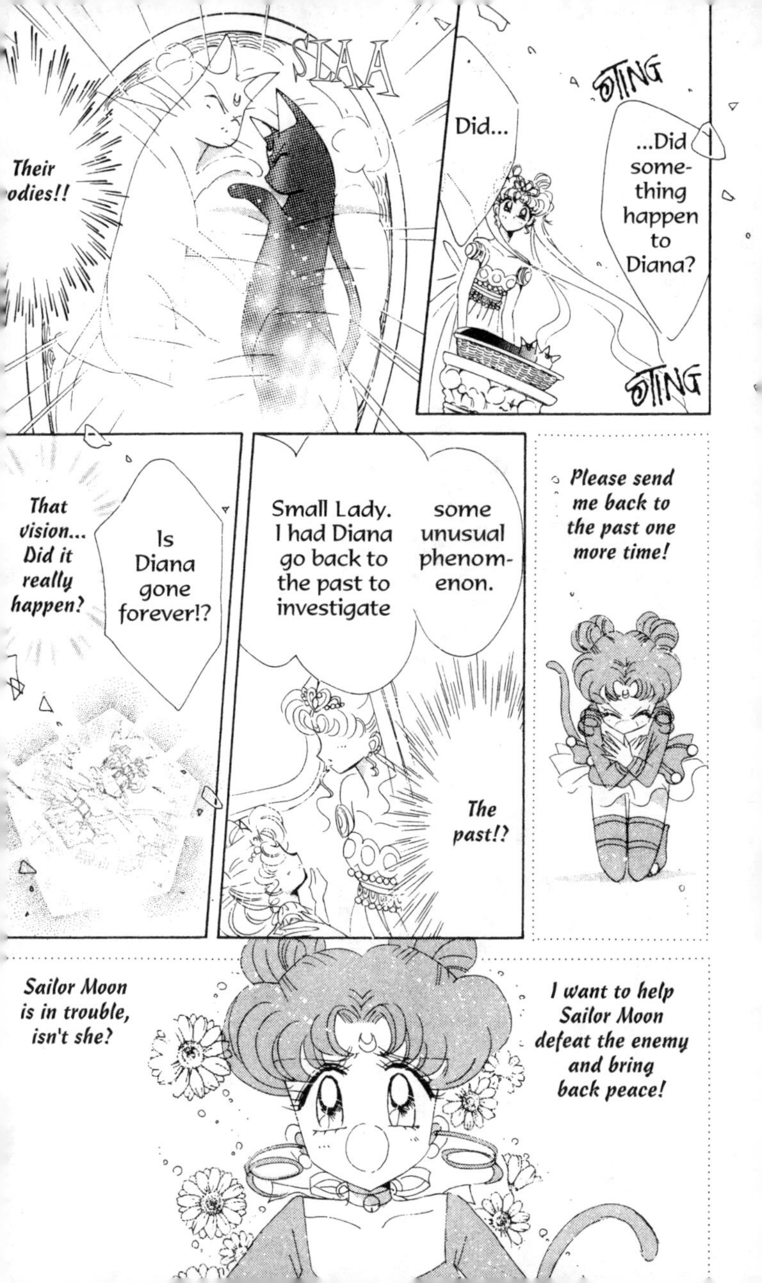

Their odies!!
SLAA
Did...
...Did something happen to Diana?
STING
STING
That vision... Did it really happen?
Is Diana gone forever!?
Small Lady. I had Diana go back to the past to investigate some unusual phenomenon.
The past!?
Please send me back to the past one more time!
Sailor Moon is in trouble, isn't she?
I want to help Sailor Moon defeat the enemy and bring back peace!

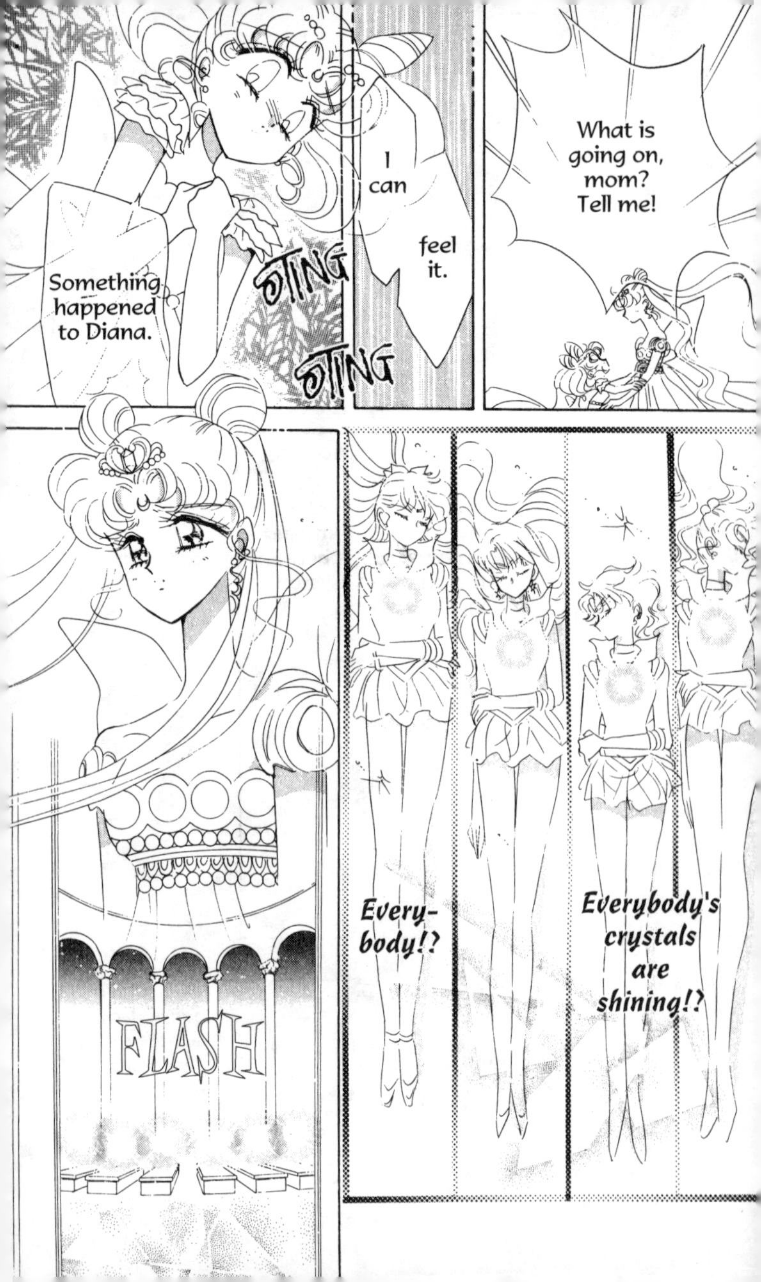

Something happened to Diana.
STING
STING
I can feel it.
What is going on, mom? Tell me!
FLASH
Every-body!?
Everybody's crystals are shining!?

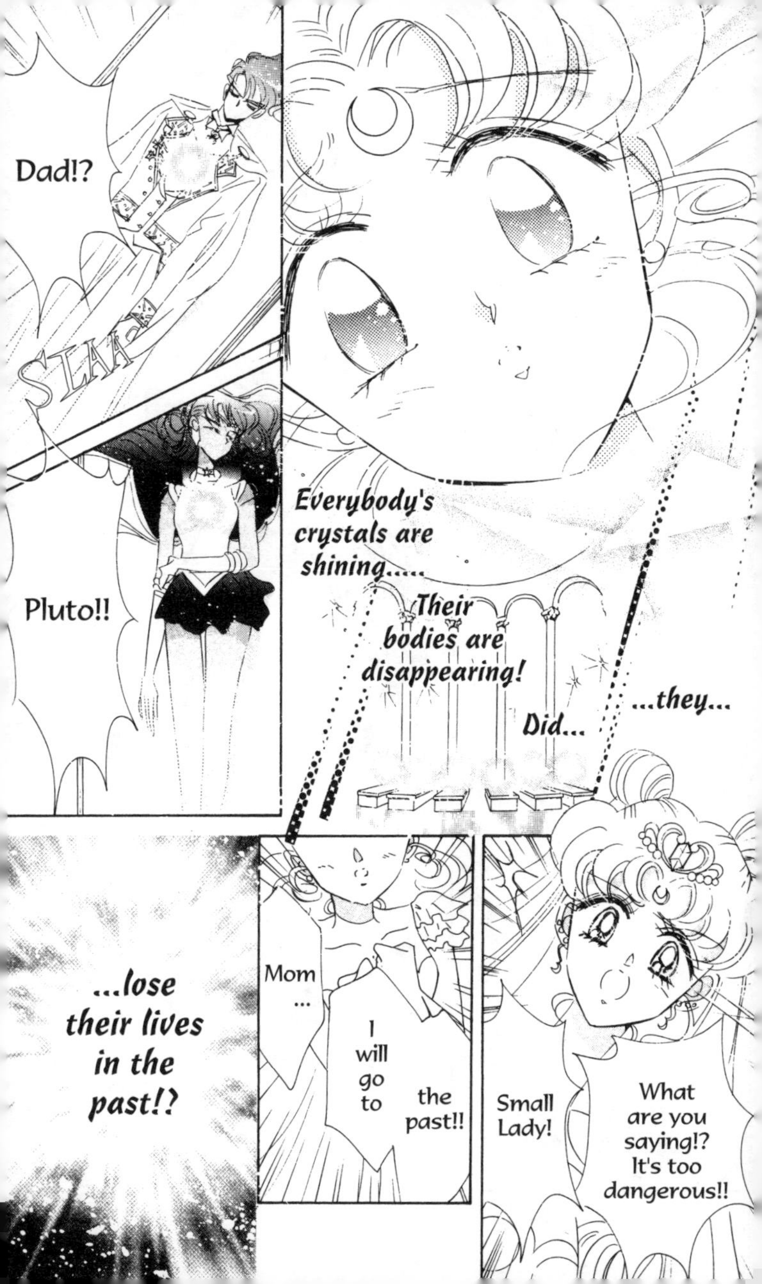
Dad!?
SLAA
Pluto!!
Everybody's crystals are shining.....
Their bodies are disappearing!
Did...
...they...
...lose their lives in the past!?
Mom...
I will go to the past!!
Small Lady!
What are you saying!? It's too dangerous!!

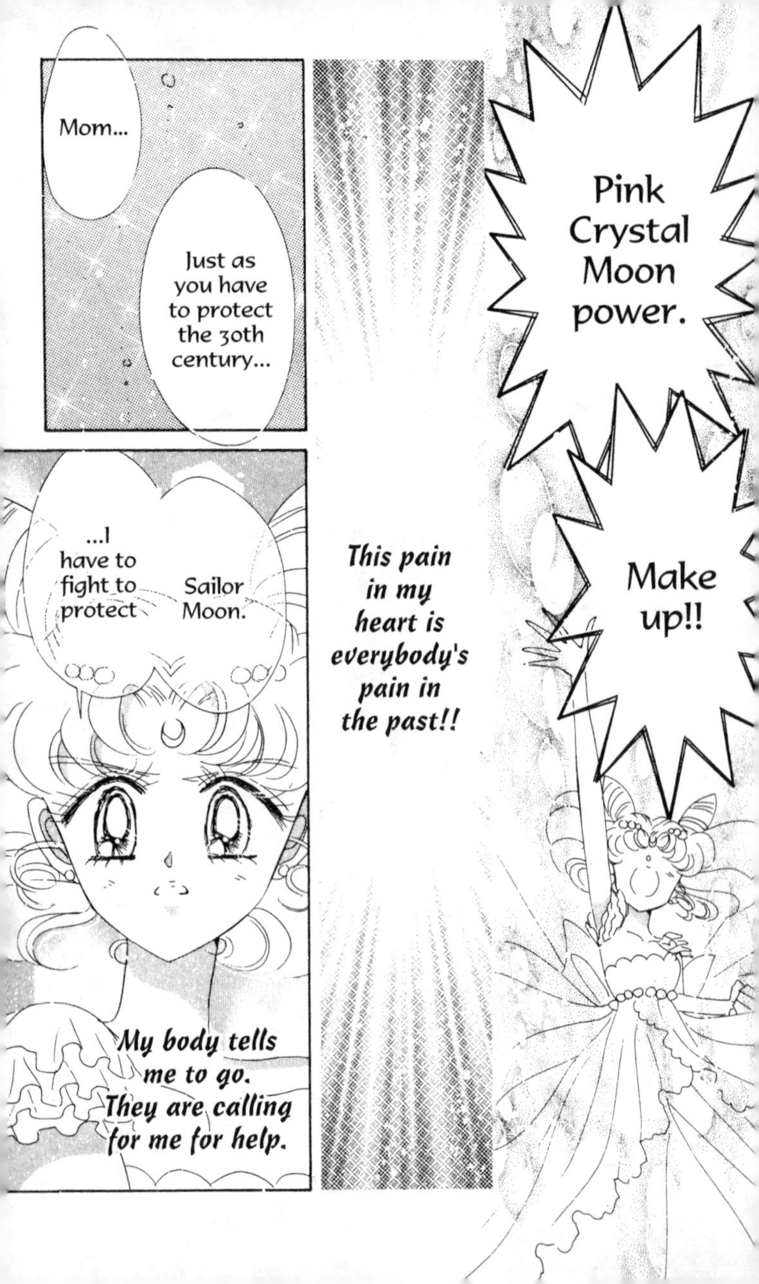
Mom...
Just as you have to protect the 30th century...
...I have to fight to protect Sailor Moon.
My body tells me to go. They are calling for me for help.
This pain in my heart is everybody's pain in the past!!
Pink Crystal Moon power.
Make up!!

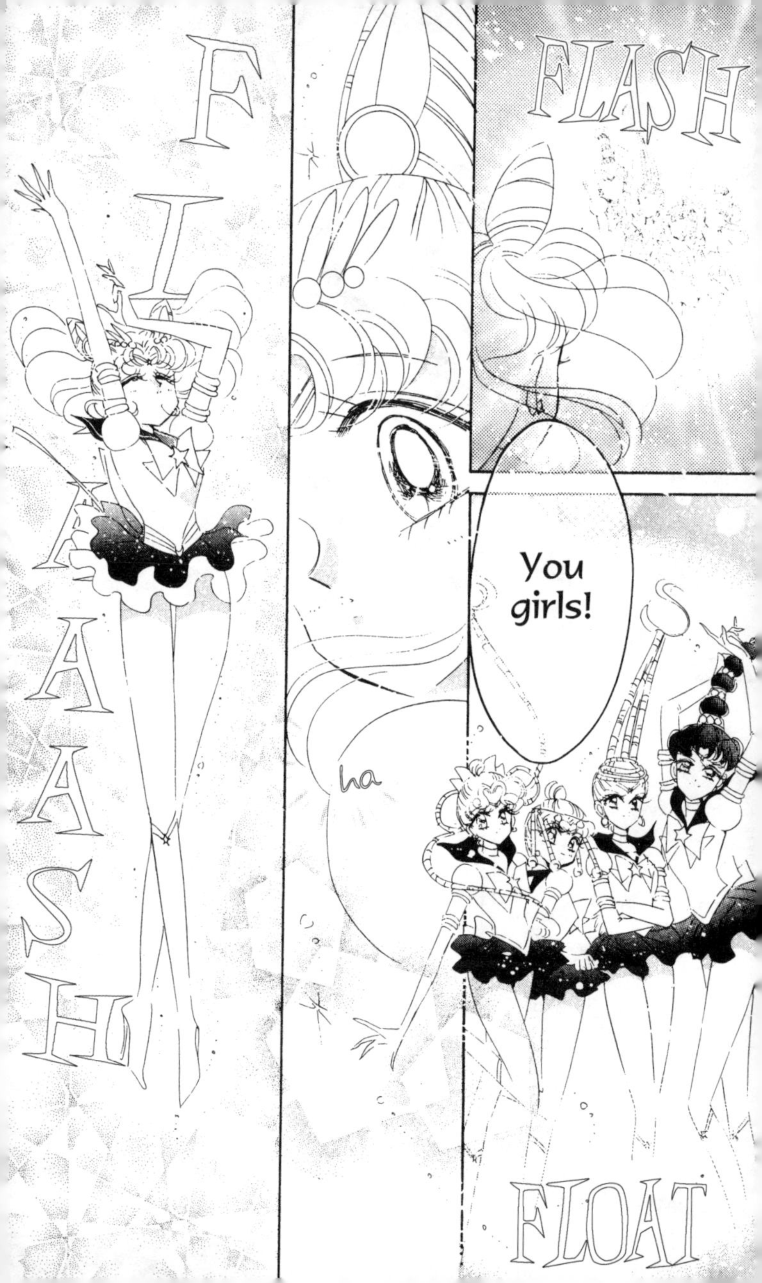
FLAAASH
ha
FLASH
You girls!
FLOAT

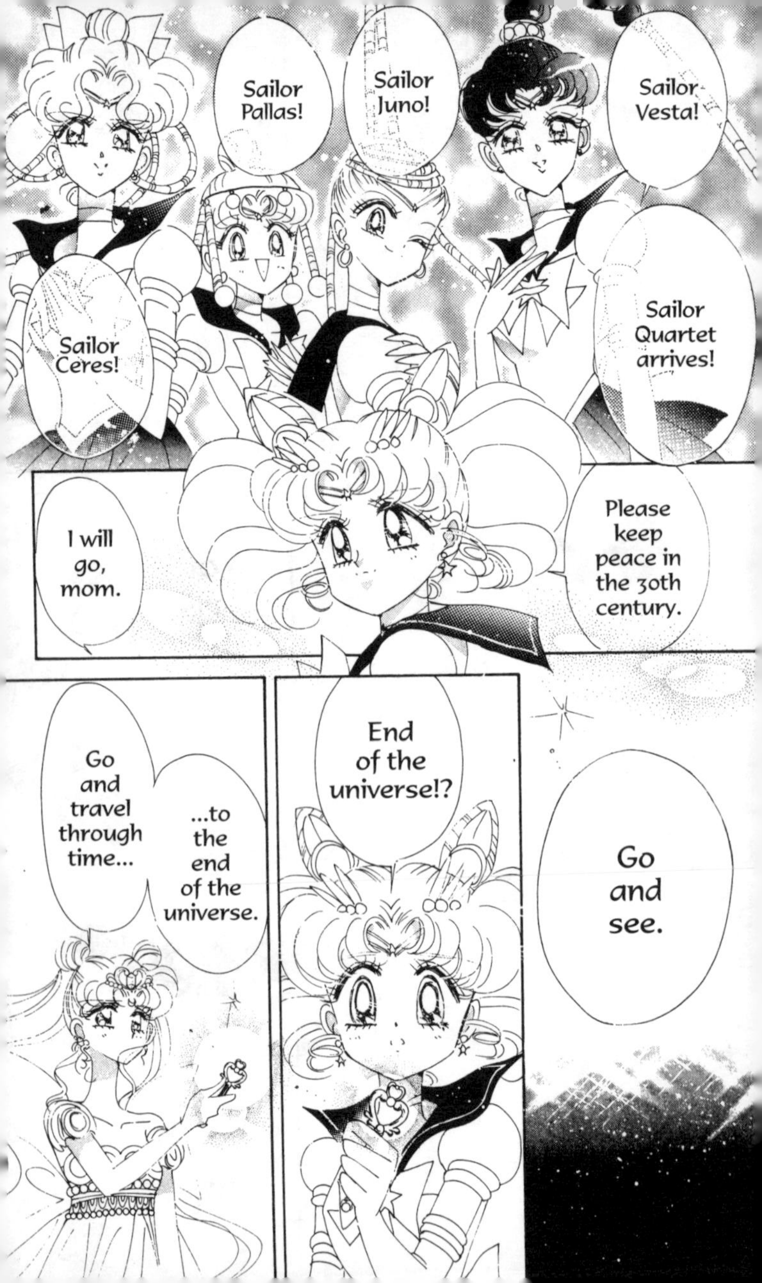
Sailor Pallas!
Sailor Juno!
Sailor Vesta!
Sailor Ceres!
Sailor Quartet arrives!
I will go, mom.
Please keep peace in the 30th century.
Go and travel through time...
...to the end of the universe.
End of the universe!?
Go and see.

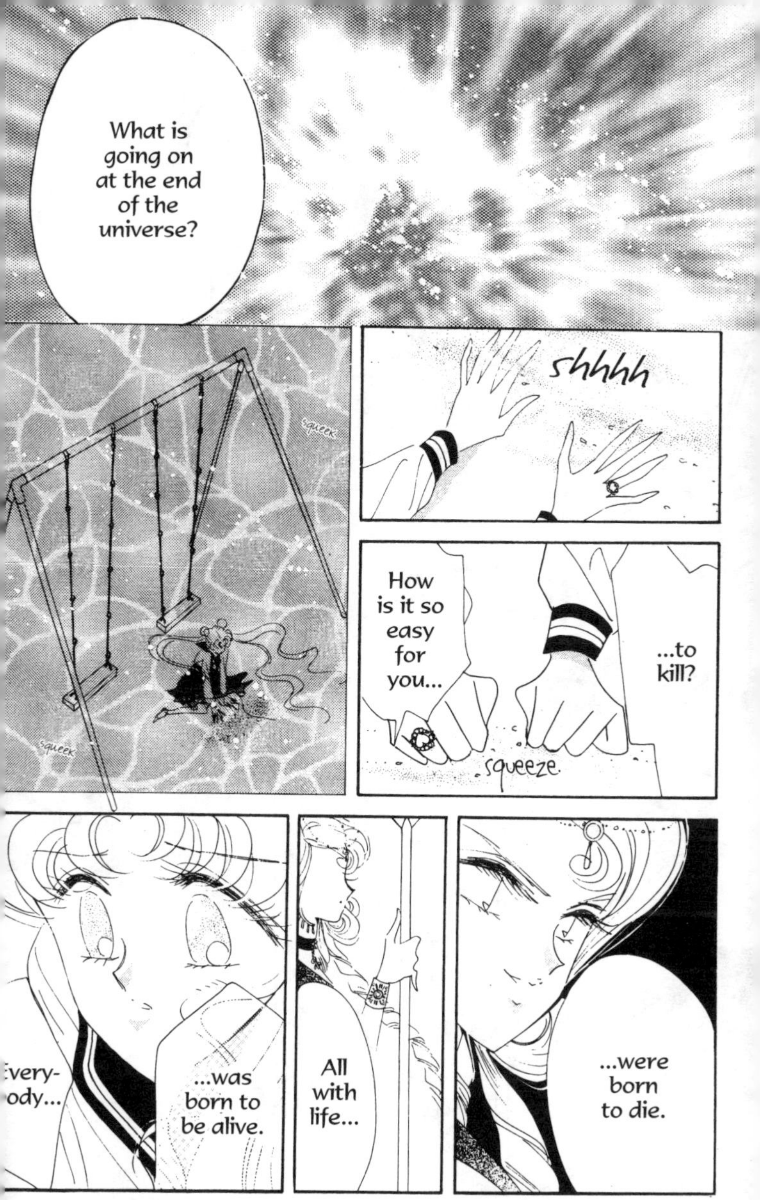
What is going on at the end of the universe?
squeek
squeek
shhhh
How is it so easy for you...
...to kill?
squeeze
Every-
ody...
...was born to be alive.
All with life...
...were born to die.

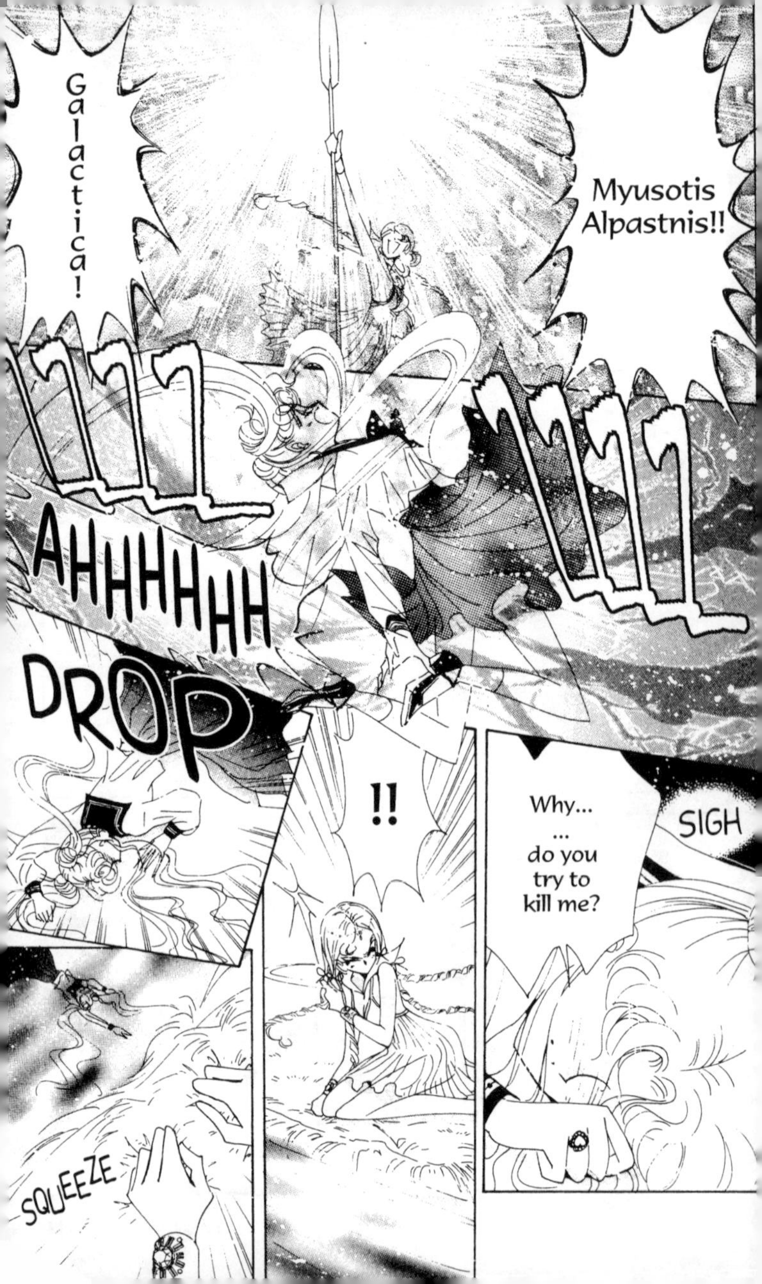
Galactica!
Myusotis Alpastnis!!
AHHHHHH
DROP
!!
Why...
...
do you
try to
kill me?
SIGH
SQUEEZE

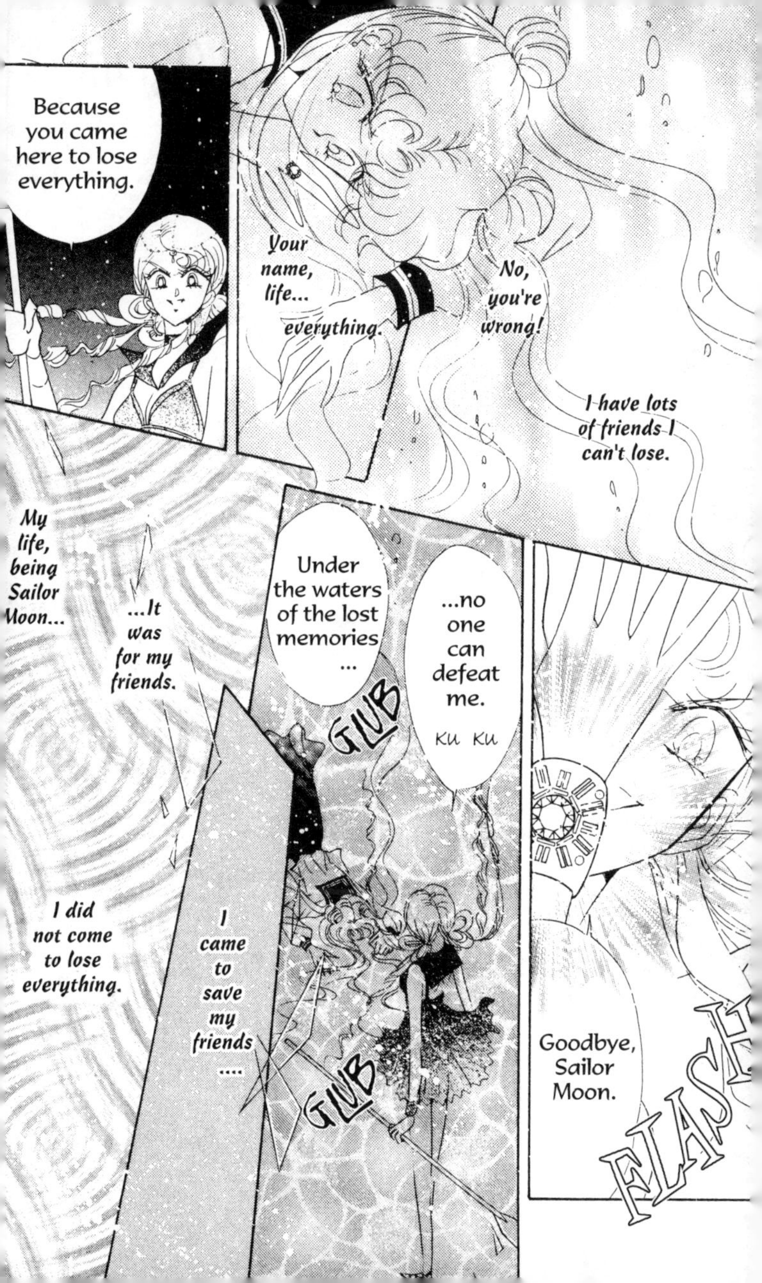
Because you came here to lose everything.
Your name, life... everything.
No, you're wrong!
I have lots of friends I can't lose.
My life, being Sailor Moon...
...It was for my friends.
I did not come to lose everything.
I came to save my friends ....
Under the waters of the lost memories ...
...no one can defeat me.
KU KU
GLUB
GLUB
Goodbye, Sailor Moon.
FLASH

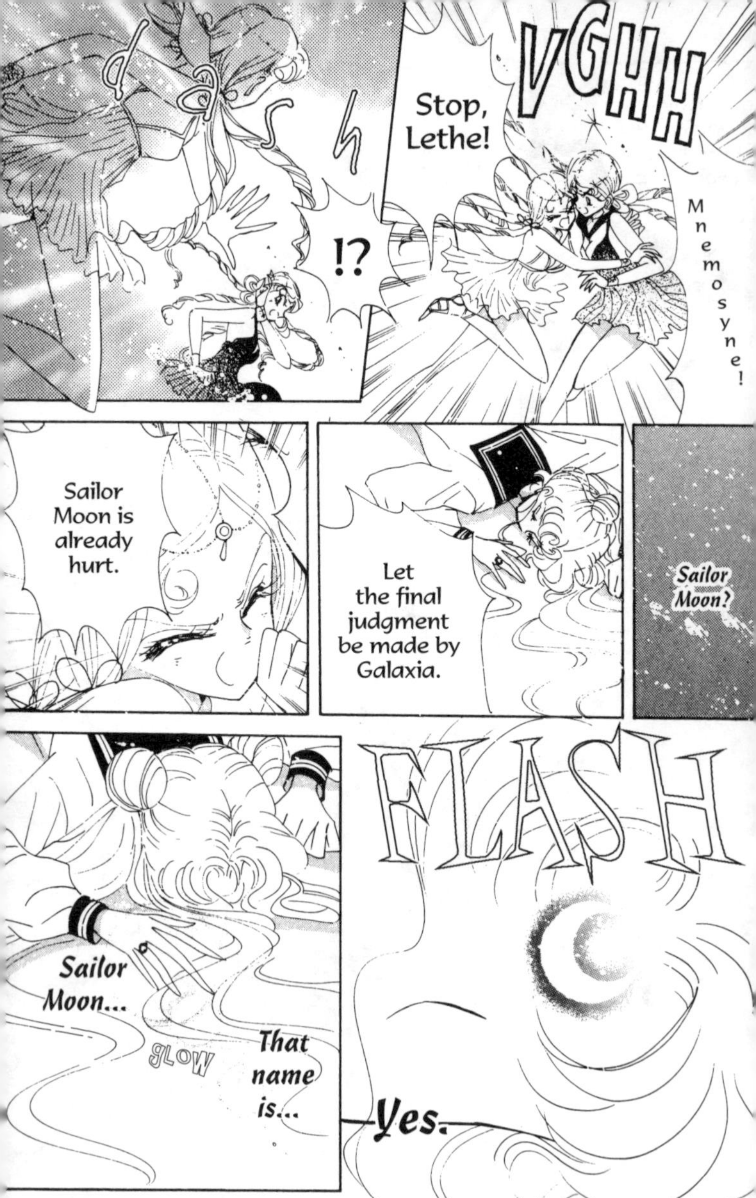
dash
!?
Stop, Lethe!
VGHH
Mnemosyne!
Sailor Moon is already hurt.
Let the final judgment be made by Galaxia.
Sailor Moon?
Sailor Moon...
glow
That name is...
FLASH
Yes.

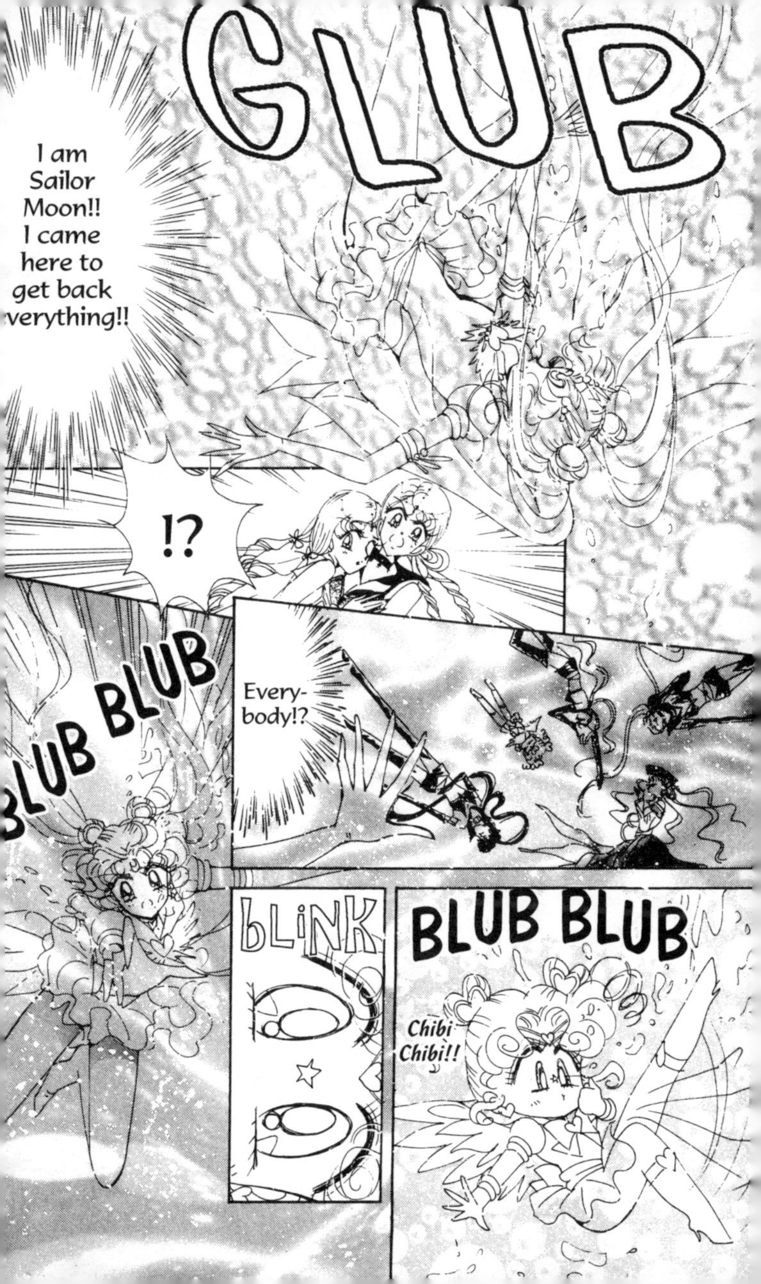
GLUB
I am Sailor Moon!! I came here to get back verything!!
!?
BLUB BLUB
Every-body!?
bLiNK
BLUB BLUB
Chibi Chibi!!

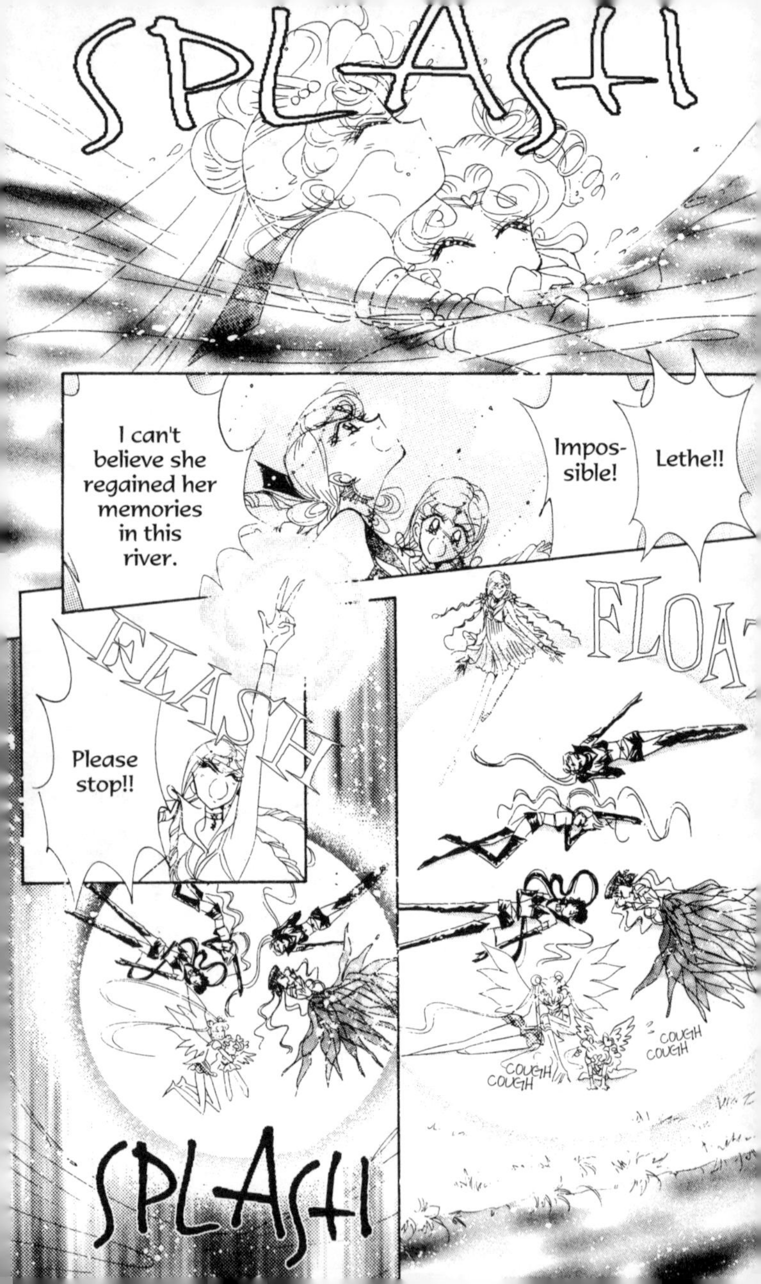
SPLASH
I can't believe she regained her memories in this river.
Impos-sible!
Lethe!!
FLASH
Please stop!!
SPLASH
FLOAT
COUGH COUGH
COUGH COUGH

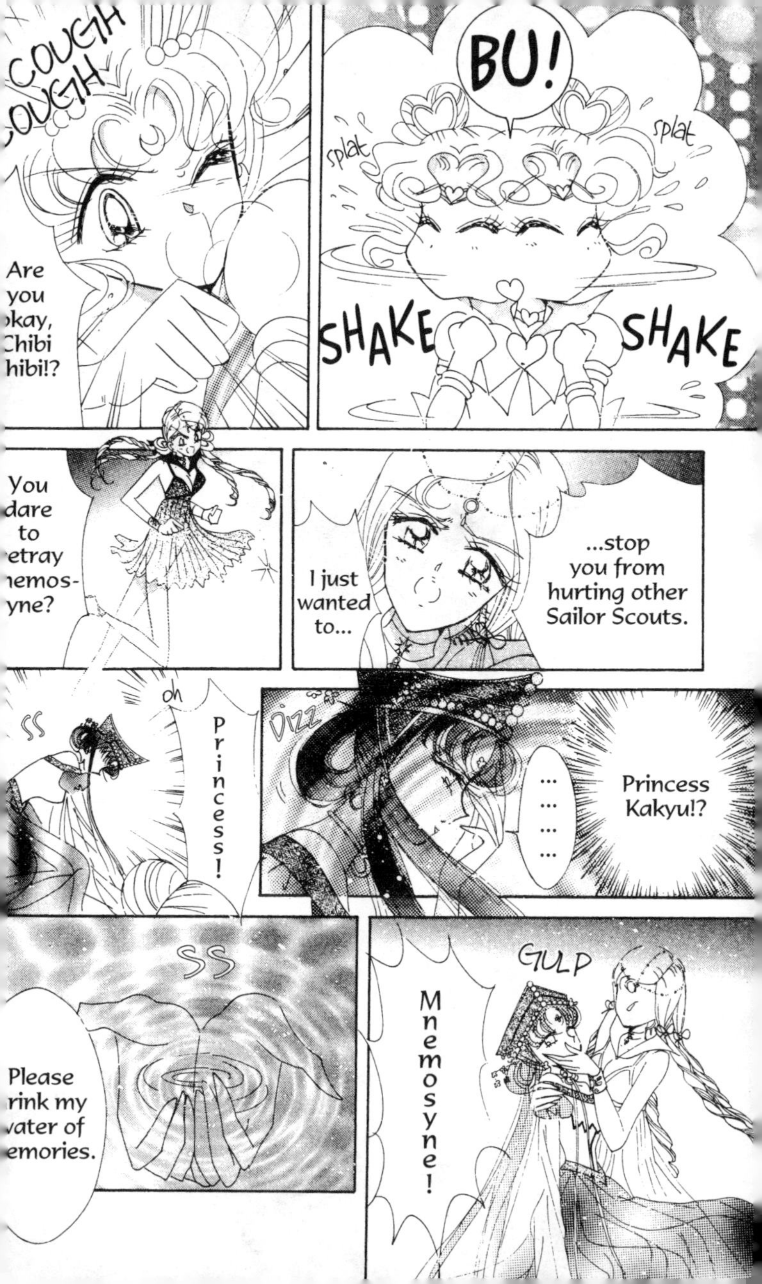
COUGH
COUGH
Are you okay, Chibi Chibi!?
BU!
splat
splat
SHAKE
SHAKE
You dare to betray Mnemosyne?
I just wanted to...
...stop you from hurting other Sailor Scouts.
ss
oh
Princess!
Dizz
....
Princess Kakyu!?
ss
Please drink my water of memories.
GULP
Mnemosyne!

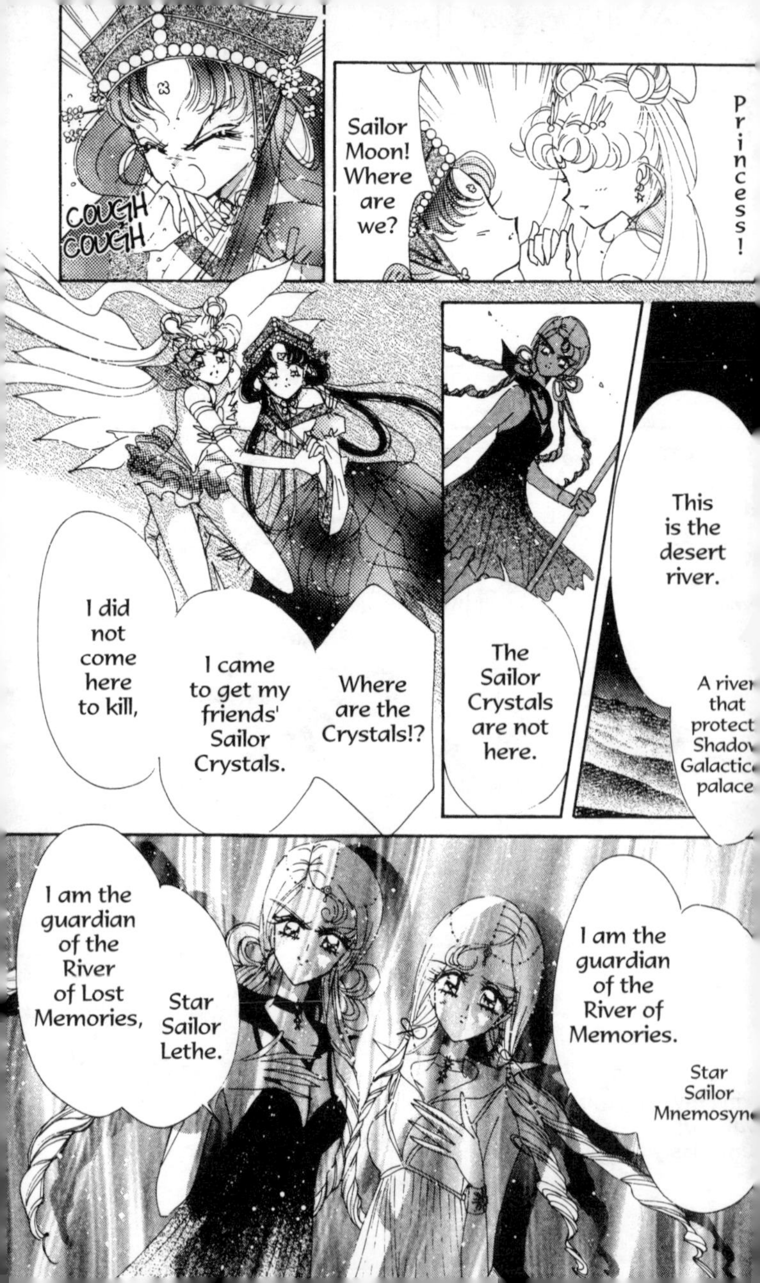
COUGH COUGH
Sailor Moon! Where are we?
Princess!
I did not come here to kill,
I came to get my friends' Sailor Crystals.
Where are the Crystals!?
The Sailor Crystals are not here.
This is the desert river.
A river that protect Shadov Galactic palace
I am the guardian of the River of Lost Memories,
Star Sailor Lethe.
I am the guardian of the River of Memories.
Star Sailor Mnemosyn

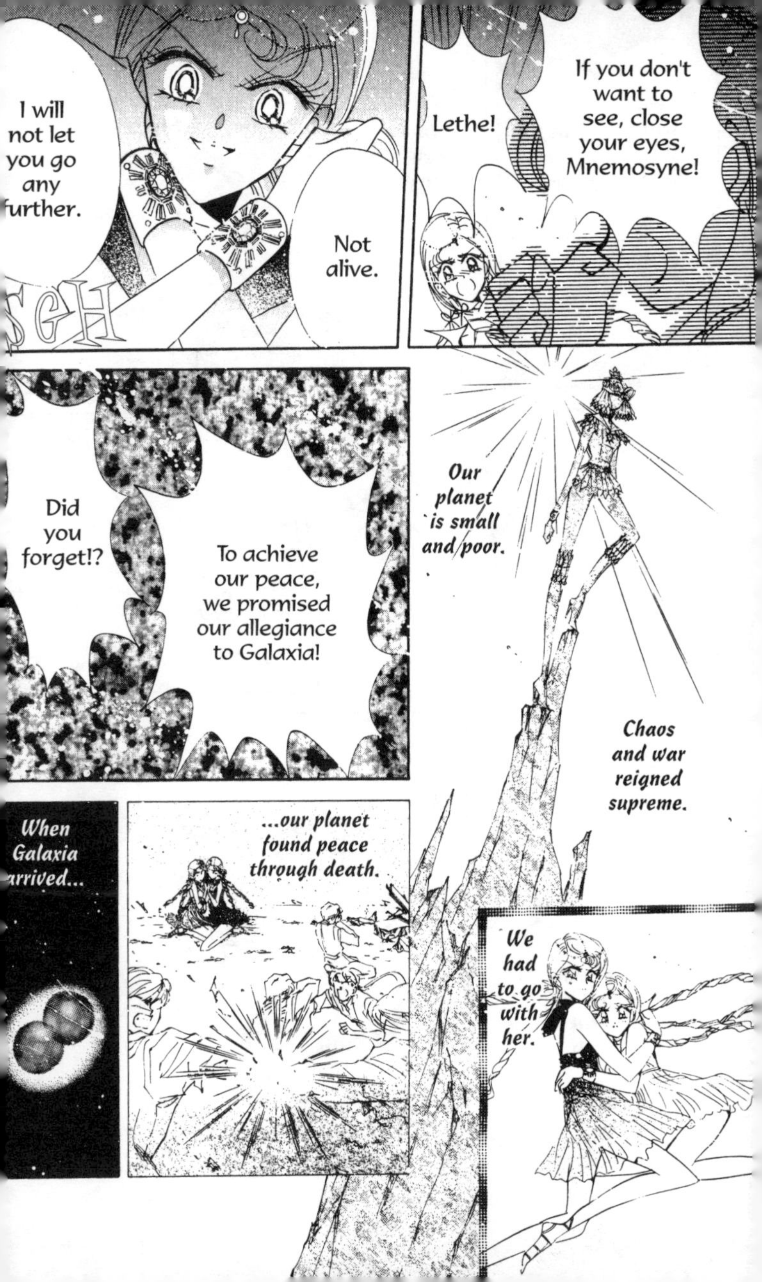
I will not let you go any further.
SGH
Not alive.
Lethe!
If you don't want to see, close your eyes, Mnemosyne!
Did you forget!?
To achieve our peace, we promised our allegiance to Galaxia!
Our planet is small and poor.
Chaos and war reigned supreme.
When Galaxia arrived...
...our planet found peace through death.
We had to go with her.

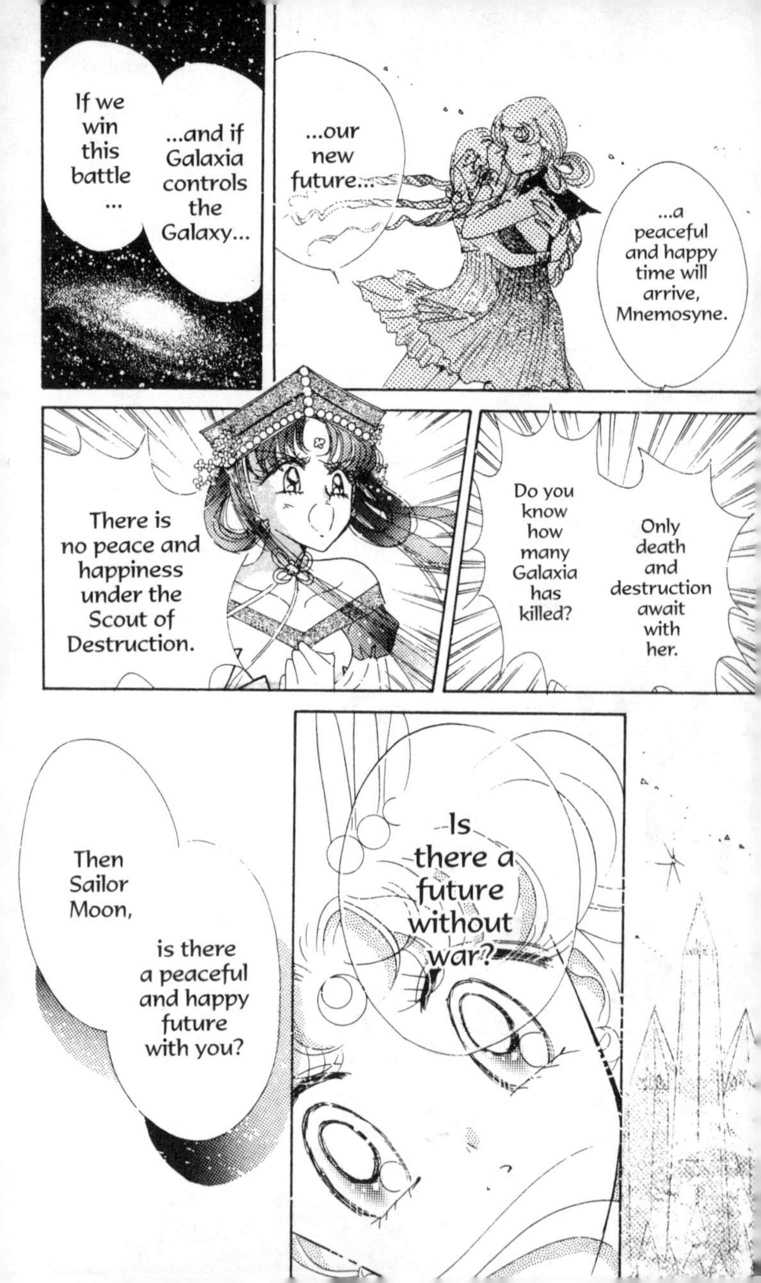
If we win this battle ...
...and if Galaxia controls the Galaxy...
...our new future...
...a peaceful and happy time will arrive, Mnemosyne.
There is no peace and happiness under the Scout of Destruction.
Do you know how many Galaxia has killed?
Only death and destruction await with her.
Then Sailor Moon,
is there a peaceful and happy future with you?
Is there a future without war?

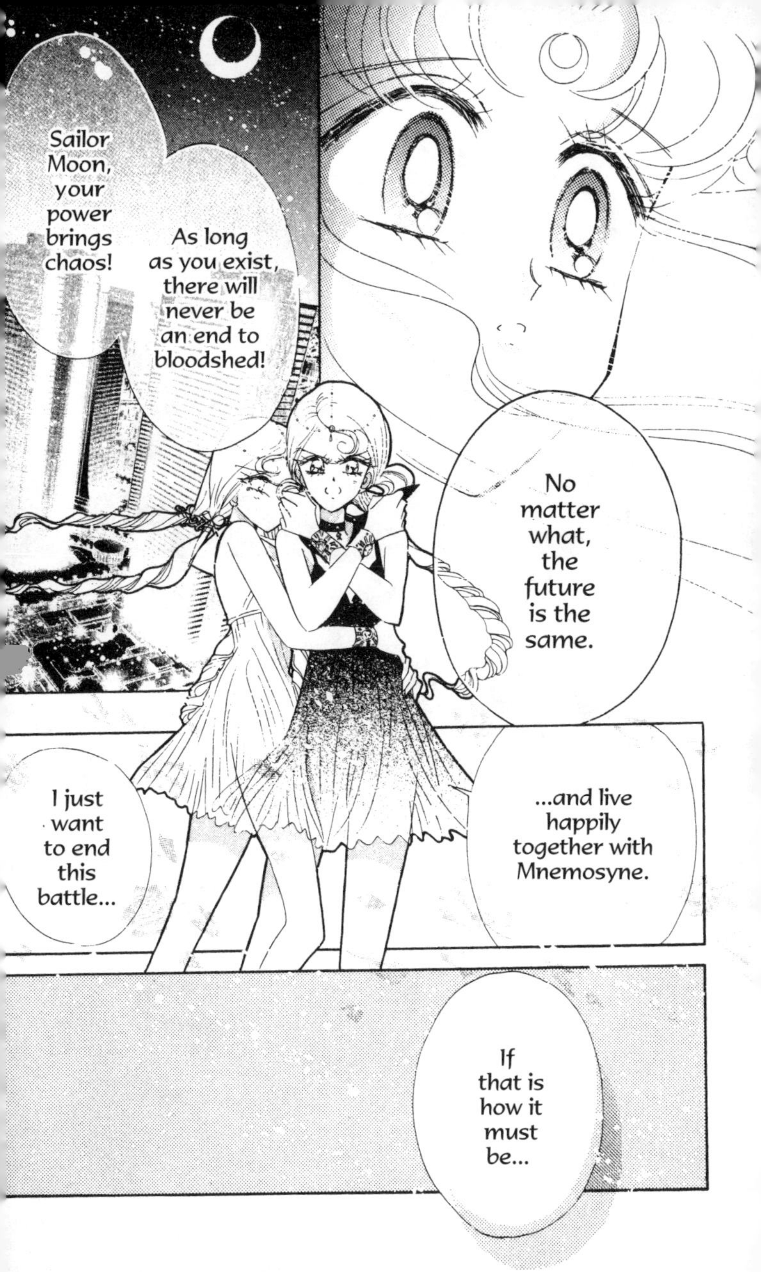
Sailor Moon, your power brings chaos!
As long as you exist, there will never be an end to bloodshed!
No matter what, the future is the same.
I just want to end this battle...
...and live happily together with Mnemosyne.
If that is how it must be...

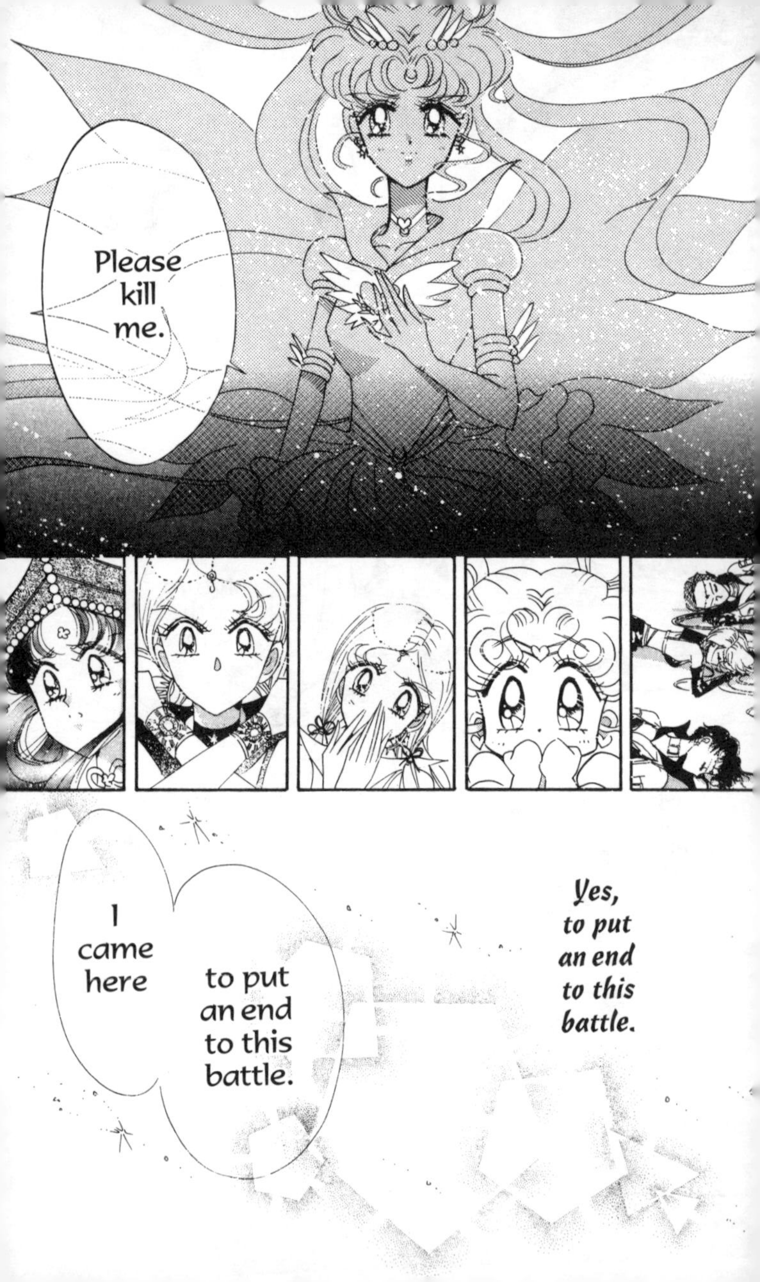
Please kill me.
I came here to put an end to this battle.
Yes, to put an end to this battle.

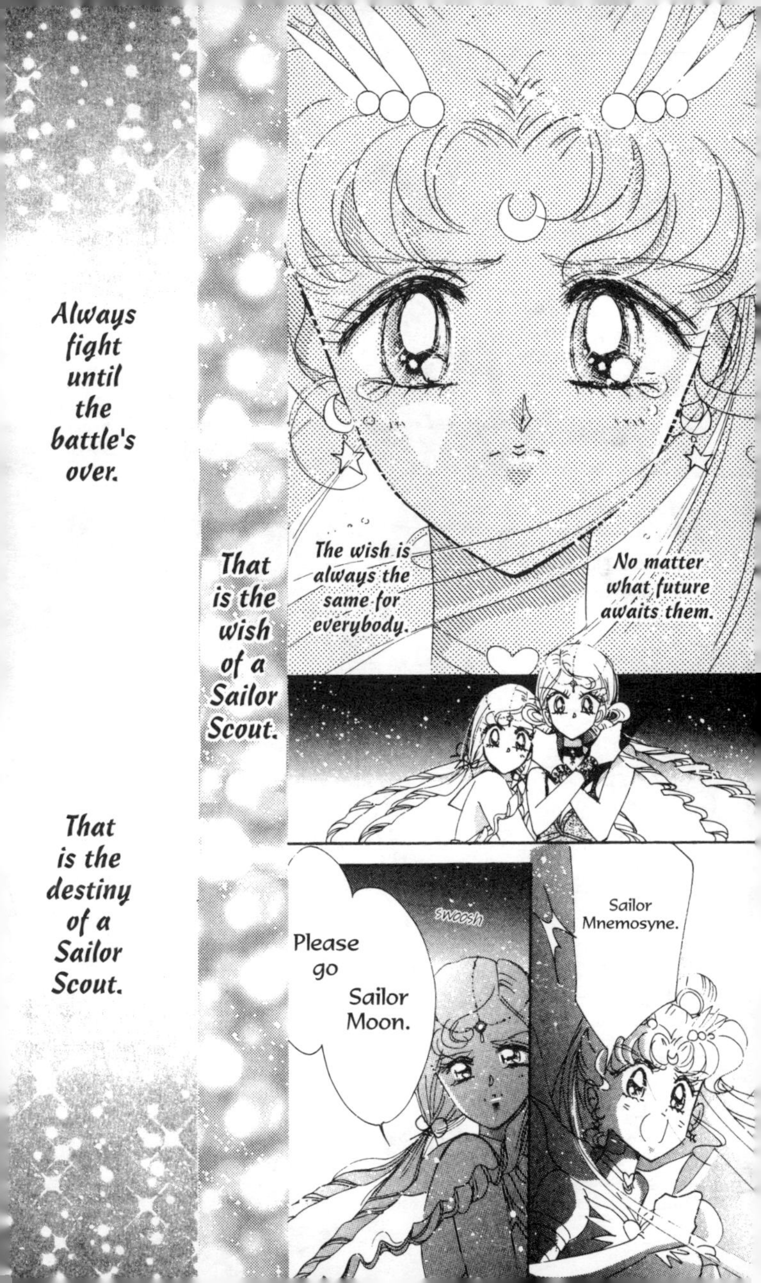
Always fight until the battle's over.
That is the destiny of a Sailor Scout.
That is the wish of a Sailor Scout.
The wish is always the same for everybody.
No matter what future awaits them.
swoosh
Please go Sailor Moon.
Sailor Mnemosyne.

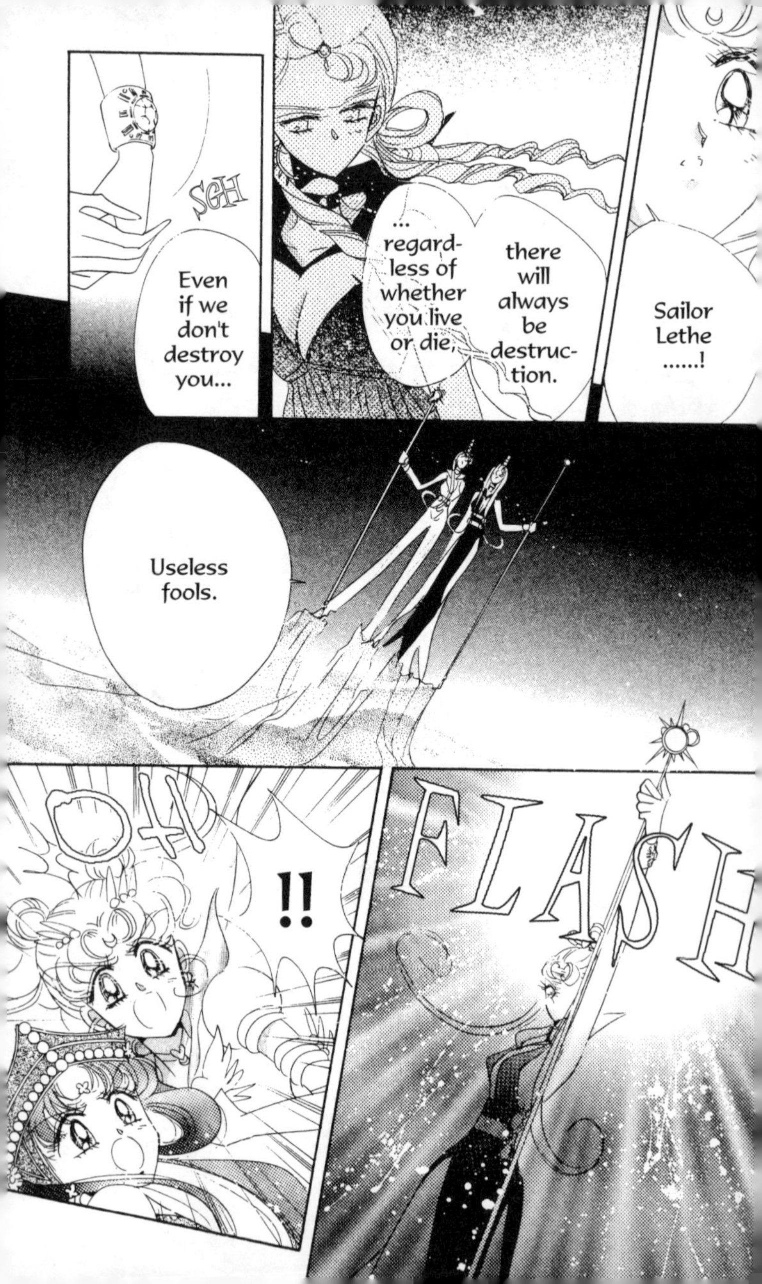

SGH
Even if we don't destroy you...
... regardless of whether you live or die,
there will always be destruction.
Sailor Lethe ......!
Useless fools.
!!
FLASH

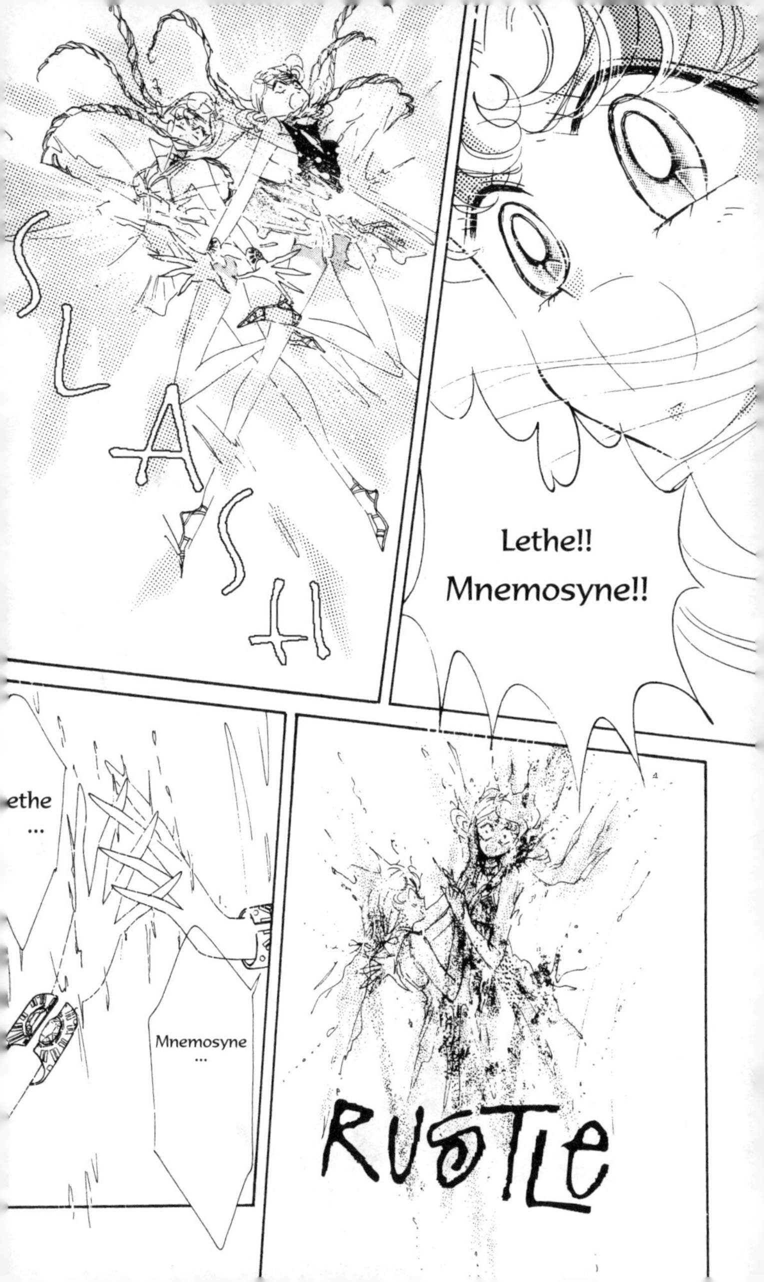
SLASH!
Lethe!!
Mnemosyne!!
ethe
...
Mnemosyne
...
RUSTLE

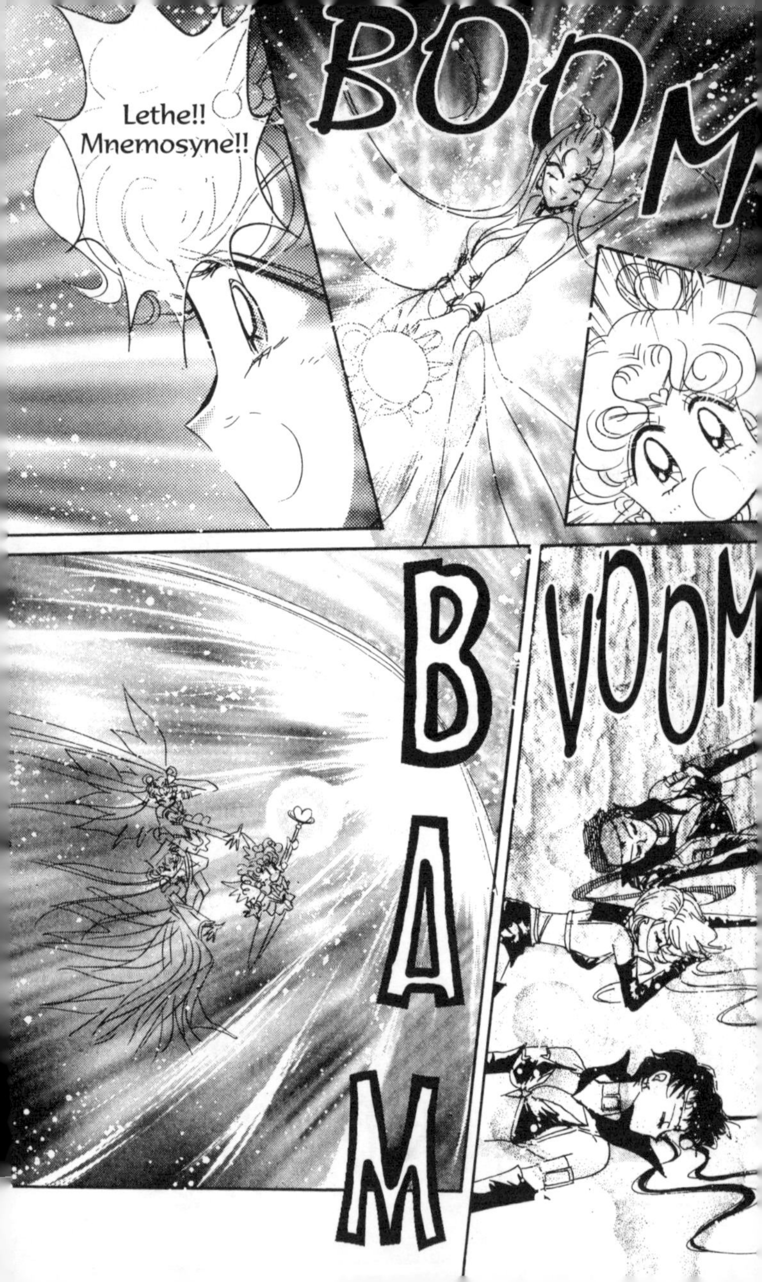

Lethe!!
Mnemosyne!!
BOOM
BVOOM
BAM

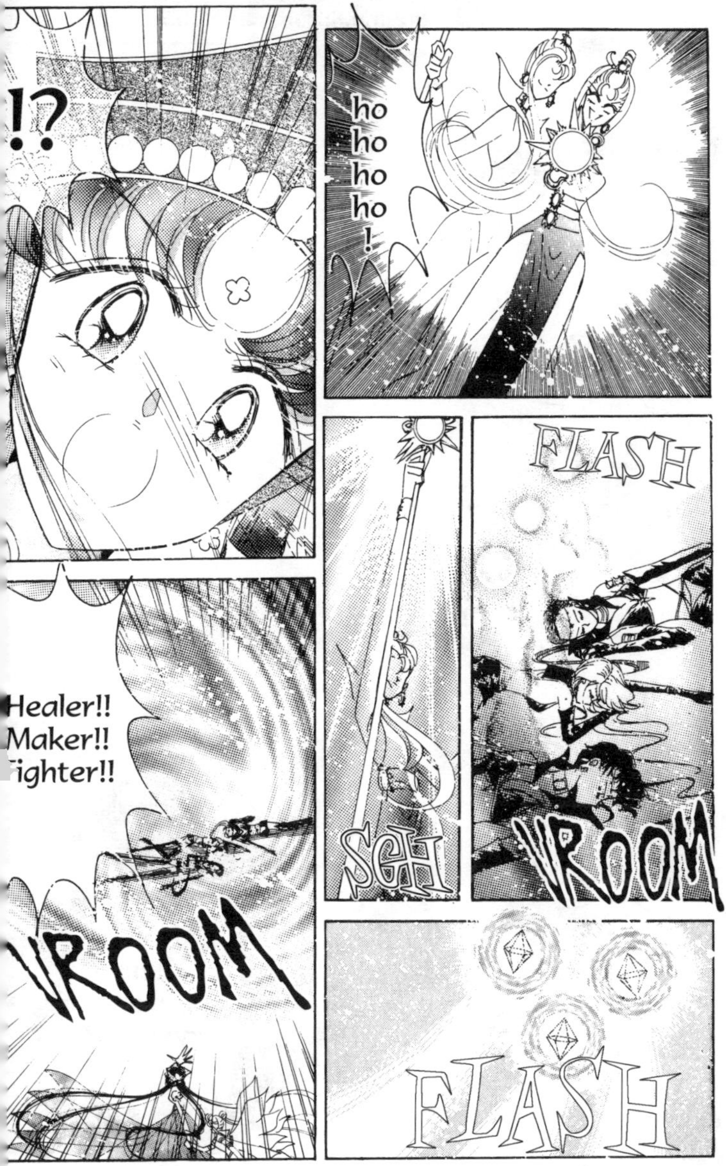
!?
ho ho ho ho !
Healer!! Maker!! Fighter!!
VROOM
SCH
FLASH
VROOM
FLASH

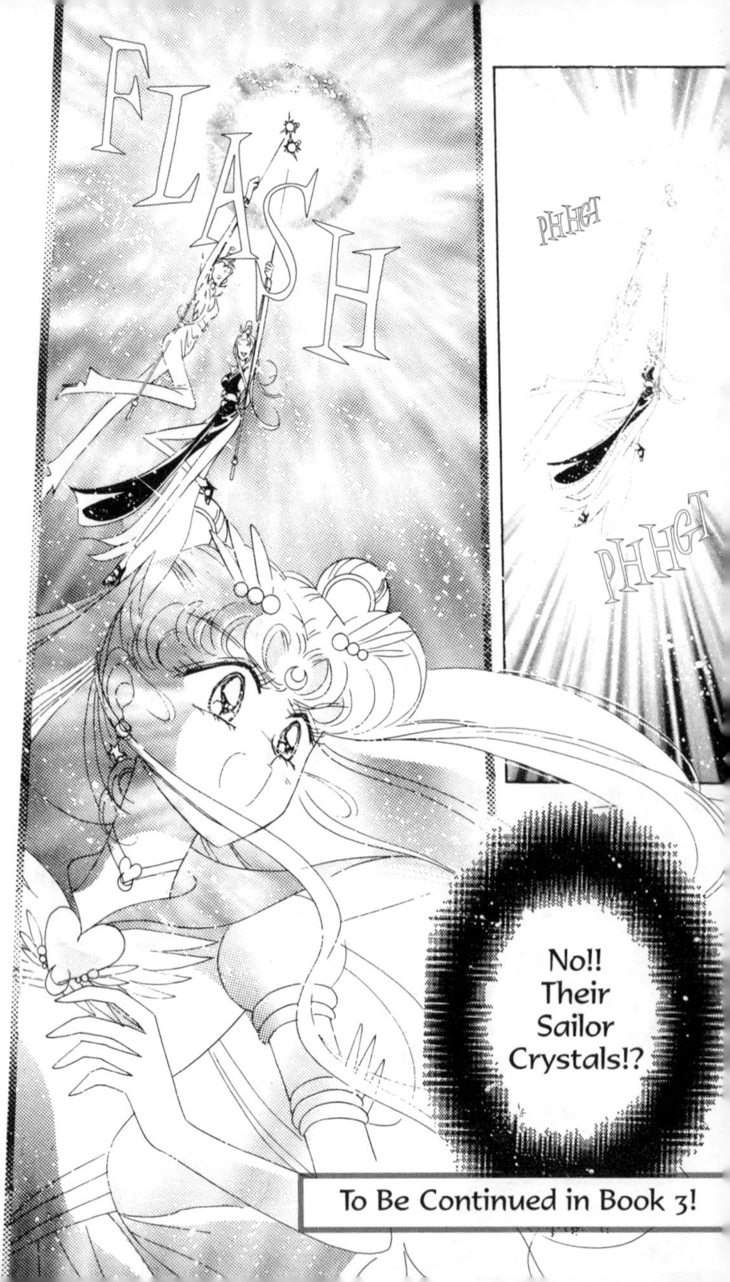
FLASH
PHHGT
PHHGT
No!! Their Sailor Crystals!?
To Be Continued in Book 3!

RINI'S PICTURE DIARY!

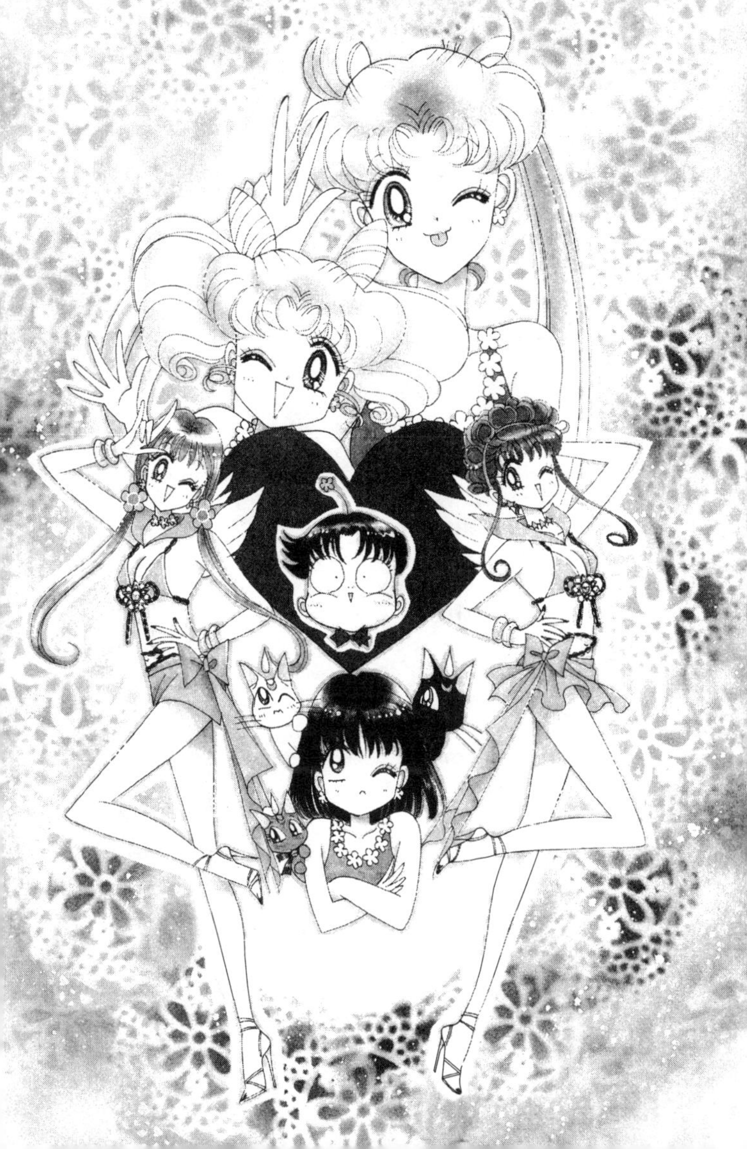

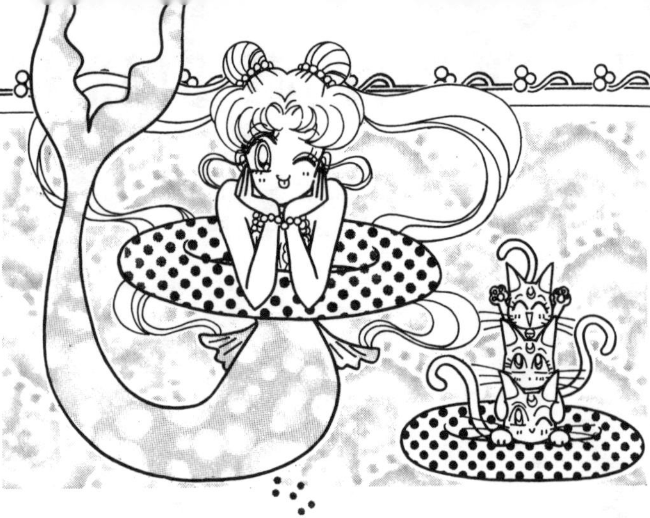

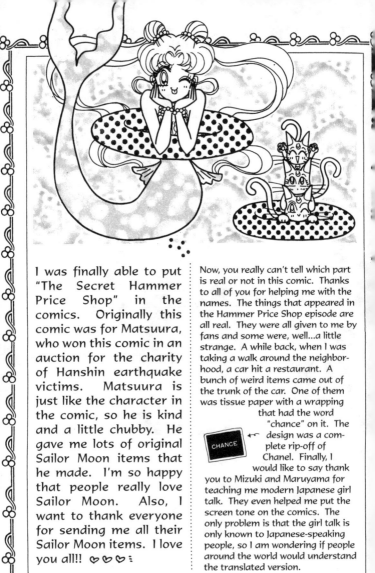

I was finally able to put "The Secret Hammer Price Shop" in the comics. Originally this comic was for Matsuura, who won this comic in an auction for the charity of Hanshin earthquake victims. Matsuura is just like the character in the comic, so he is kind and a little chubby. He gave me lots of original Sailor Moon items that he made. I'm so happy that people really love Sailor Moon. Also, I want to thank everyone for sending me all their Sailor Moon items. I love you all!! ♡♡♡

Now, you really can't tell which part is real or not in this comic. Thanks to all of you for helping me with the names. The things that appeared in the Hammer Price Shop episode are all real. They were all given to me by fans and some were, well...a little strange. A while back, when I was taking a walk around the neighborhood, a car hit a restaurant. A bunch of weird items came out of the trunk of the car. One of them was tissue paper with a wrapping that had the word "chance" on it. The design was a complete rip-off of Chanel.

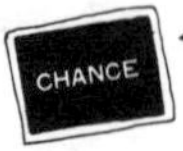
CHANCE

Finally, I would like to say thank you to Mizuki and Maruyama for teaching me modern Japanese girl talk. They even helped me put the screen tone on the comics. The only problem is that the girl talk is only known to Japanese-speaking people, so I am wondering if people around the world would understand the translated version.

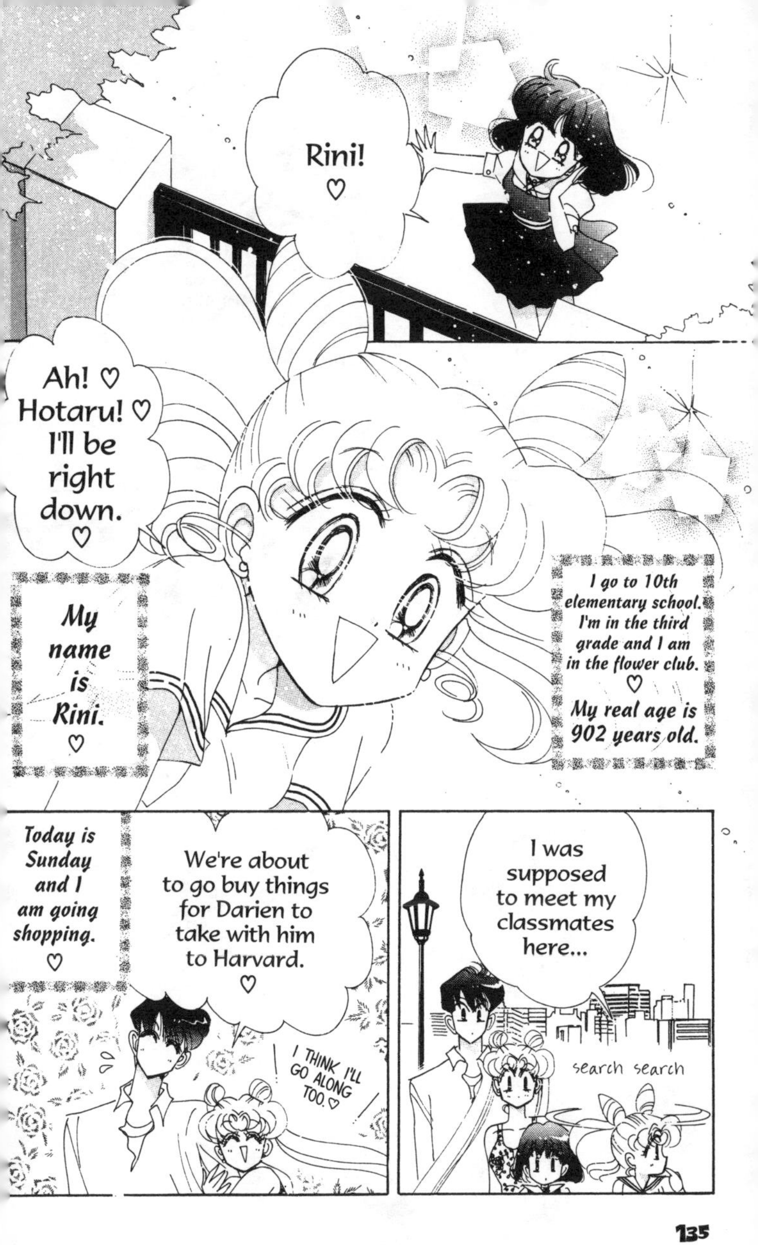

Rini! ♡
Ah! ♡ Hotaru! ♡ I'll be right down. ♡
My name is Rini. ♡
I go to 10th elementary school. I'm in the third grade and I am in the flower club. ♡ My real age is 902 years old.
Today is Sunday and I am going shopping. ♡
We're about to go buy things for Darien to take with him to Harvard. ♡
I THINK I'LL GO ALONG TOO. ♡
I was supposed to meet my classmates here...
search search

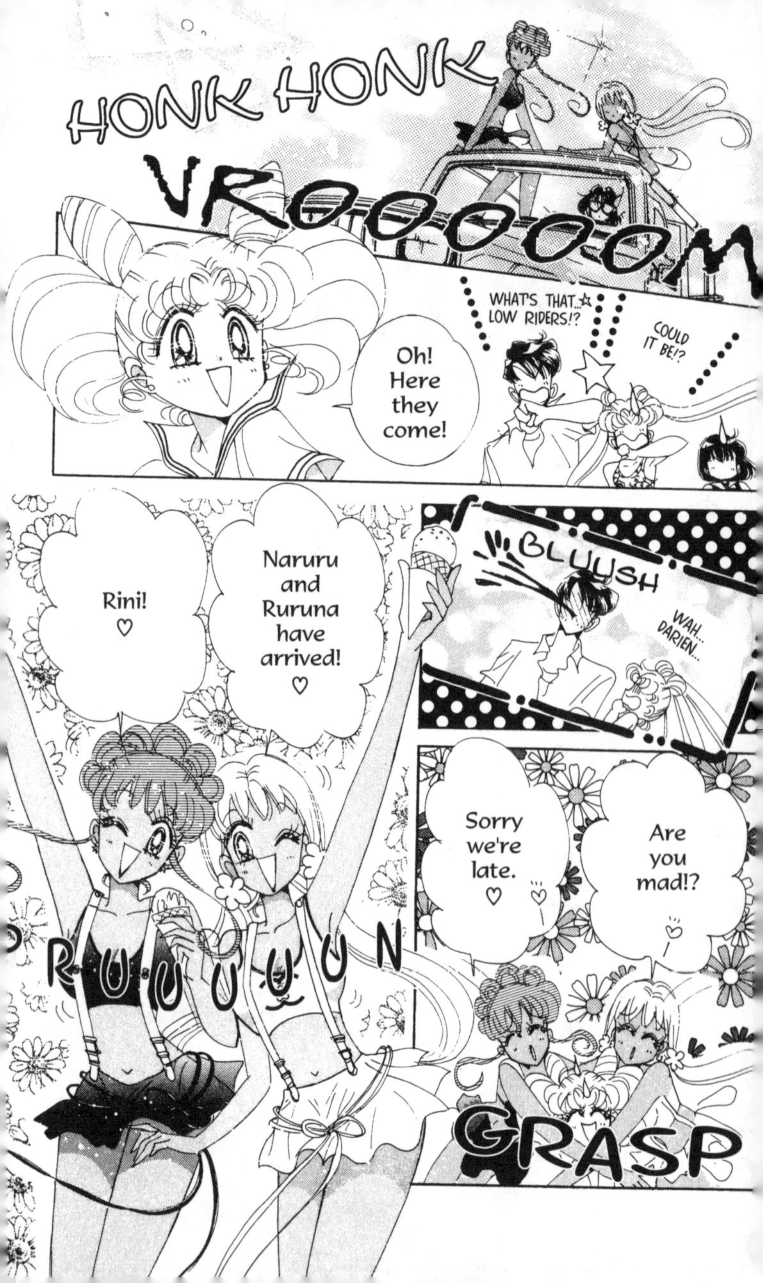
HONK HONK
VROOOOOOM
Oh! Here they come!
WHAT'S THAT...☆ LOW RIDERS!?
COULD IT BE!?
Rini! ♡
Naruru and Ruruna have arrived! ♡
DRUUUUN
BLUUSH
WAH... DARIEN...
Sorry we're late. ♡
Are you mad!?
GRASP

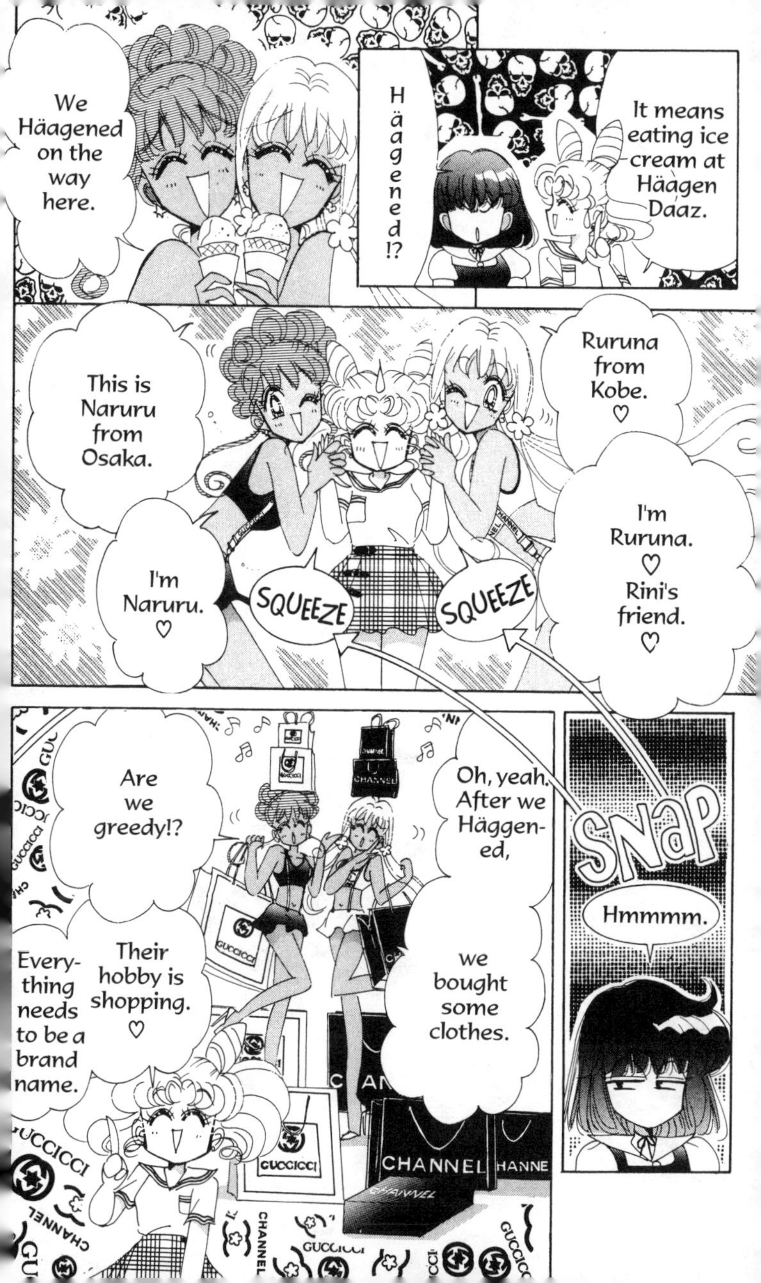

We Häagened on the way here.
Häagened!?
It means eating ice cream at Häagen Daaz.
This is Naruru from Osaka.
Ruruna from Kobe. ♡
I'm Naruru. ♡
SQUEEZE
SQUEEZE
I'm Ruruna. ♡ Rini's friend. ♡
Are we greedy!?
Oh, yeah. After we Häggen-ed,
we bought some clothes.
Their hobby is shopping. ♡
Every-thing needs to be a brand name.
SNAP
Hmmmm.

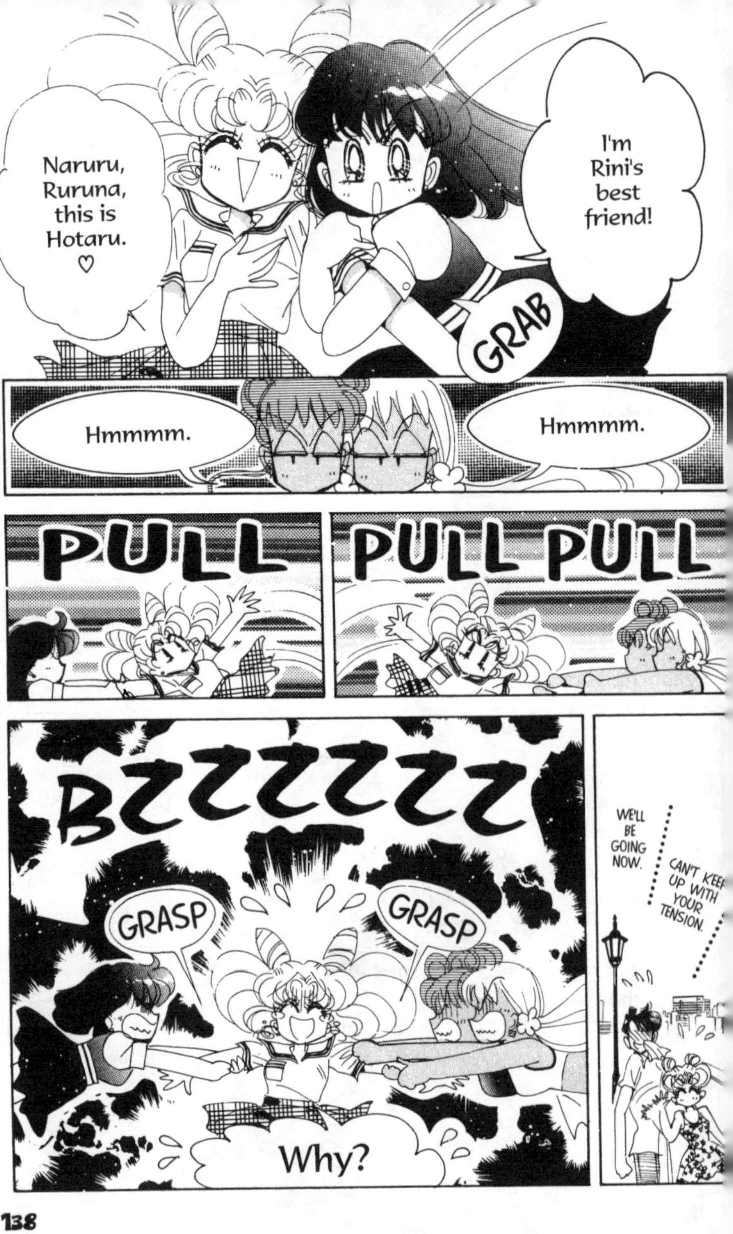

Naruru, Ruruna, this is Hotaru. ♡
I'm Rini's best friend!
GRAB
Hmmmm.
Hmmmm.
PULL
PULL PULL
BZZZZZZ
GRASP
GRASP
Why?
WE'LL BE GOING NOW.
CAN'T KEEP UP WITH YOUR TENSION.

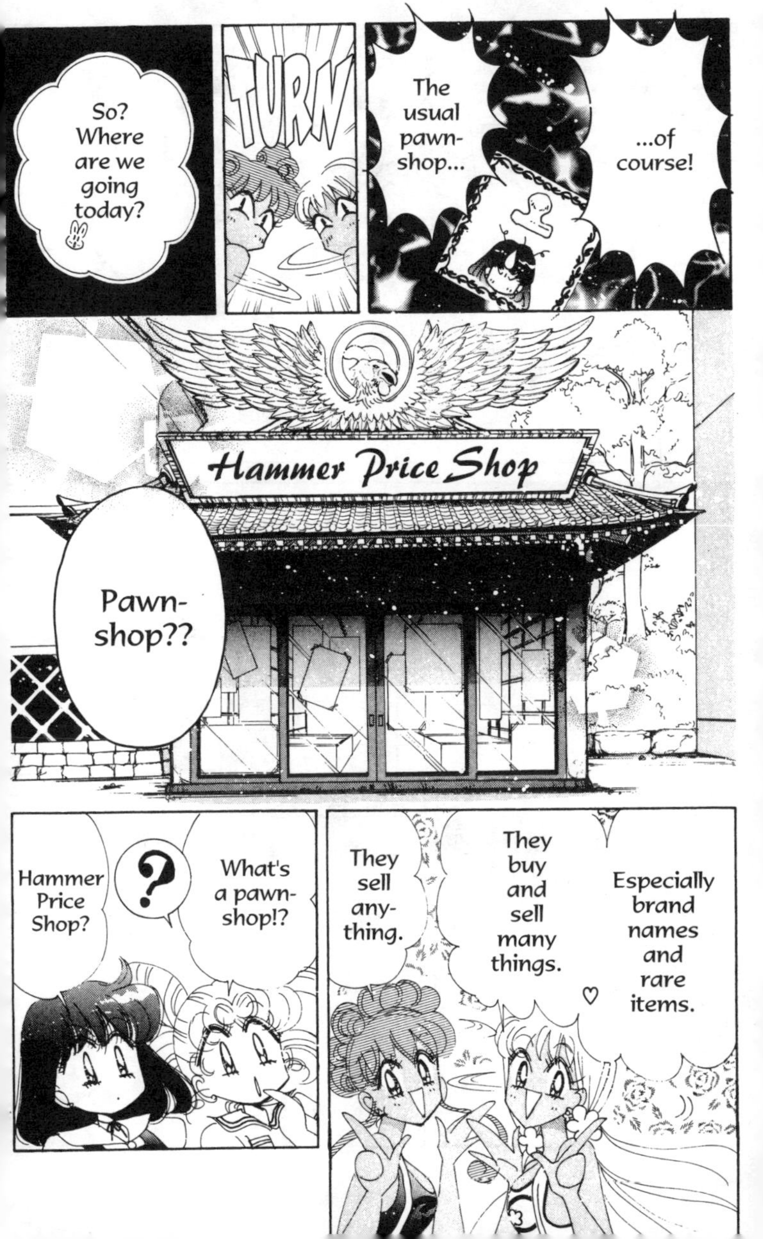
So? Where are we going today?
TURN
The usual pawn-shop...
...of course!
Hammer Price Shop
Pawn-shop??
Hammer Price Shop?
?
What's a pawn-shop!?
They sell any-thing.
They buy and sell many things.
Especially brand names and rare items.

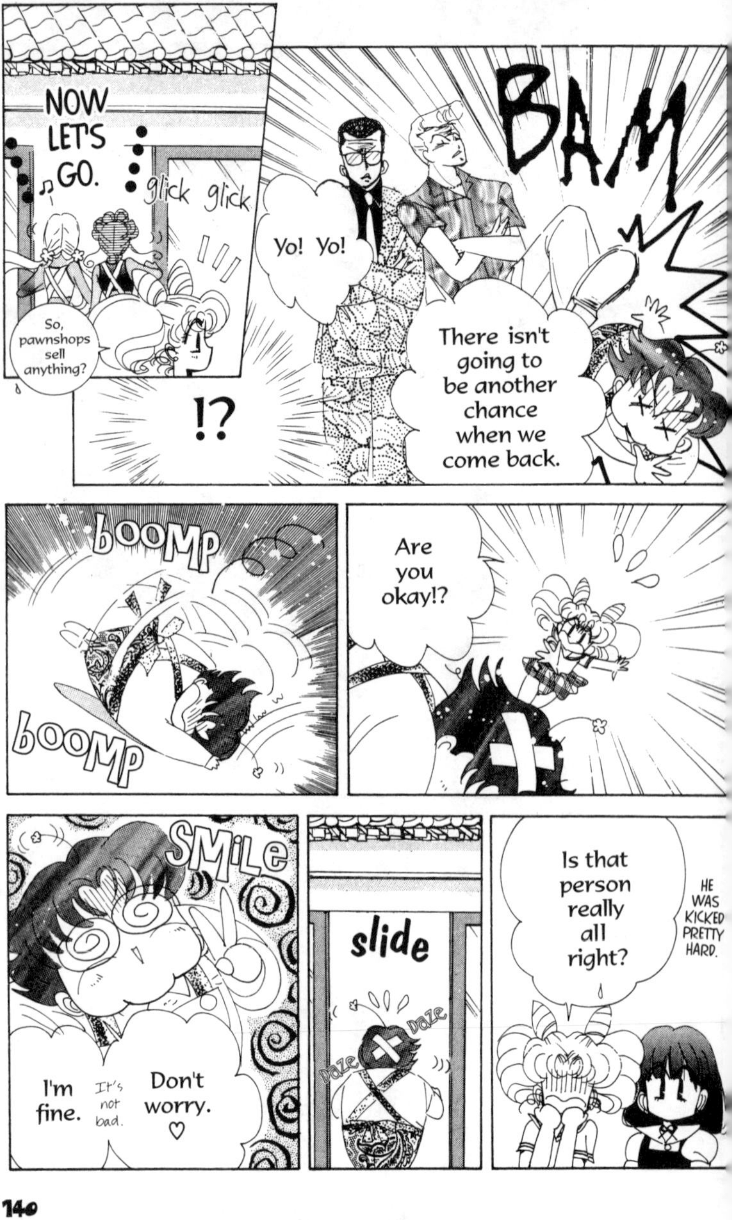

NOW LET'S GO.
glick glick
So, pawnshops sell anything?
!?
Yo! Yo!
BAM
There isn't going to be another chance when we come back.
boomp
boomp
Are you okay!?
SMILE
I'm fine.
It's not bad.
Don't worry. ♡
slide
DAZE
DAZE
Is that person really all right?
HE WAS KICKED PRETTY HARD.

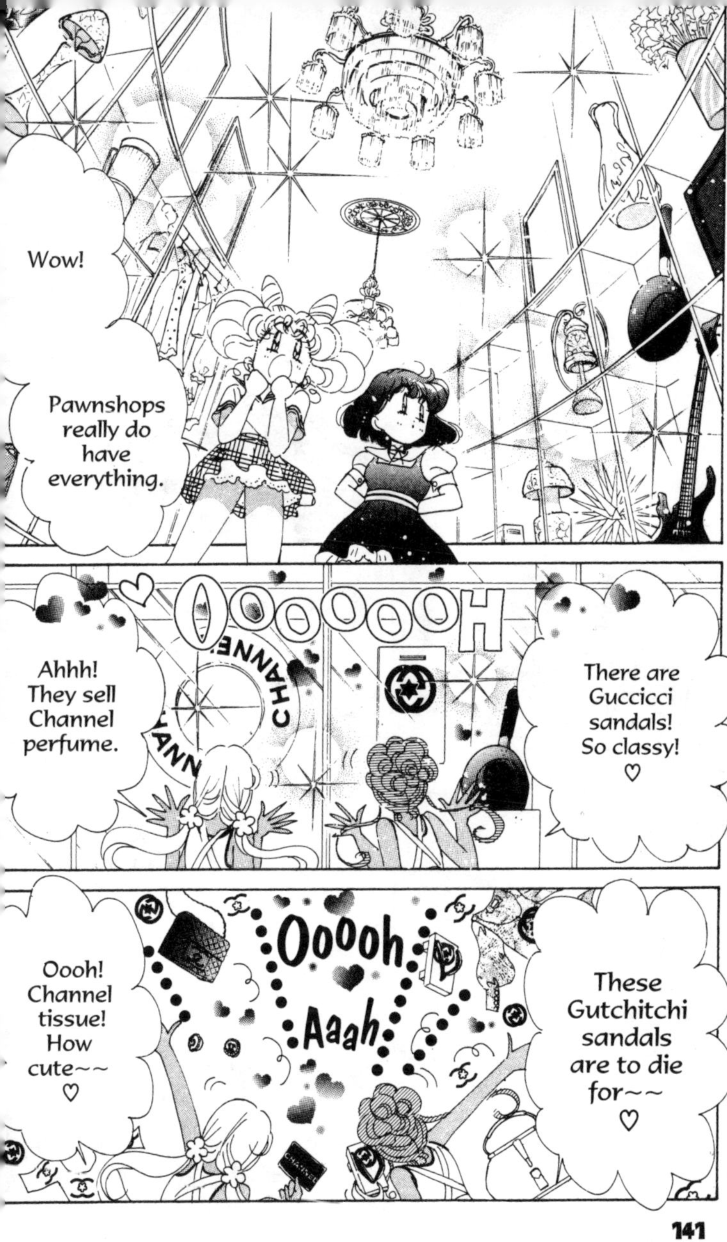
Wow!
Pawnshops really do have everything.
OOOOOOH
Ahhh! They sell Channel perfume.
There are Guccicci sandals! So classy! ♡
Ooooh
Aaah
Oooh! Channel tissue! How cute~~ ♡
These Gutchitchi sandals are to die for~~ ♡

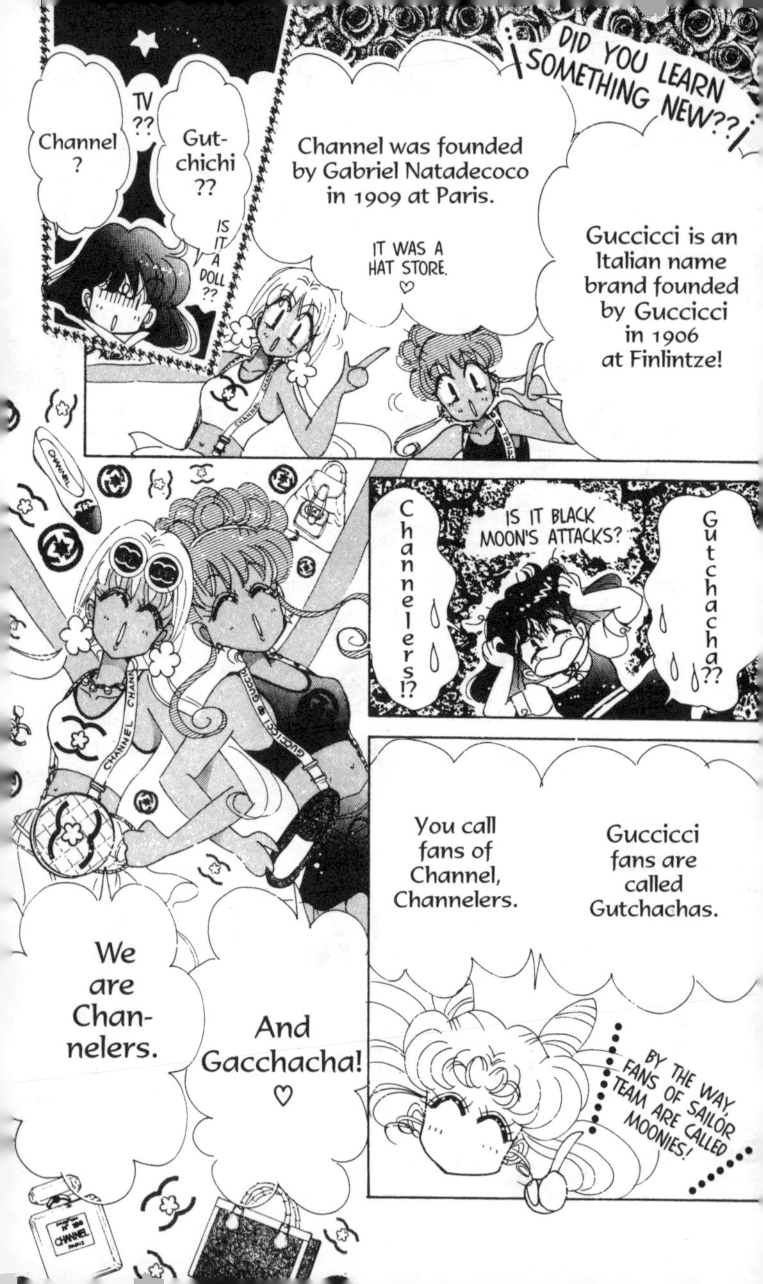

Channel ?
TV ??
Gut-chichi ??
IS IT A DOLL ??
DID YOU LEARN SOMETHING NEW??
Channel was founded by Gabriel Natadecoco in 1909 at Paris.
IT WAS A HAT STORE. ♡
Guccicci is an Italian name brand founded by Guccicci in 1906 at Finlintze!
We are Chan-nelers.
And Gacchacha! ♡
Channelers!?
IS IT BLACK MOON'S ATTACKS?
Gutchacha??
You call fans of Channel, Channelers.
Guccicci fans are called Gutchachas.
BY THE WAY, FANS OF SAILOR TEAM ARE CALLED MOONIES!

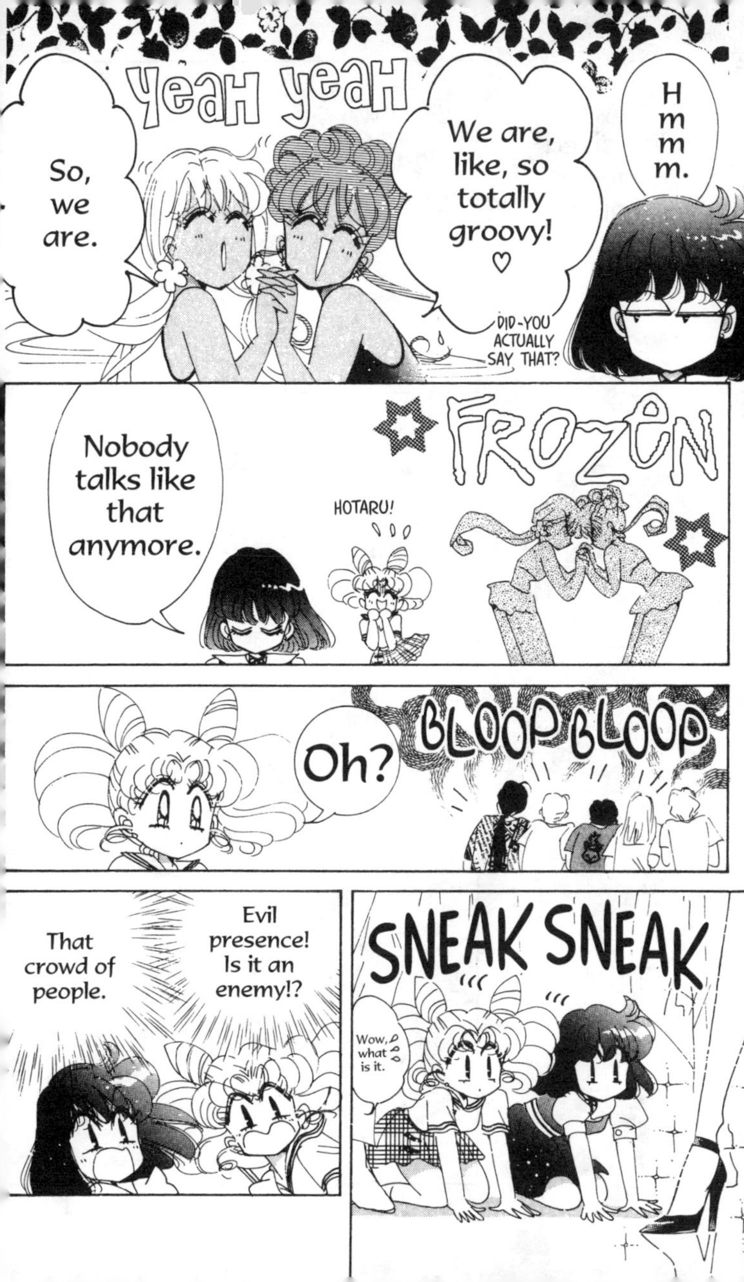
So, we are.
YEAH YEAH
We are, like, so totally groovy! ♡
Hmmm.
DID-YOU ACTUALLY SAY THAT?
Nobody talks like that anymore.
FROZEN
HOTARU!
Oh?
BLOOP BLOOP
That crowd of people.
Evil presence! Is it an enemy!?
SNEAK SNEAK
Wow, what is it.

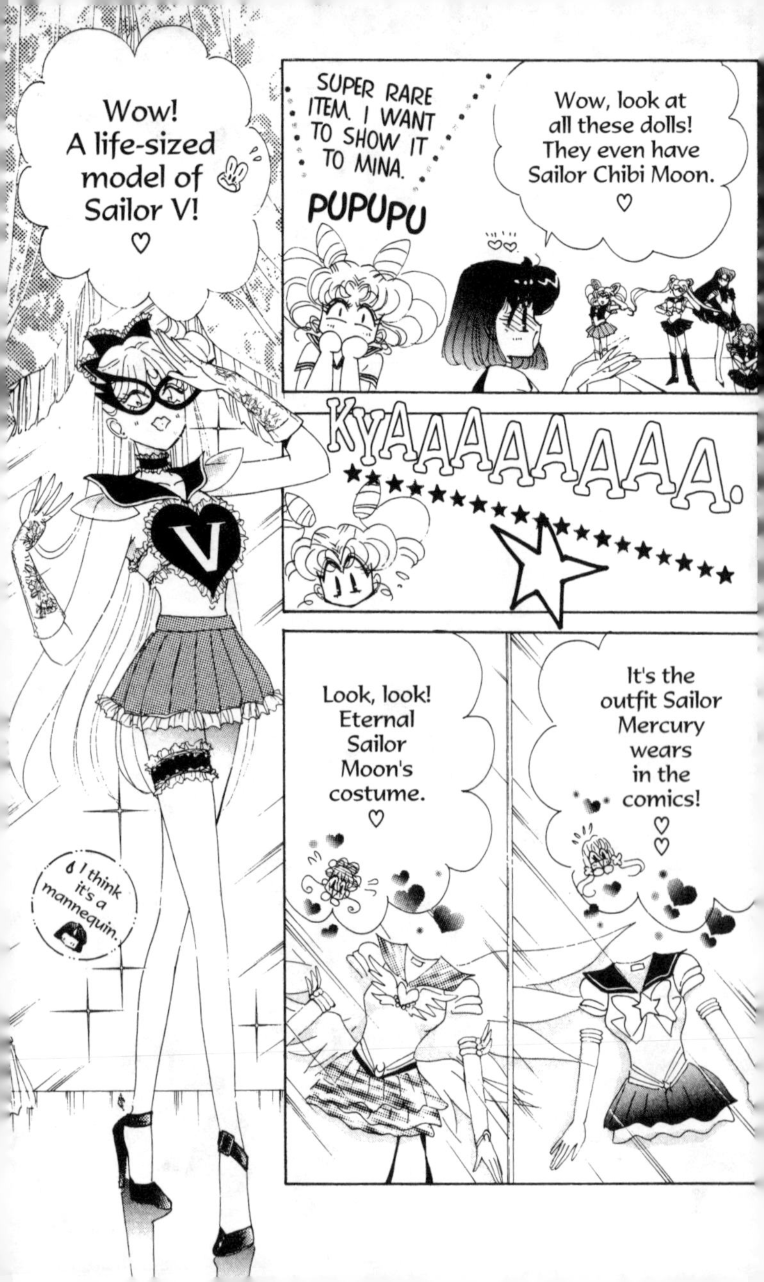
Wow! A life-sized model of Sailor V! ♡
I think it's a mannequin.
SUPER RARE ITEM. I WANT TO SHOW IT TO MINA.
PUPUPU
Wow, look at all these dolls! They even have Sailor Chibi Moon. ♡
KYAAAAAAAAA.
Look, look! Eternal Sailor Moon's costume. ♡
It's the outfit Sailor Mercury wears in the comics! ♡ ♡

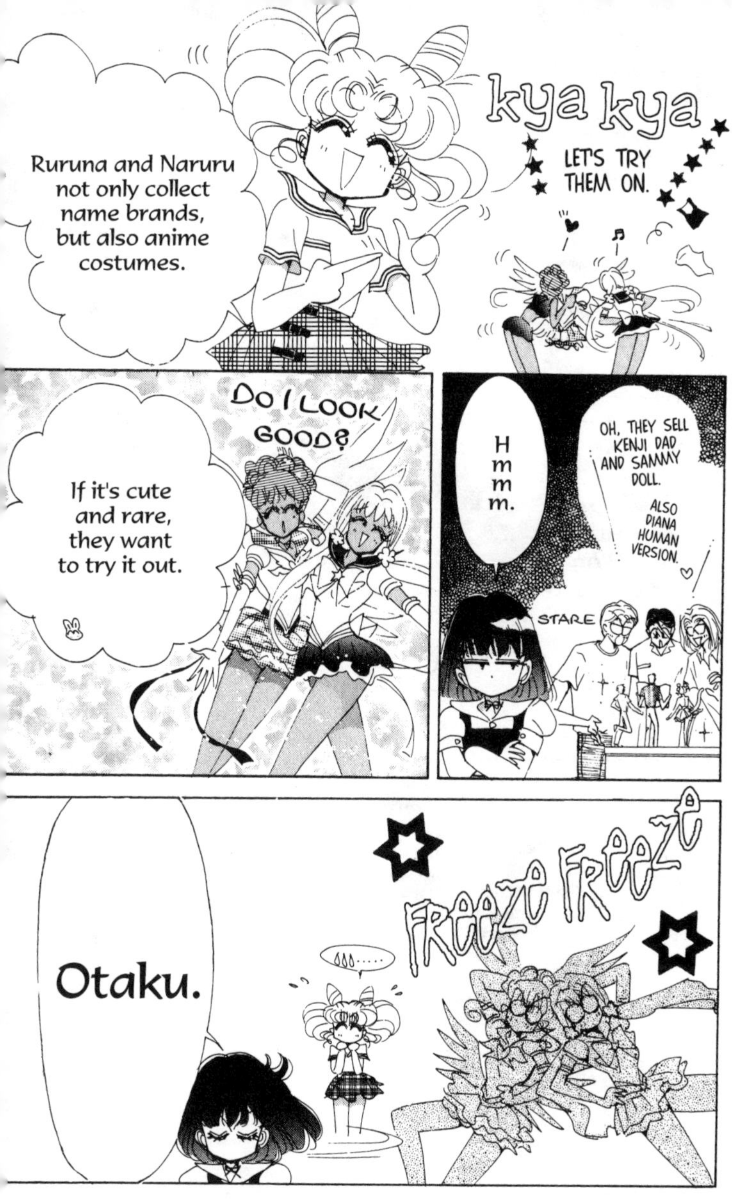

Ruruna and Naruru not only collect name brands, but also anime costumes.
kya kya
LET'S TRY THEM ON.
DO I LOOK GOOD?
If it's cute and rare, they want to try it out.
Hmmm.
OH, THEY SELL KENJI DAD AND SAMMY DOLL.
ALSO DIANA HUMAN VERSION.
STARE
Otaku.
Freeze Freeze

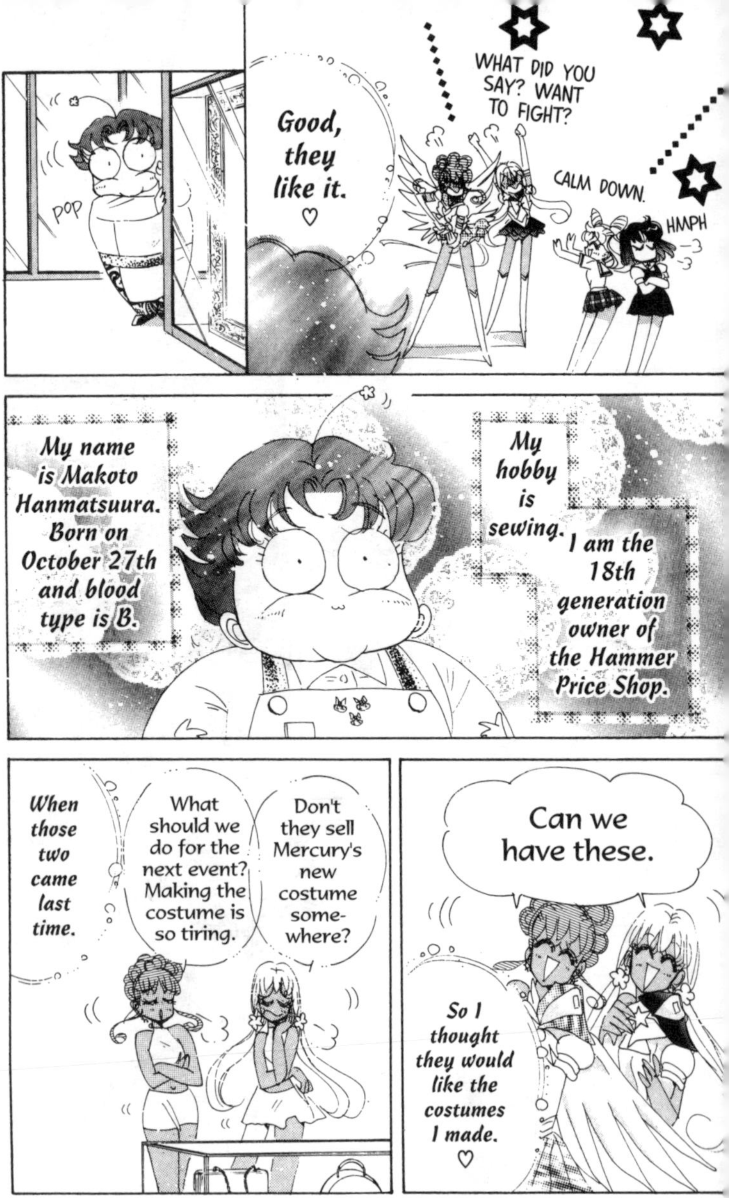

POP
Good, they like it. ♡
WHAT DID YOU SAY? WANT TO FIGHT?
CALM DOWN.
HMPH
My name is Makoto Hanmatsuura. Born on October 27th and blood type is B.
My hobby is sewing.
I am the 18th generation owner of the Hammer Price Shop.
When those two came last time.
What should we do for the next event? Making the costume is so tiring.
Don't they sell Mercury's new costume some-where?
Can we have these.
So I thought they would like the costumes I made. ♡

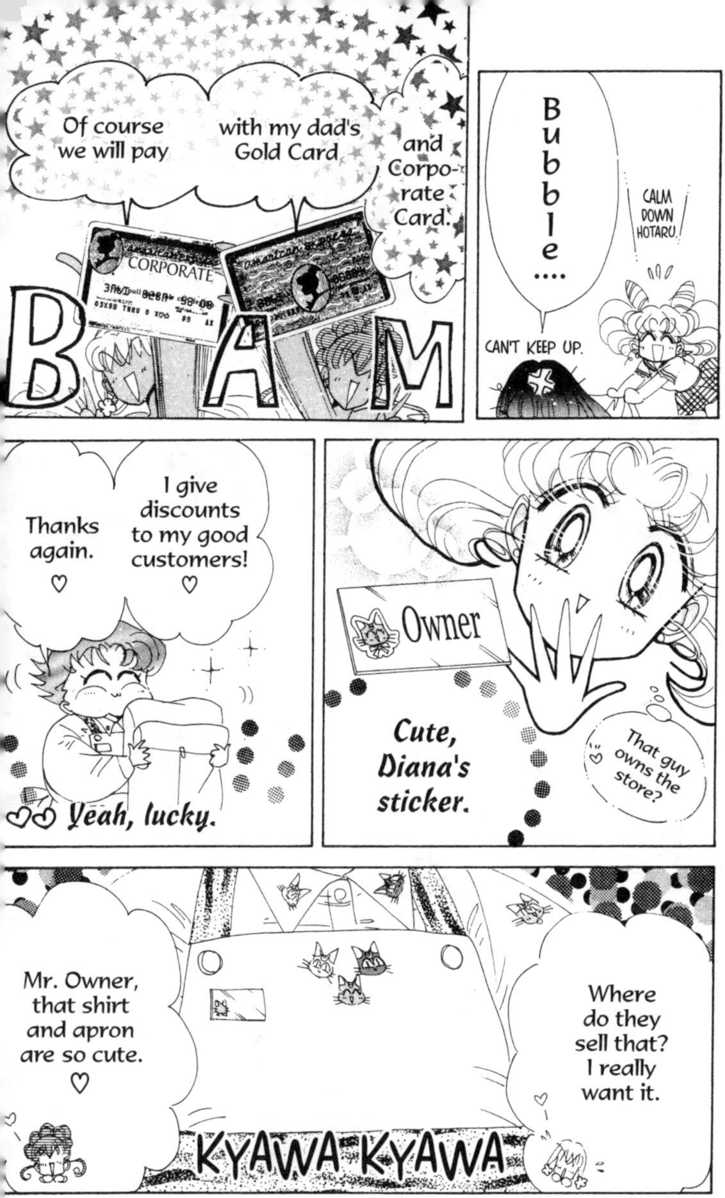

Of course we will pay
with my dad's Gold Card
and Corpo-rate Card.
CORPORATE
BAM
Bubble....
CALM DOWN HOTARU.
CAN'T KEEP UP.
Thanks again. ♡
I give discounts to my good customers! ♡
Yeah, lucky.
Owner
Cute, Diana's sticker.
That guy owns the store?
Mr. Owner, that shirt and apron are so cute. ♡
Where do they sell that? I really want it.
KYAWA KYAWA

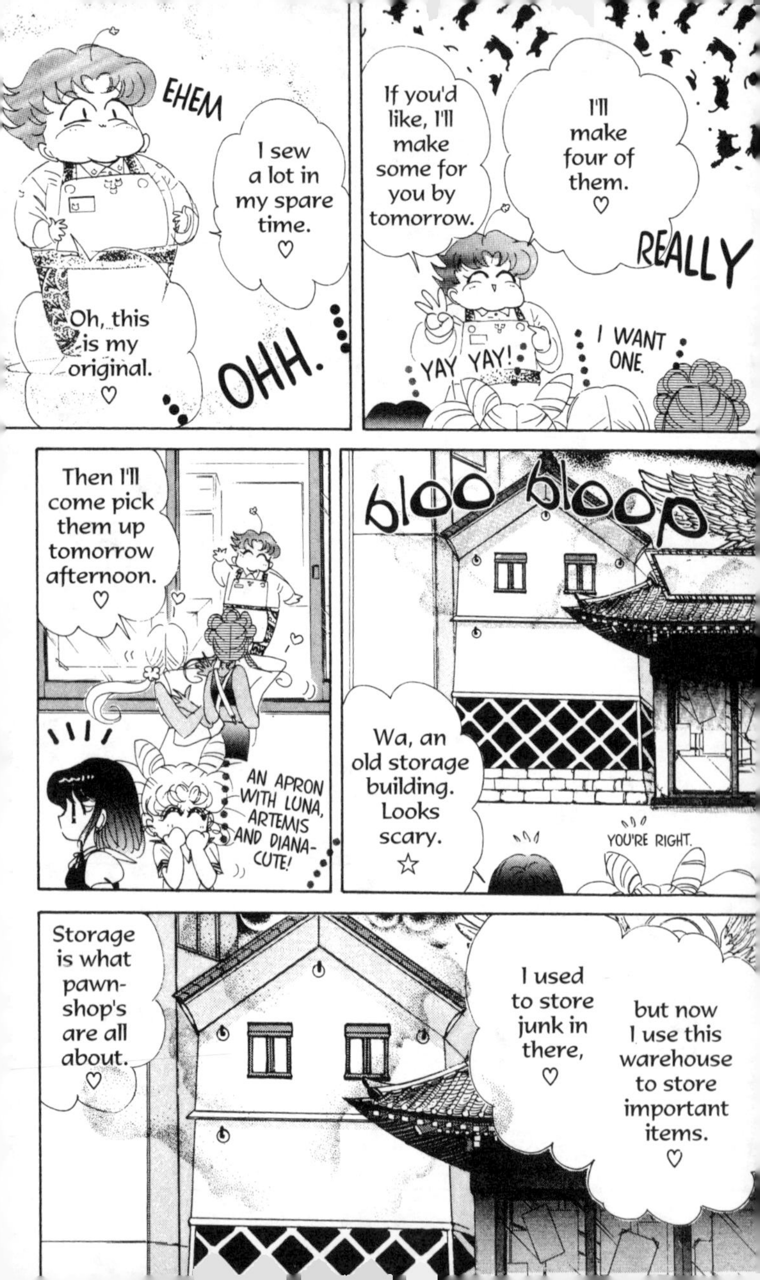
EHEM
I sew a lot in my spare time. ♡
Oh, this is my original. ♡
OHH.
If you'd like, I'll make some for you by tomorrow.
I'll make four of them. ♡
REALLY
YAY YAY!
I WANT ONE.
Then I'll come pick them up tomorrow afternoon. ♡
AN APRON WITH LUNA, ARTEMIS AND DIANA-CUTE!
bloo bloop
Wa, an old storage building. Looks scary. ☆
YOU'RE RIGHT.
Storage is what pawn-shop's are all about. ♡
I used to store junk in there, ♡
but now I use this warehouse to store important items. ♡

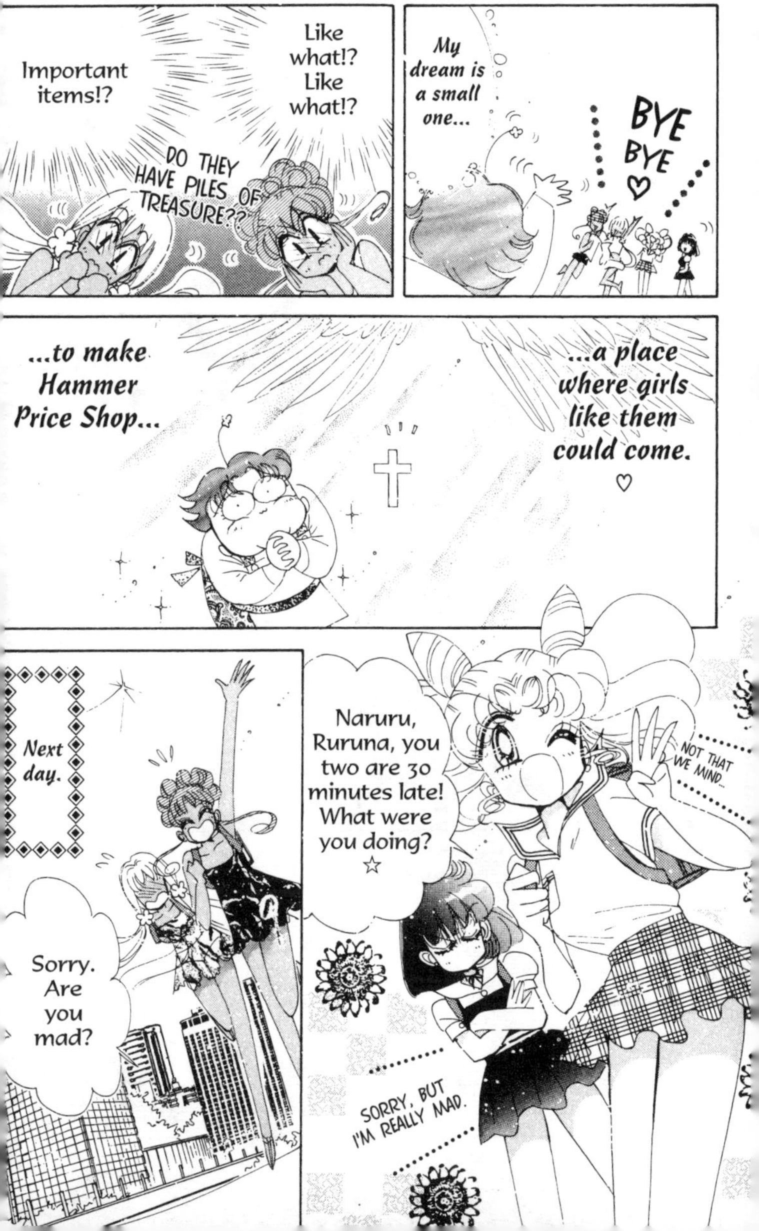

Important items!?
Like what!? Like what!?
DO THEY HAVE PILES OF TREASURE??
My dream is a small one...
BYE BYE ♡
...to make Hammer Price Shop...
...a place where girls like them could come. ♡
Next day.
Sorry. Are you mad?
Naruru, Ruruna, you two are 30 minutes late! What were you doing? ☆
NOT THAT WE MIND...
SORRY, BUT I'M REALLY MAD.

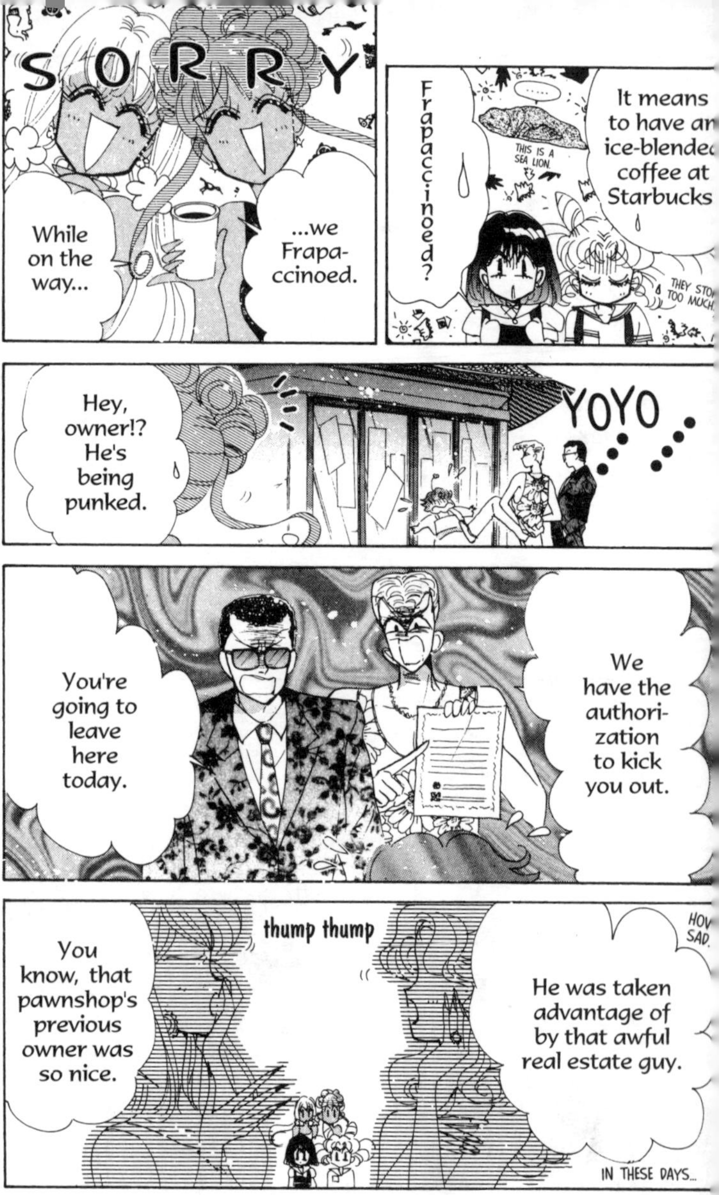

SORRY
While on the way...
...we Frapaccinoed.
Frapaccinoed?
......
THIS IS A SEA LION.
It means to have a ice-blende coffee at Starbucks
THEY STO TOO MUCH
Hey, owner!? He's being punked.
YOYO
You're going to leave here today.
We have the authorization to kick you out.
thump thump
You know, that pawnshop's previous owner was so nice.
He was taken advantage of by that awful real estate guy.
HOV SAD.
IN THESE DAYS...

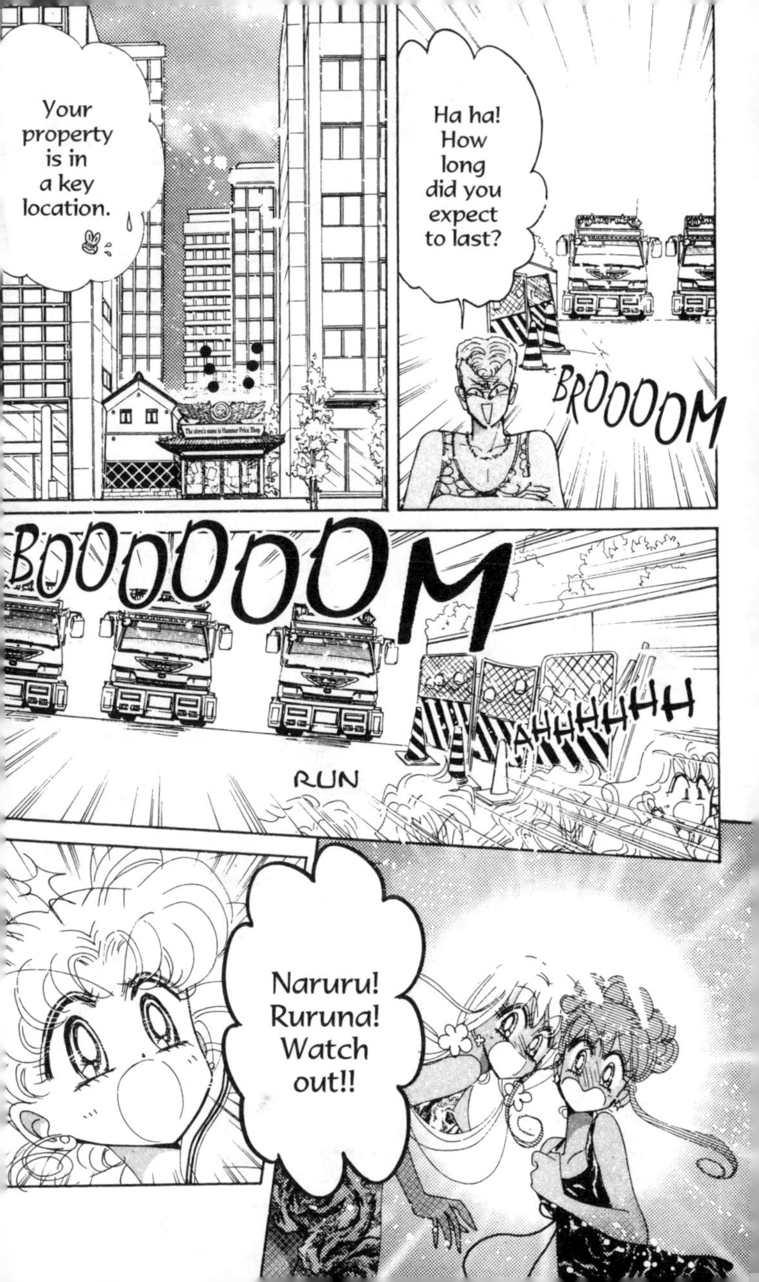
Your property is in a key location.
The store's name is Hammer Price Shop
Ha ha! How long did you expect to last?
BROOOOM
BOOOOOOM
AHHHHHHH
RUN
Naruru! Ruruna! Watch out!!

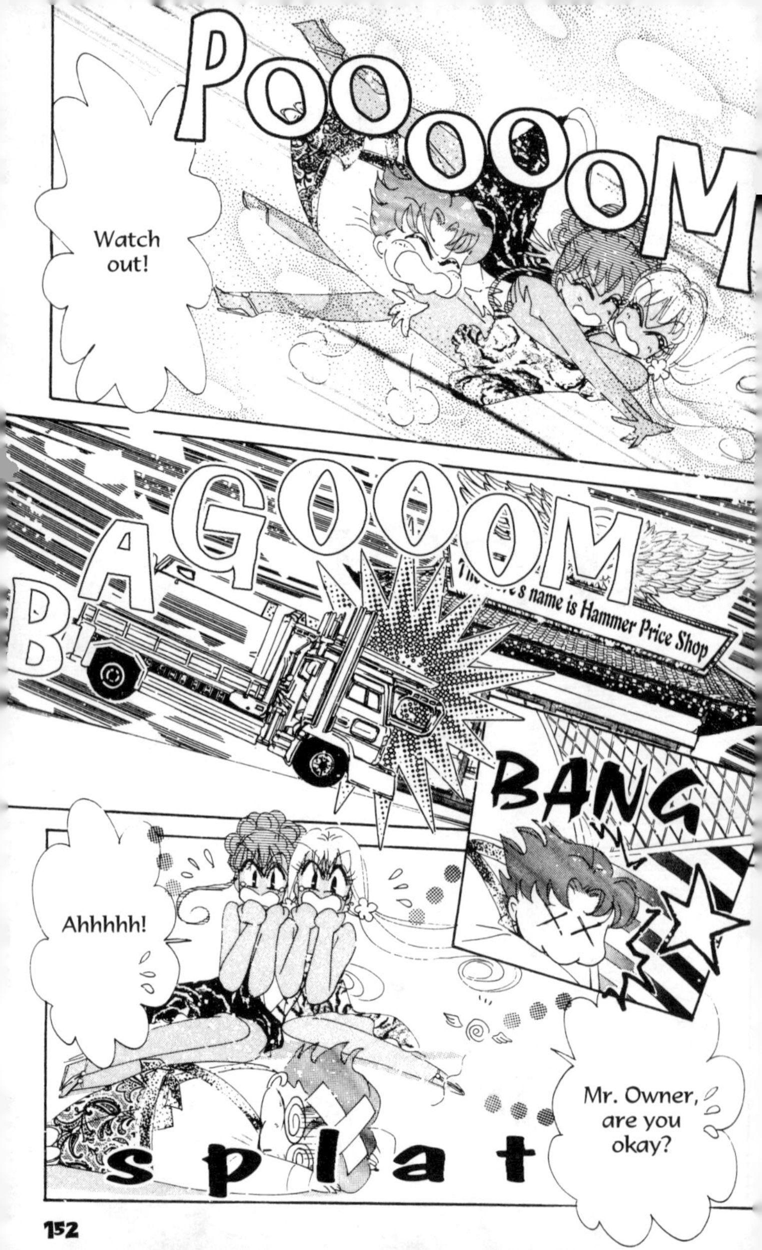

Watch out!
POOOOOOM
BAGOOOM
s name is Hammer Price Shop
BANG
Ahhhhh!
splat
Mr. Owner, are you okay?

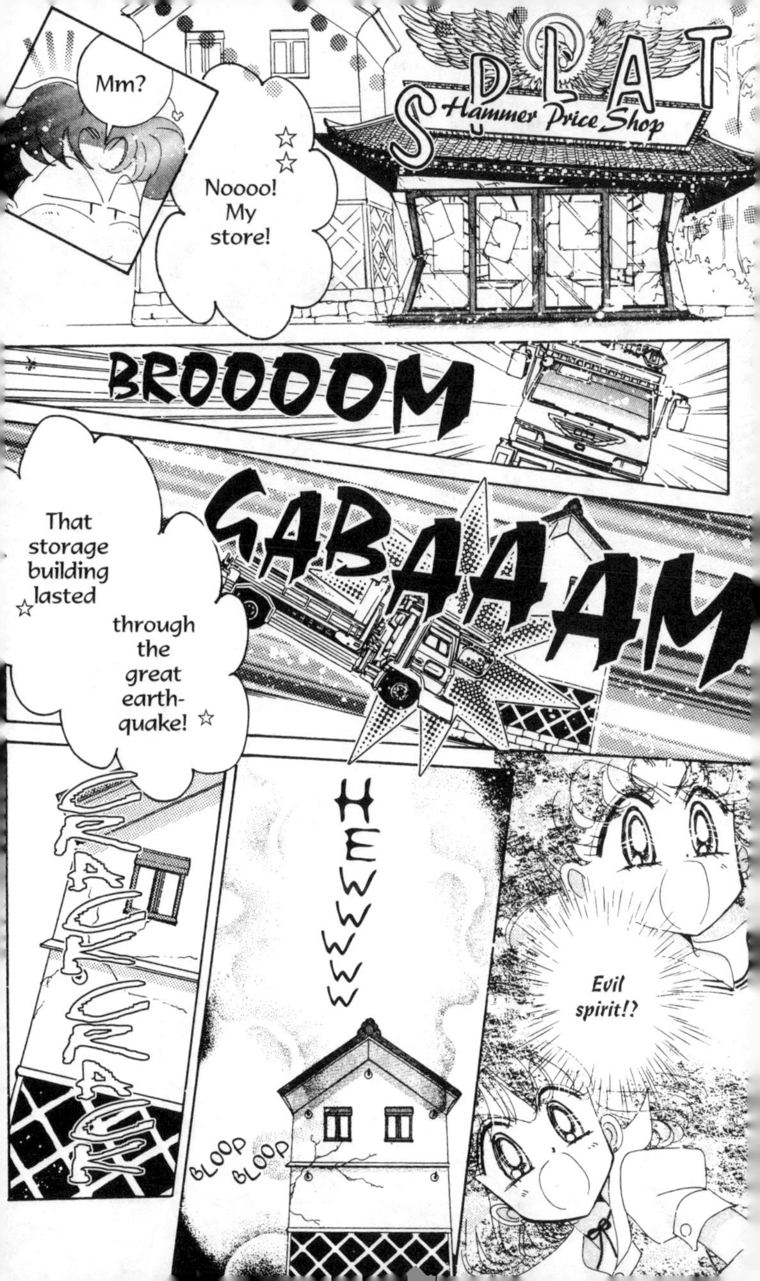
Mm?
Noooo! My store!
SPLAT
Hammer Price Shop
BROOOOM
That storage building lasted through the great earthquake!
GABAAAM
HEWWWWW
BLOOP BLOOP
Evil spirit!?

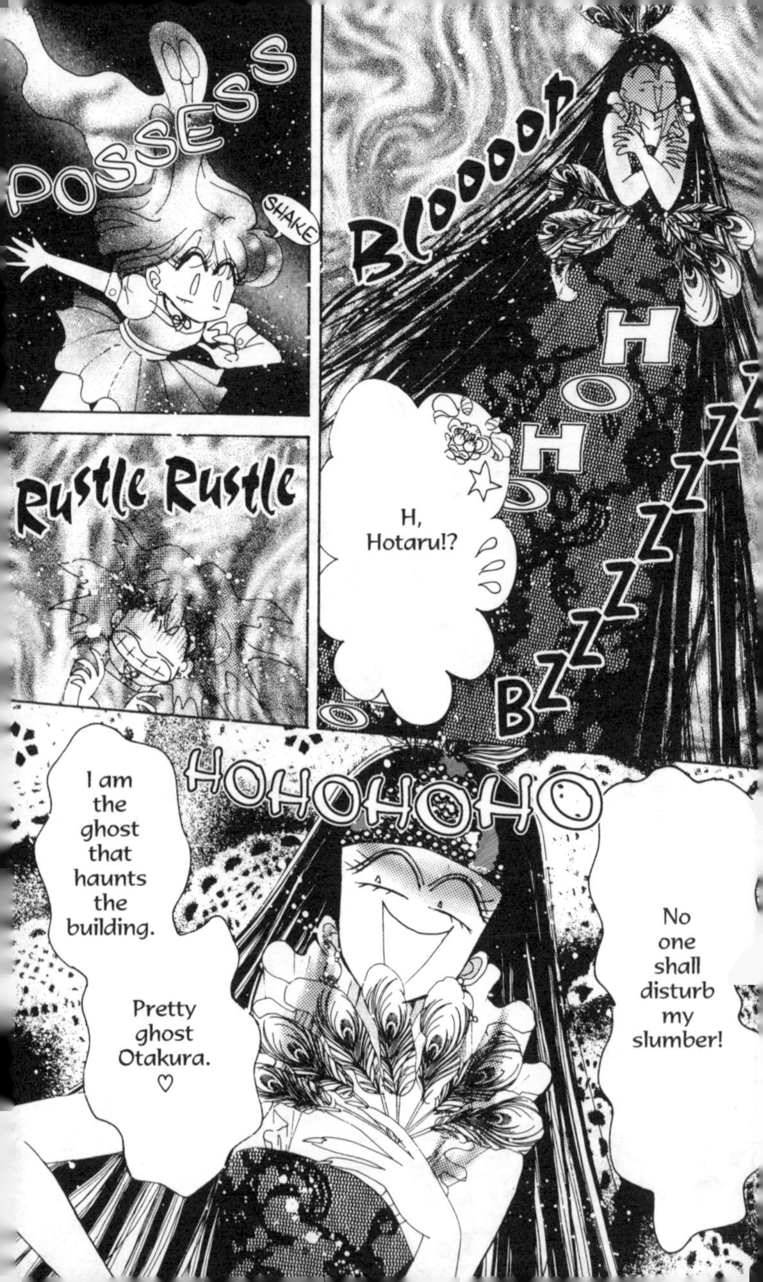
POSSESS
SHAKE
Rustle Rustle
Bloooop
H, Hotaru!?
HOHO
BZZZZZZZZZ
HOHOHOHOHO
I am the ghost that haunts the building.
Pretty ghost Otakura. ♡
No one shall disturb my slumber!

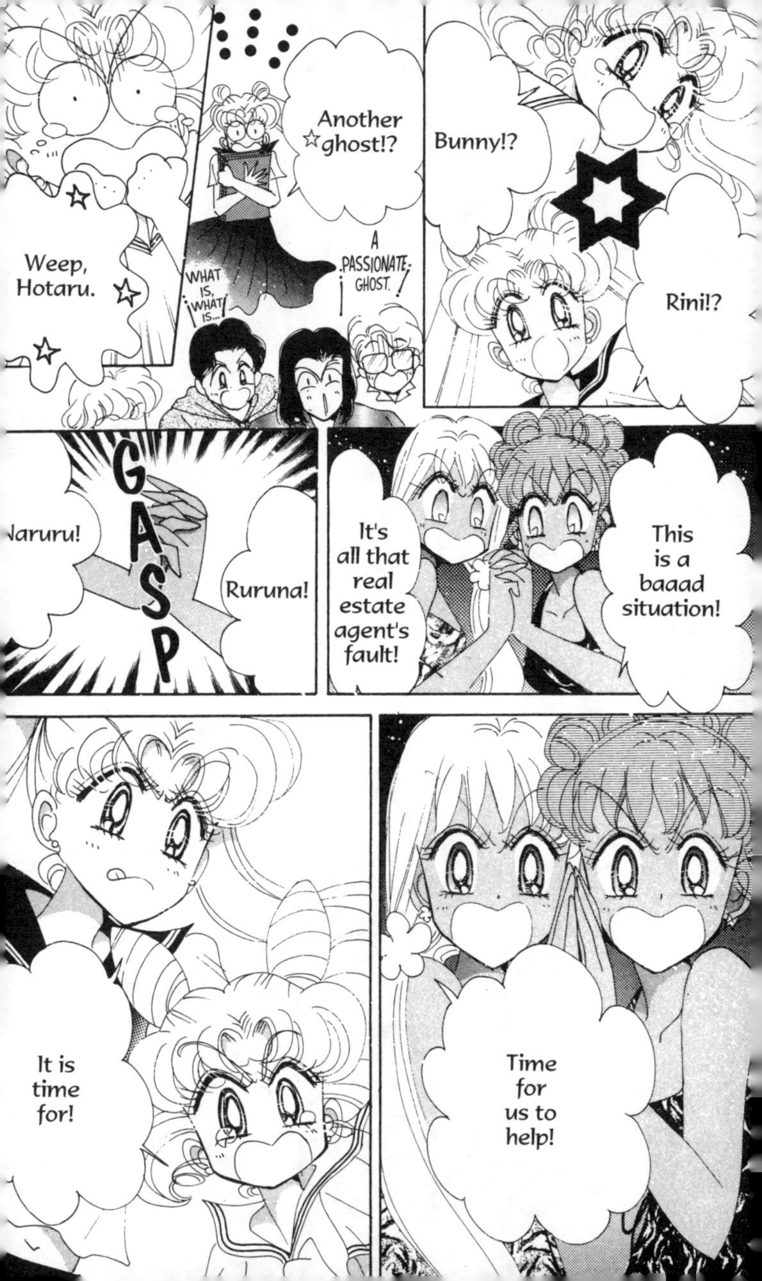
Weep, Hotaru.
Another ghost!?
WHAT IS, WHAT IS...
A PASSIONATE GHOST.
Bunny!?
Rini!?
Naruru!
GASP
Ruruna!
It's all that real estate agent's fault!
This is a baaad situation!
It is time for!
Time for us to help!

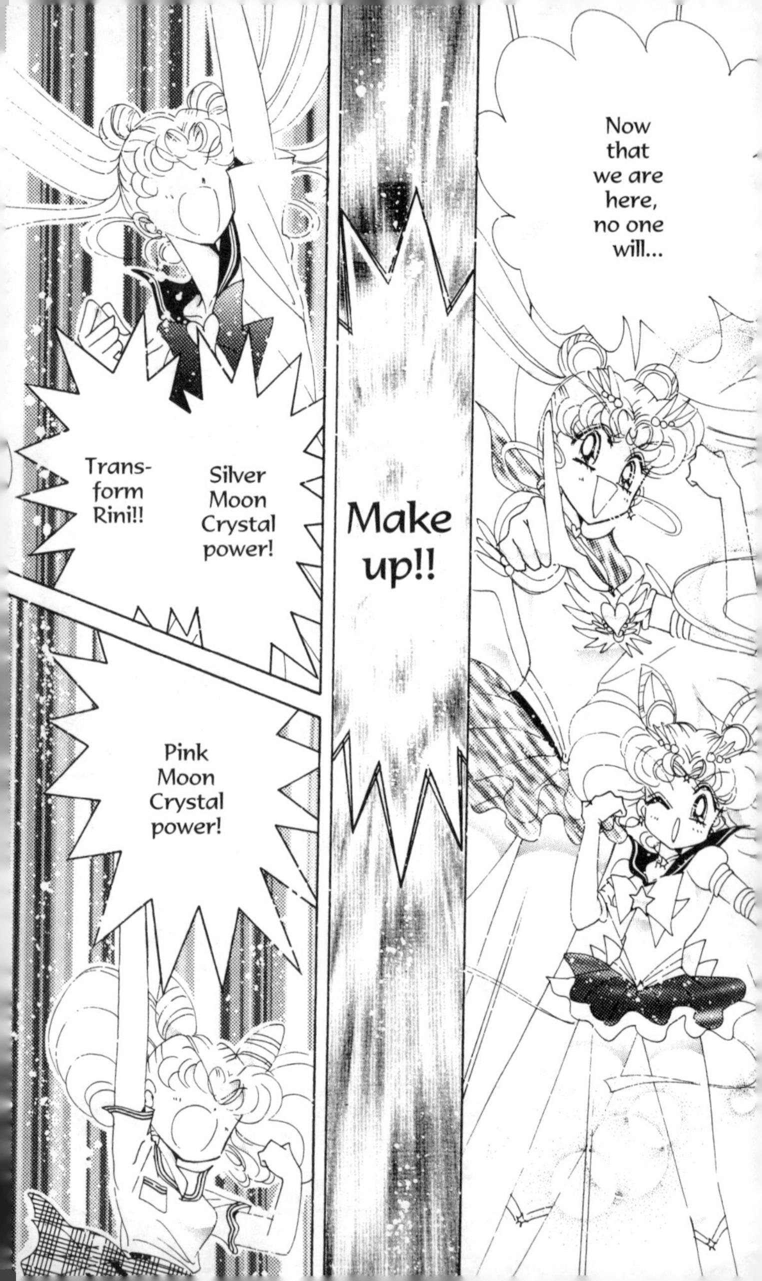
Trans-form Rini!!
Silver Moon Crystal power!
Pink Moon Crystal power!
Make up!!
Now that we are here, no one will...

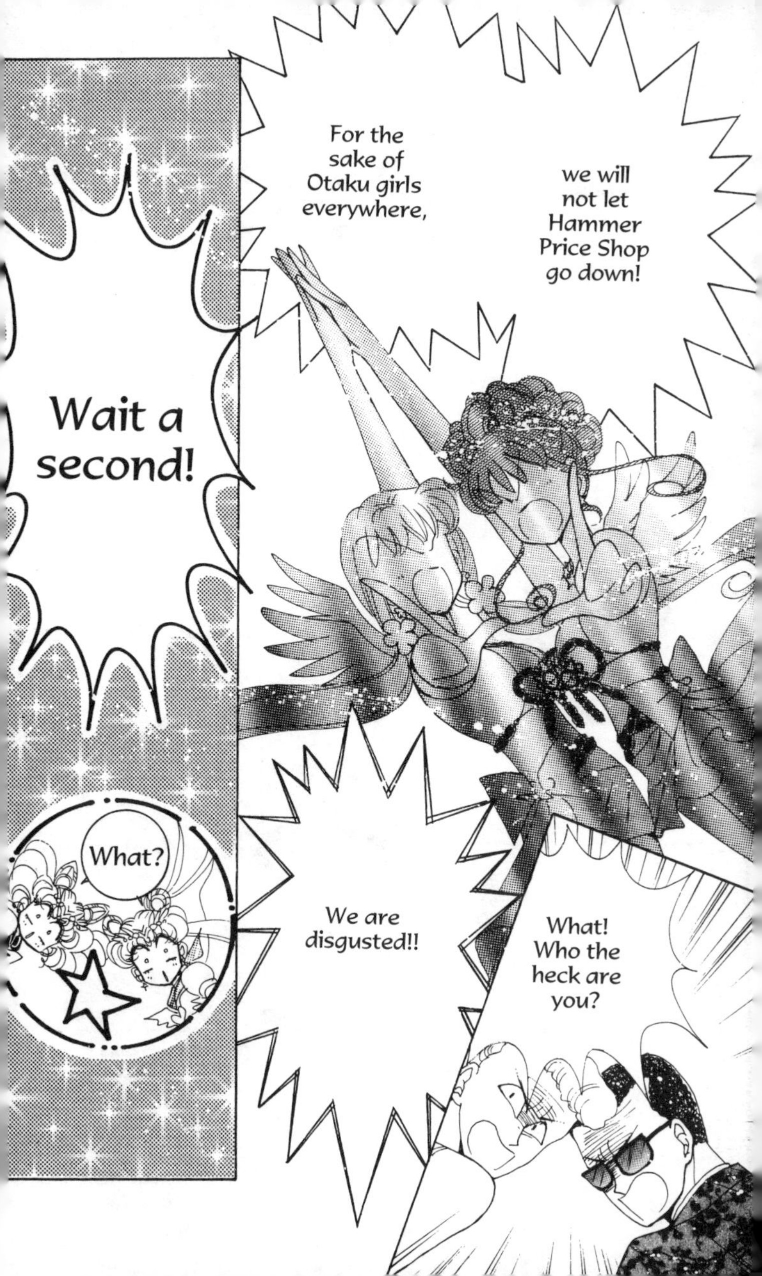
Wait a second!
What?
For the sake of Otaku girls everywhere,
we will not let Hammer Price Shop go down!
We are disgusted!!
What! Who the heck are you?

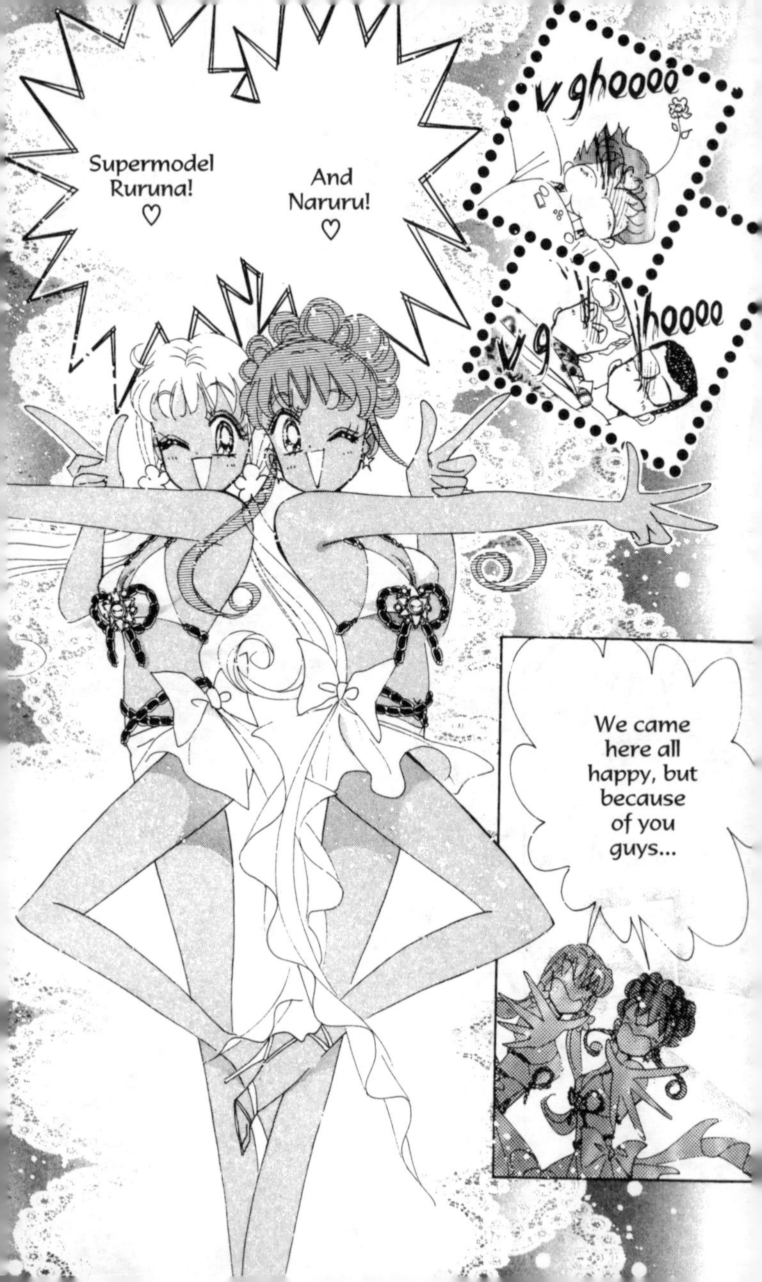

Supermodel Ruruna! ♡
And Naruru! ♡
vghoooo
vg hoooo
We came here all happy, but because of you guys...

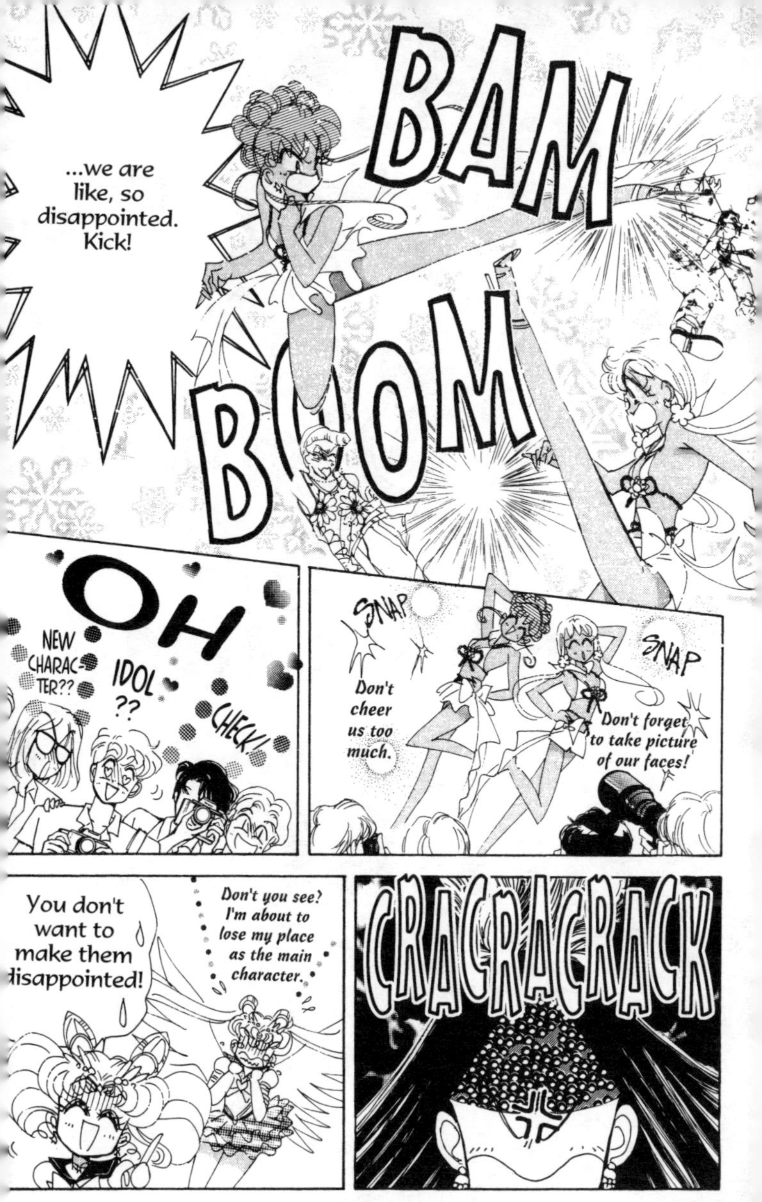
...we are like, so disappointed. Kick!
BAM
BOOM
OH
NEW CHARACTER??
IDOL ??
CHECK!
SNAP
Don't cheer us too much.
SNAP
Don't forget to take picture of our faces!
You don't want to make them disappointed!
Don't you see? I'm about to lose my place as the main character.
CRACRACRACK

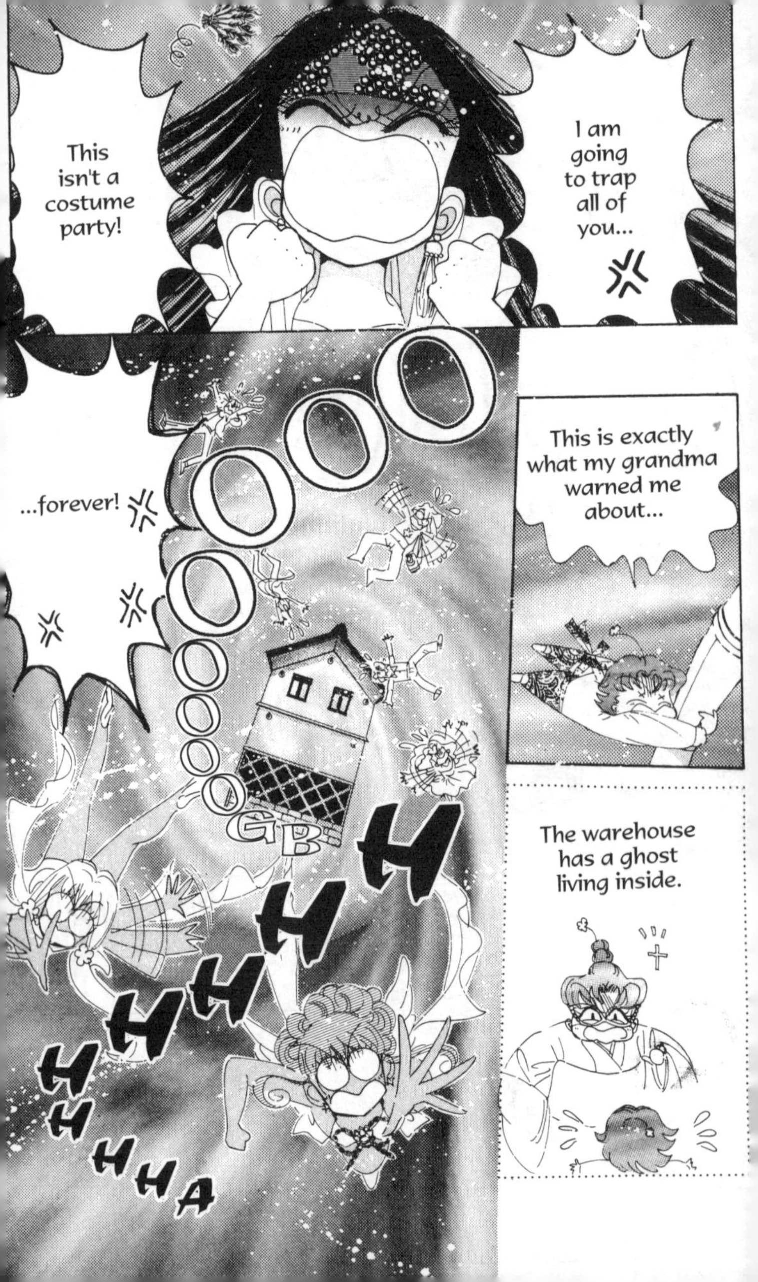
This isn't a costume party!
I am going to trap all of you...
...forever!
OOOOOOOOOOOGBHHHHHHHHHHA
This is exactly what my grandma warned me about...
The warehouse has a ghost living inside.

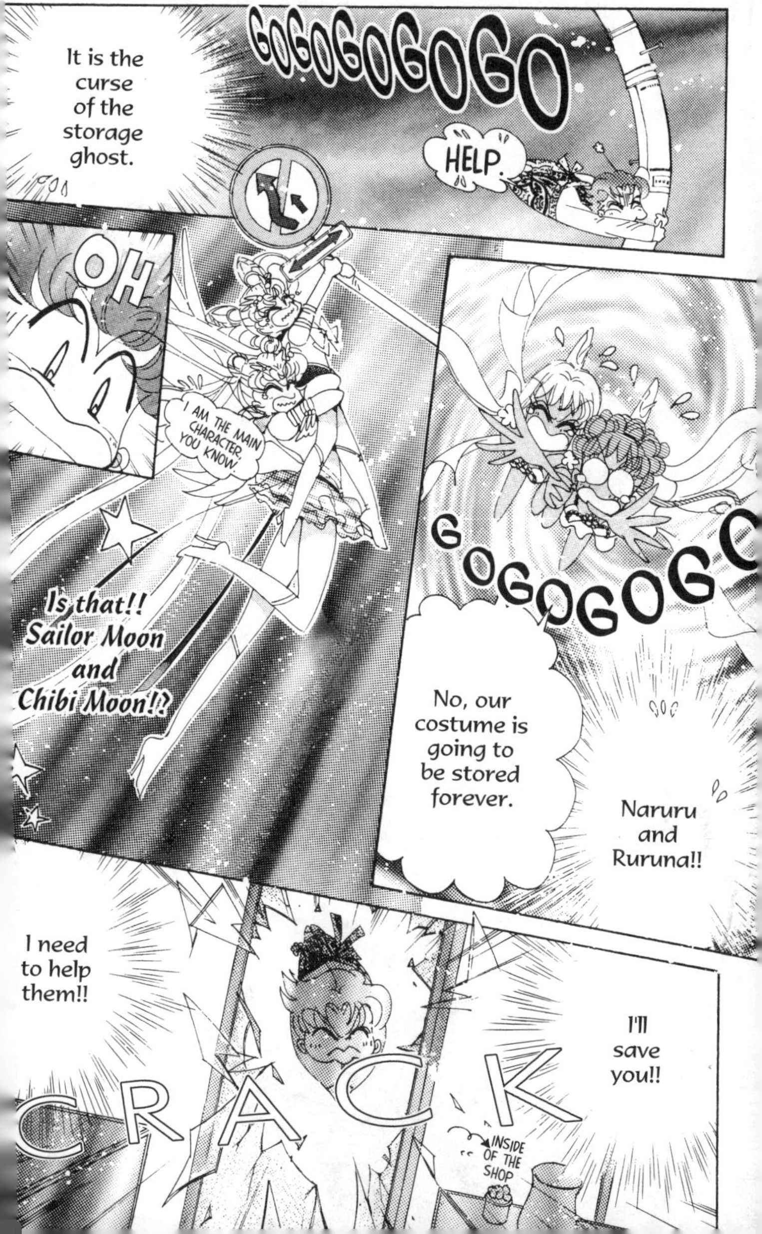
It is the curse of the storage ghost.
GOGOGOGOGO
HELP.
OH
I AM THE MAIN CHARACTER, YOU KNOW.
Is that!! Sailor Moon and Chibi Moon!?
GOGOGOGOGO
No, our costume is going to be stored forever.
Naruru and Ruruna!!
I need to help them!!
CRACK
INSIDE OF THE SHOP
I'll save you!!

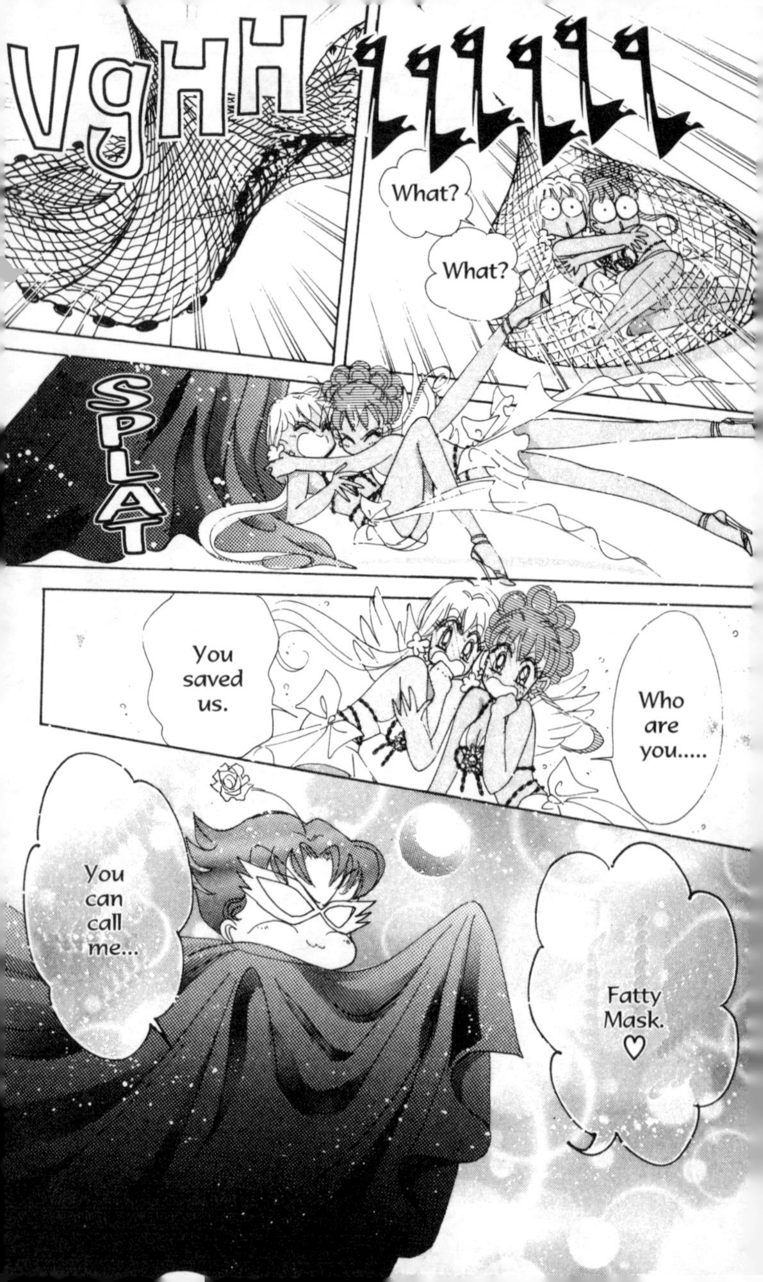
VgHH
What?
What?
SPLAT
You saved us.
Who are you.....
You can call me...
Fatty Mask. ♡

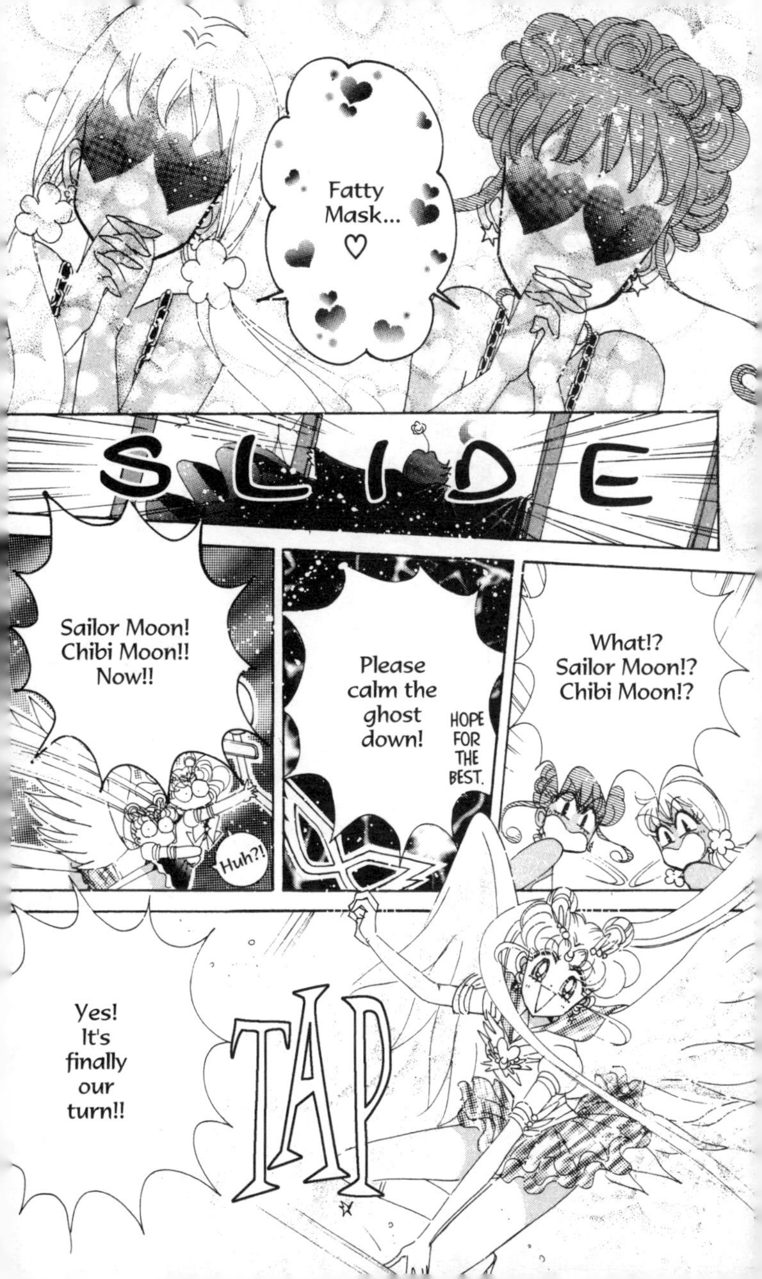

Fatty Mask... ♡
SLIDE
Sailor Moon! Chibi Moon!! Now!!
Huh?!
Please calm the ghost down!
HOPE FOR THE BEST.
What!? Sailor Moon!? Chibi Moon!?
Yes! It's finally our turn!!
TAP

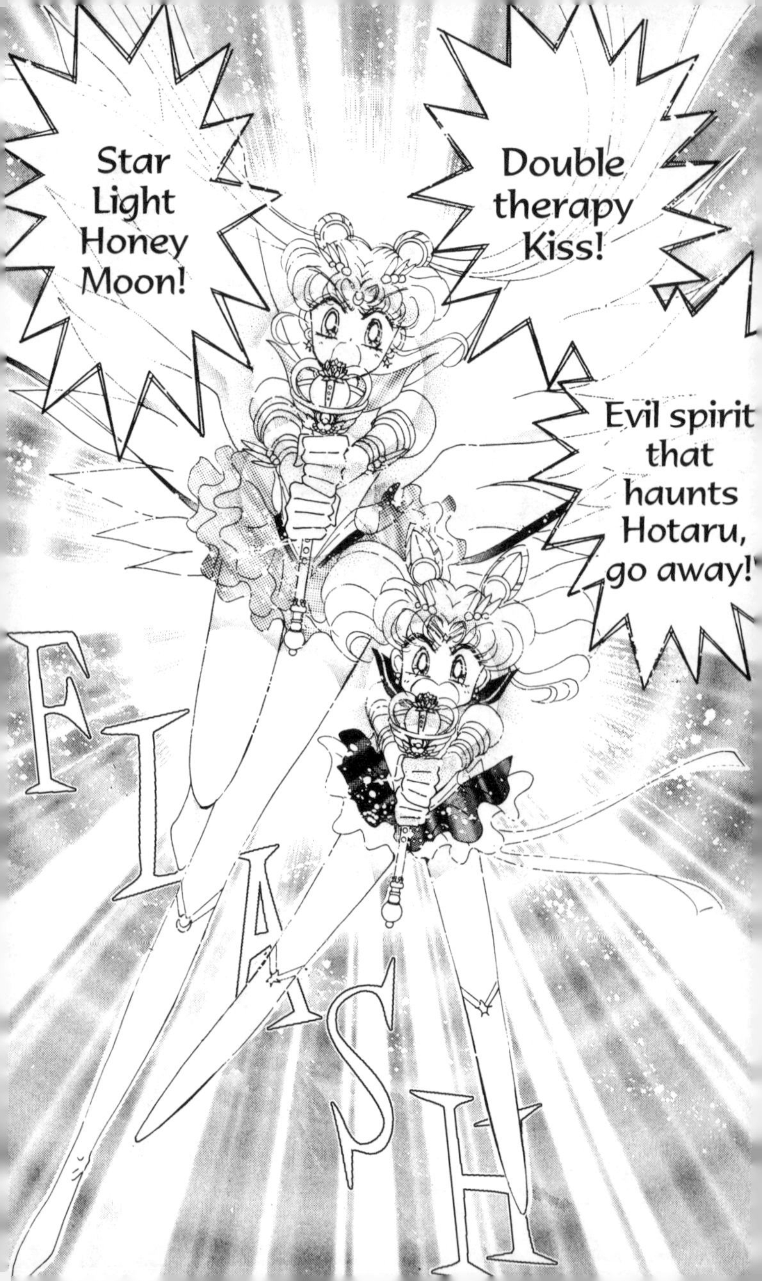
Star Light Honey Moon!
Double therapy Kiss!
Evil spirit that haunts Hotaru, go away!
FLASH

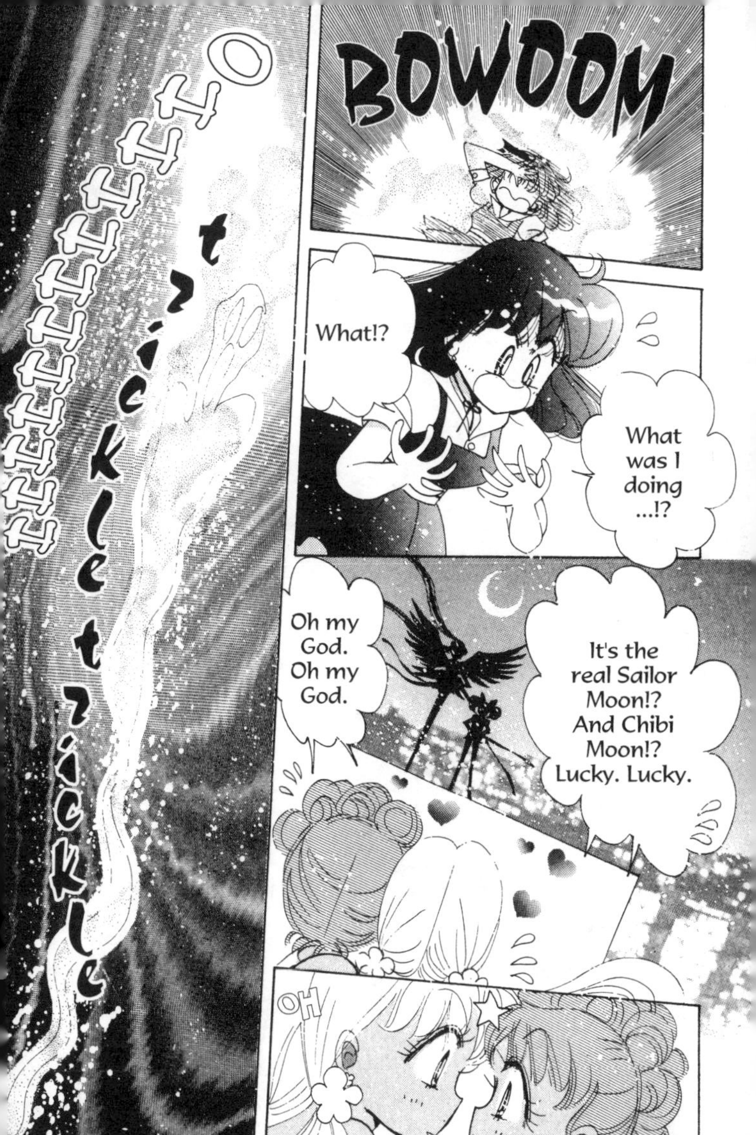
tzickle tzickle
BOWOOM
What!?
What was I doing ...!?
Oh my God. Oh my God.
It's the real Sailor Moon!? And Chibi Moon!? Lucky. Lucky.
OH
OH

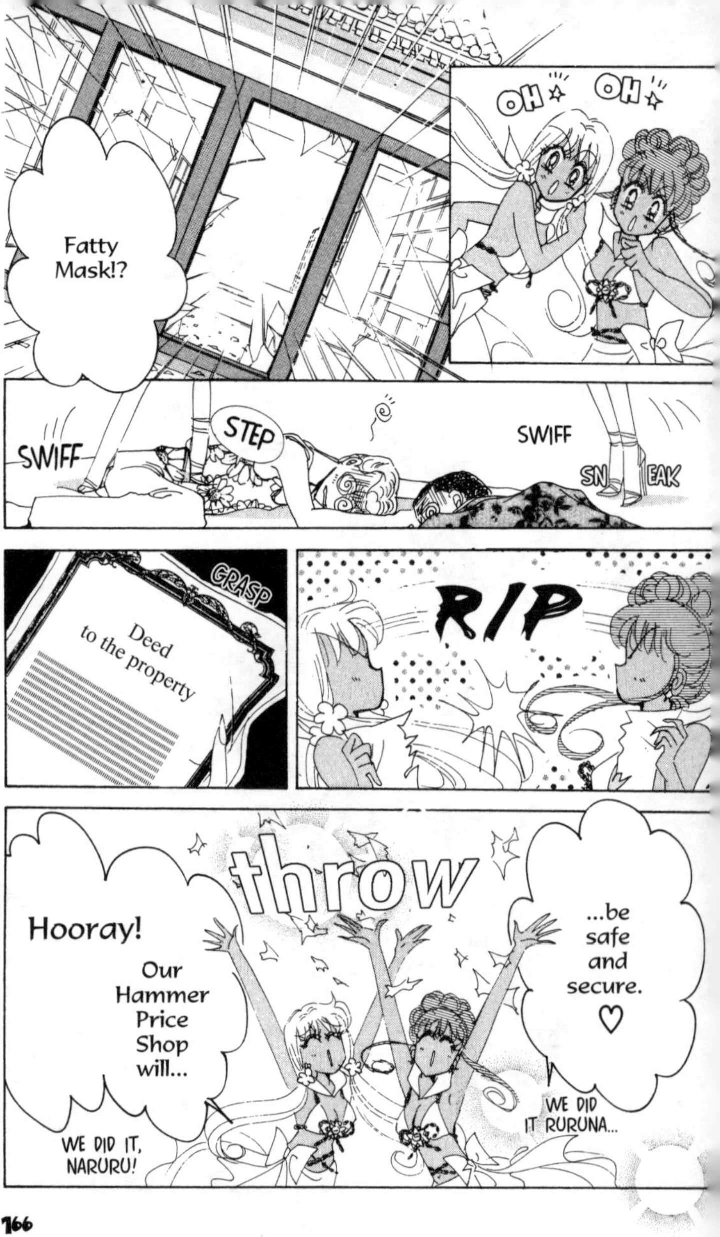
Fatty Mask!?
OH OH
SWIFF
STEP
SWIFF
SN EAK
Deed to the property
GRASP
RIP
Hooray! Our Hammer Price Shop will...
throw
...be safe and secure. ♡
WE DID IT, NARURU!
WE DID IT RURUNA...

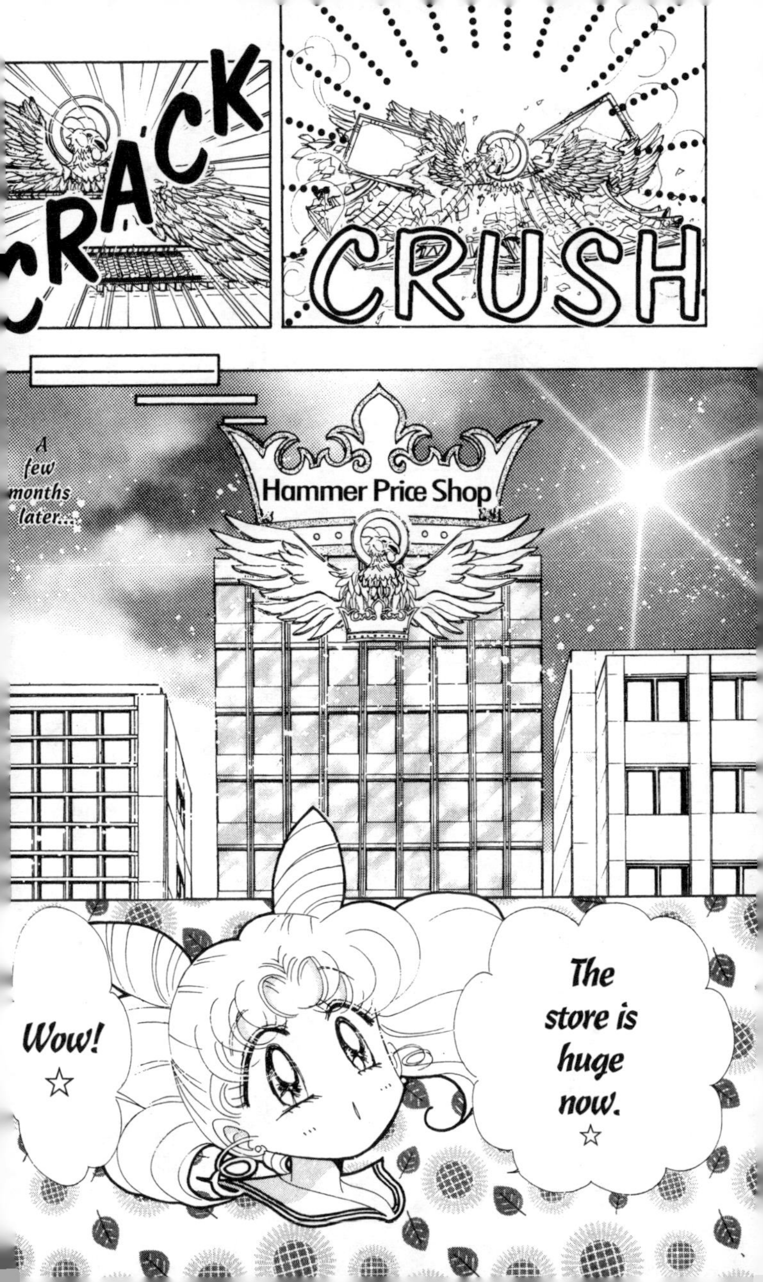

CRACK
CRUSH
A few months later...
Hammer Price Shop
Wow! ☆
The store is huge now. ☆

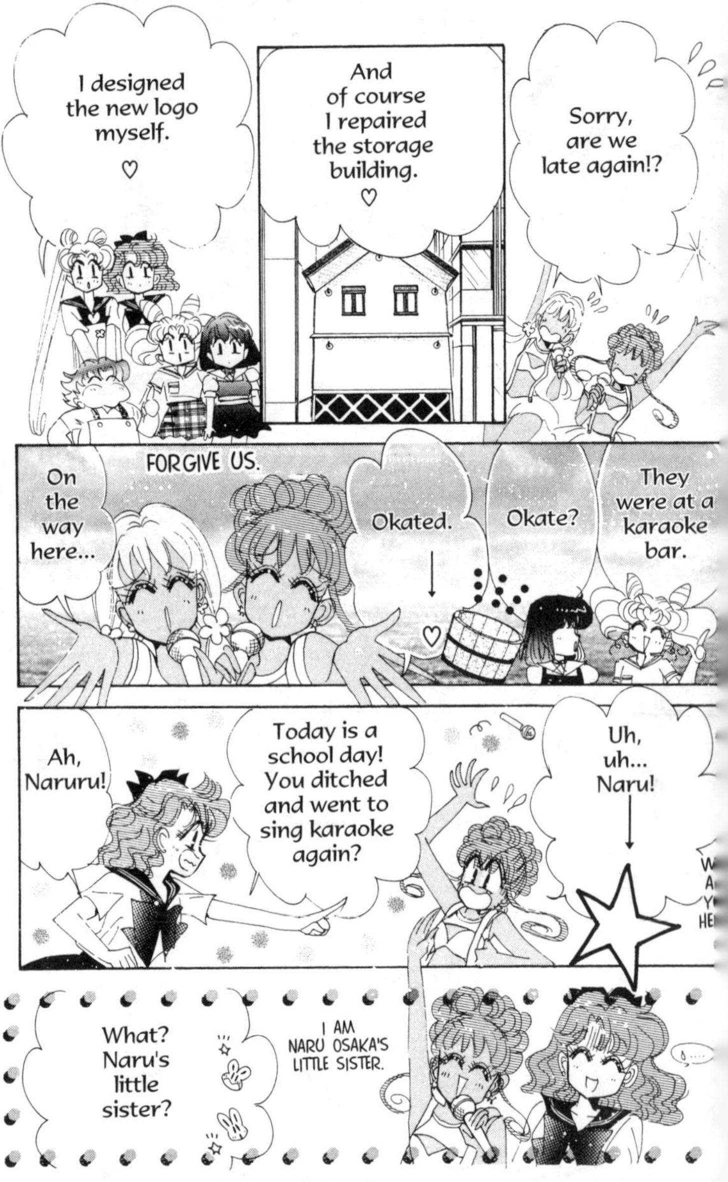

I designed the new logo myself. ♡
And of course I repaired the storage building. ♡
Sorry, are we late again!?
On the way here...
FORGIVE US.
Okated.
Okate?
They were at a karaoke bar.
Ah, Naruru!
Today is a school day! You ditched and went to sing karaoke again?
Uh, uh... Naru!
What? Naru's little sister?
I AM NARU OSAKA'S LITTLE SISTER.

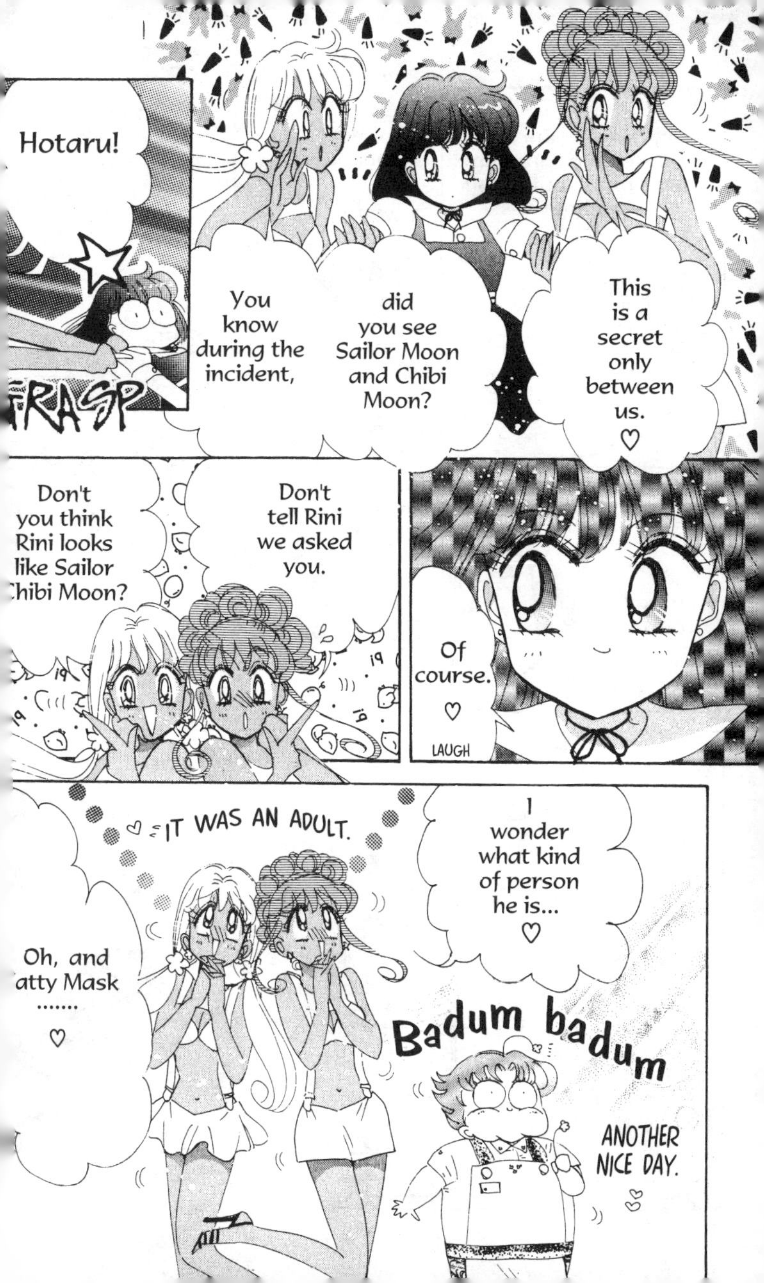
Hotaru!
GRASP
You know during the incident,
did you see Sailor Moon and Chibi Moon?
This is a secret only between us. ♡
Don't you think Rini looks like Sailor Chibi Moon?
Don't tell Rini we asked you.
Of course. ♡
LAUGH
IT WAS AN ADULT.
I wonder what kind of person he is... ♡
Oh, and atty Mask .... ♡
Badum badum
ANOTHER NICE DAY.

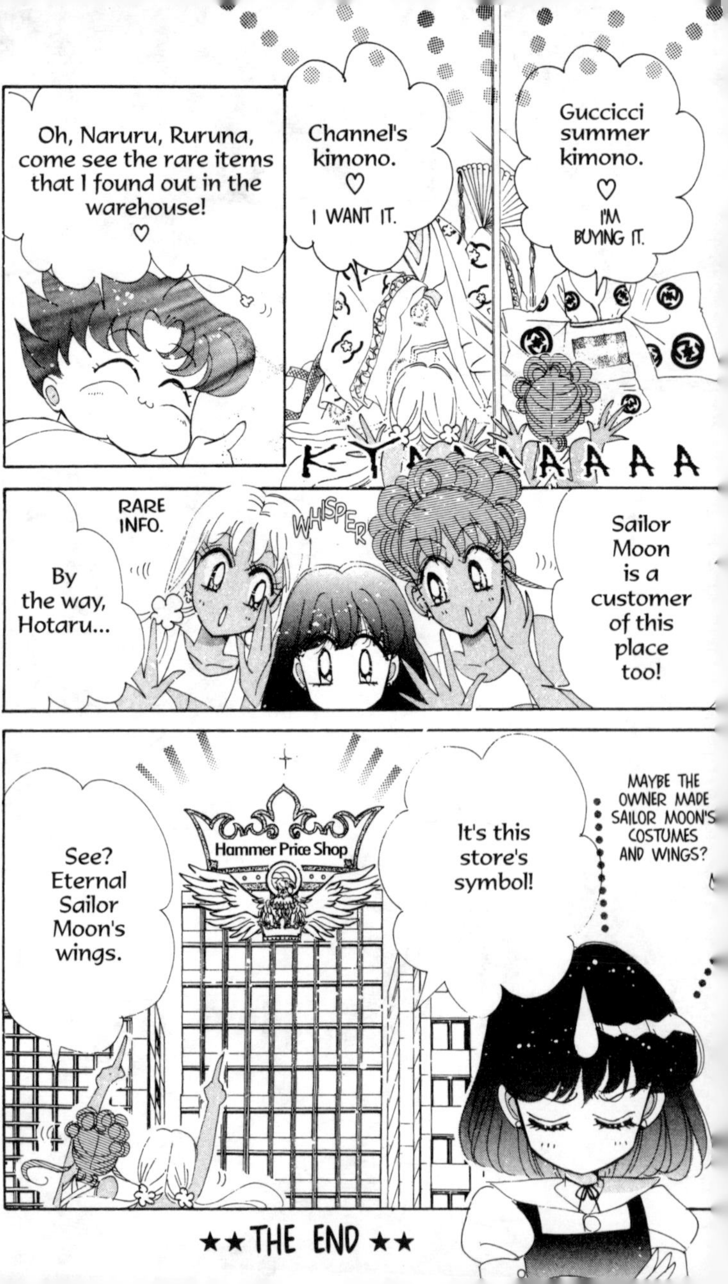

Oh, Naruru, Ruruna, come see the rare items that I found out in the warehouse! ♡
Channel's kimono. ♡
I WANT IT.
Guccicci summer kimono. ♡
I'M BUYING IT.
KYAAAAAAA
RARE INFO.
By the way, Hotaru...
WHISPER
Sailor Moon is a customer of this place too!
See? Eternal Sailor Moon's wings.
Hammer Price Shop
It's this store's symbol!
MAYBE THE OWNER MADE SAILOR MOON'S COSTUMES AND WINGS?

★★THE END★★

EXTRA

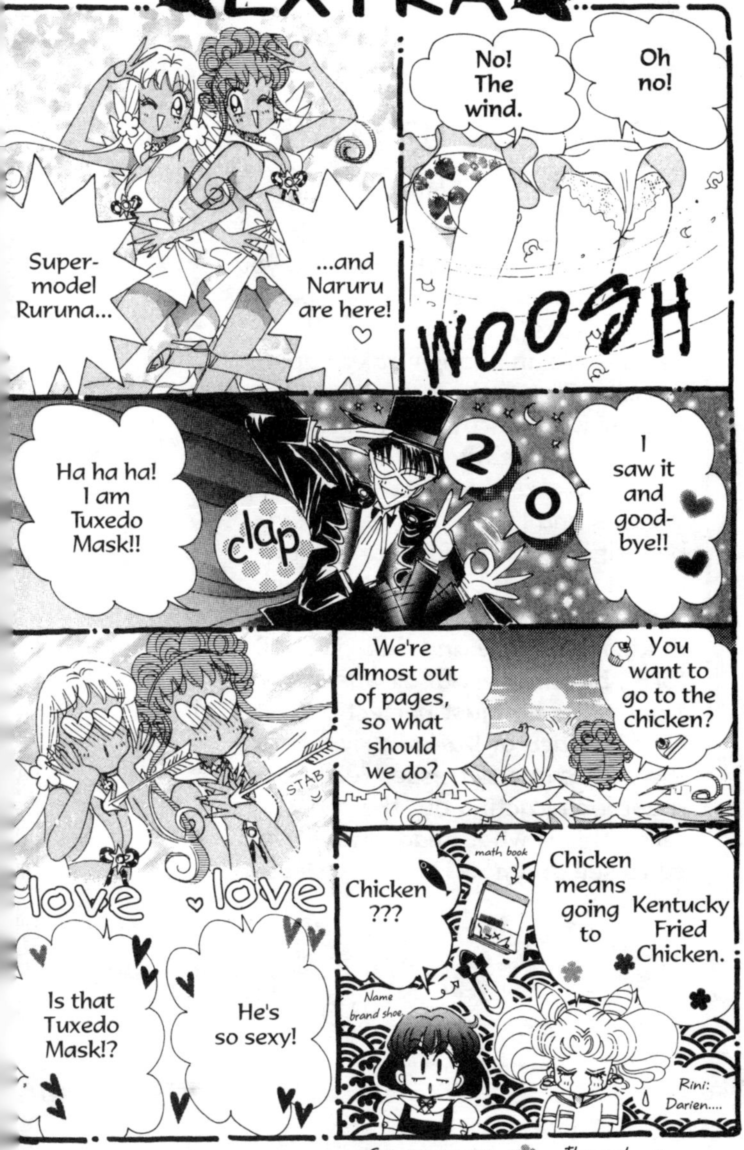

Super-model Ruruna...
...and Naruru are here!
No! The wind.
Oh no!
WOOSH
Ha ha ha! I am Tuxedo Mask!!
clap
2
0
I saw it and good-bye!!
love love
Is that Tuxedo Mask!?
He's so sexy!
STAB
We're almost out of pages, so what should we do?
You want to go to the chicken?
Chicken ???
A math book
Chicken means going to Kentucky Fried Chicken.
Name brand shoe
Rini: Darien....

Surprise surprise ✿ The end. ♡

96 11/3 - Today at AkeAzu, I saw the Musical Stars Super Live Show. They had lots of songs and skits that were a lot of fun!

THERE IS NO BETTER SHOW THAN SAILOR MOON!!

In 1996, the Sailor Moon's Musical Show was in its fourth year. Did you see the '96 summer musical special, "Sailor Stars"?

I was there, in Shenshuraku, Japan. I'm actually a little embarrassed to see my work on T.V. or on a show. In the intro of the musical show, they had Haruka and Michiru in fabulous dresses and I thought they looked beautiful. Also, Sailor Star Lights looked so much better in the musical than in the animation. They even made Ironmouse and Galaxia in 3D form, but the best of all was Darien. They made him just perfect and I liked the idea of Darien's rival. All of the actors and actresses really did a great job of acting out the characters. This is what I had always wanted to see and now I am very pleased!!

SOME OF THE STAMPS THAT I GAVE OUT!

172

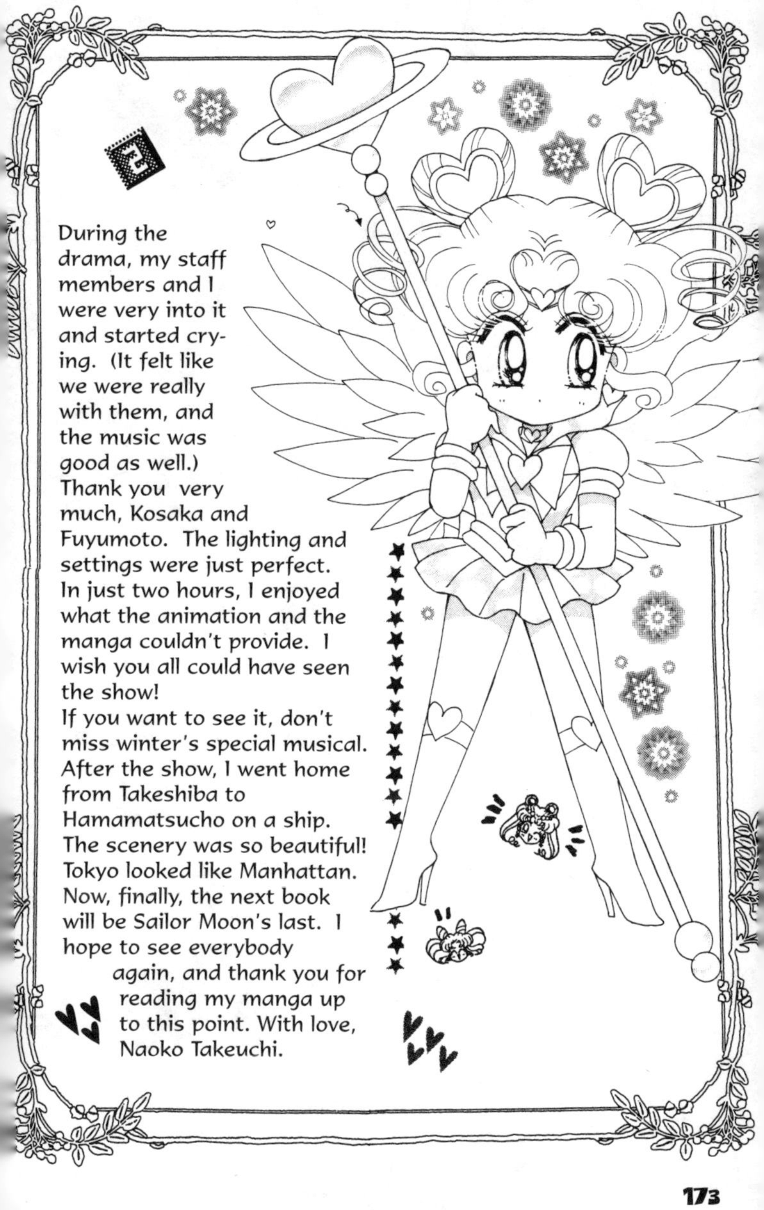

During the drama, my staff members and I were very into it and started crying. (It felt like we were really with them, and the music was good as well.) Thank you very much, Kosaka and Fuyumoto. The lighting and settings were just perfect. In just two hours, I enjoyed what the animation and the manga couldn't provide. I wish you all could have seen the show!
If you want to see it, don't miss winter's special musical. After the show, I went home from Takeshiba to Hamamatsucho on a ship. The scenery was so beautiful! Tokyo looked like Manhattan. Now, finally, the next book will be Sailor Moon's last. I hope to see everybody again, and thank you for reading my manga up to this point. With love, Naoko Takeuchi.

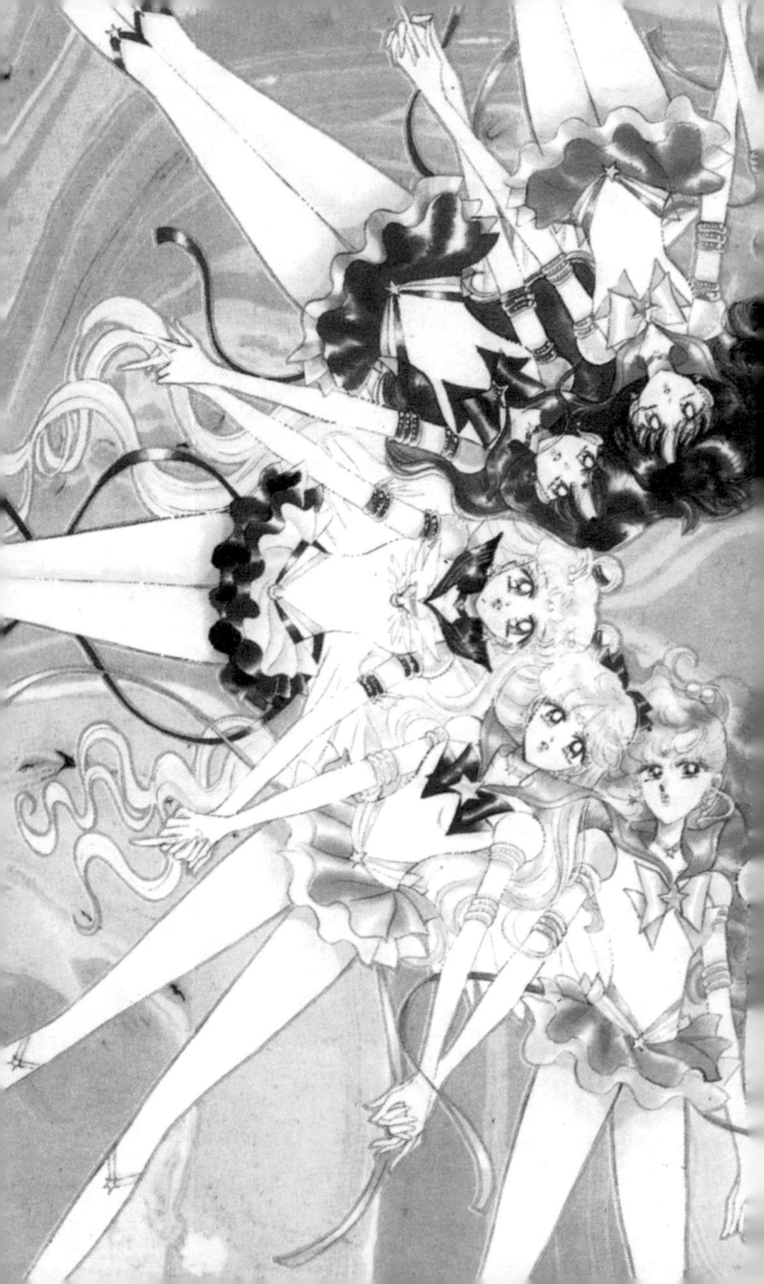

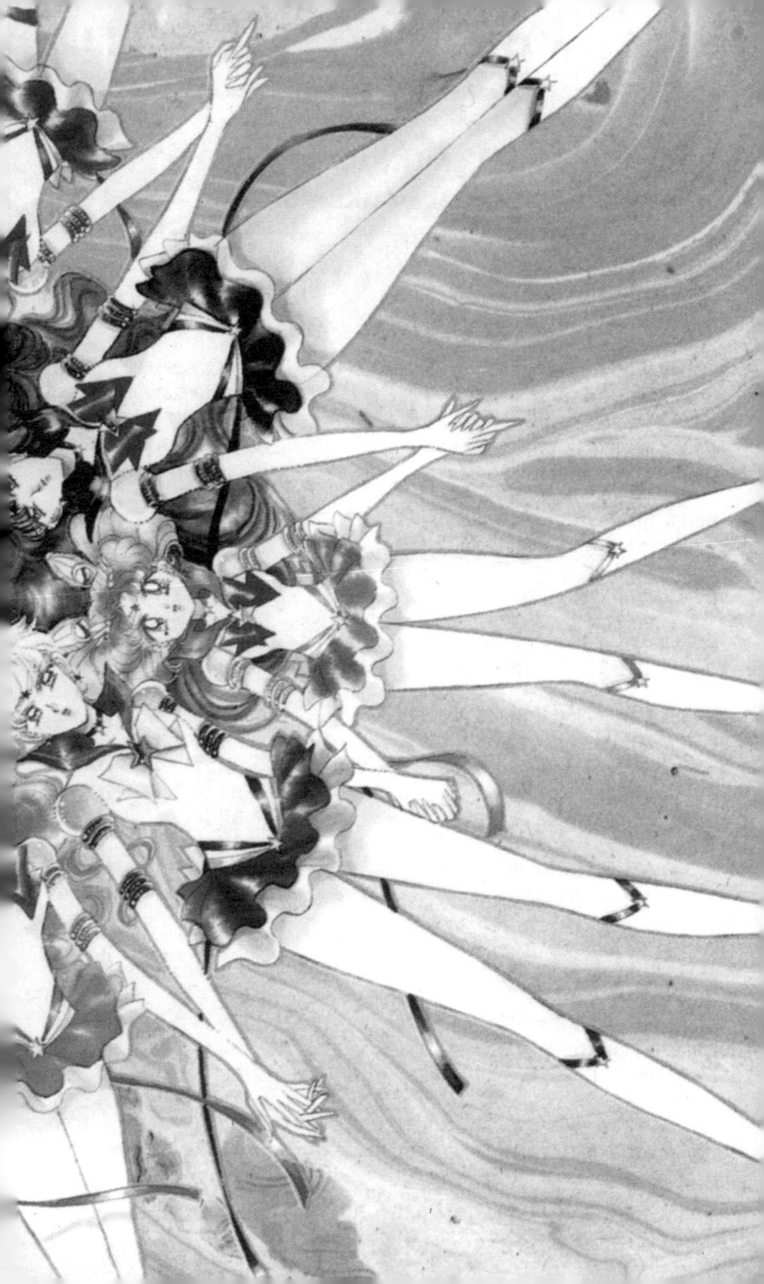